Robert Morel

Devotions to Jesus Christ: In the most holy sacrament of the altar

Robert Morel

Devotions to Jesus Christ: In the most holy sacrament of the altar

ISBN/EAN: 9783742823724

Manufactured in Europe, USA, Canada, Australia, Japa

Cover: Foto ©Lupo / pixelio.de

Manufactured and distributed by brebook publishing software (www.brebook.com)

Robert Morel

Devotions to Jesus Christ: In the most holy sacrament of the altar

DEVOTIONS

TO

JESUS CHRIST

IN THE

MOST HOLY SACRAMENT

OF

THE ALTAR:

CONTAINING

PIOUS EXERCISES FOR HONOURING THIS DIVINE MYSTERY, AND APPROACHING IT WORTHILY:

COMPOSED IN FRENCH

By the Rev. Father DOMINICK MOREL,

OF THE ORDER OF ST. BENEDICT.

THE SECOND EDITION,

CAREFULLY REVISED AND CORRECTED.

DUBLIN:

PRINTED BY J. MEHAIN, NO. 49, ESSEX-STREET, CORNER OF CRAMPTON-COURT.
AND RICHARD CROSS, NO. 28, BRIDGE-STREET.

To the Most Reverend
Dr. FRANCIS MOYLAN,
Roman Catholic Bishop of Cork:

This New Edition

OF DEVOTIONS TO JESUS CHRIST

IN THE

MOST HOLY SACRAMENT

OF THE ALTAR:

IS MOST HUMBLY INSCRIBED

By his most obedient

And most obliged Servants,

The EDITORS.

SUBSCRIBERS NAMES.

A
Timothy Allen

B
Rev. Patrick Byrne
Rev. Mr. Barry
James Bird, Efq; Drogheda, 2 books
Mr. Garrett Barry
Mr. Michael Bardon, Miltown
Mr. Patrick Byrne, Effex-ftreet
Mr. Edmond Barrett
Mrs. Catharine Burke
Mrs. Ellen Bernard
Mifs Anne Baldwin
Mifs Alice Brennan
Mifs Eleanor Barry
Mifs Catharine Barry

C
Mr. James Coftello, George's-ftreet, 22 books
Mr. Edward Coftollo
Mr. Thomas Cheevers
Mr. John Corballis, New-ftreet
Mr. Patt. Carroll, feed-merchant, Cook-ftreet
Mr. Michael Cogan
Mr. Dennis Coleman
Mr. Dennis Corcoran
Mr. Richard Cantwell
Mrs. Cahill, Rofs, 12 books
Mrs. Mary Cahill

Mrs. Mary

Mrs. Mary Callaghan, Cork
Mrs. Ellen Carroll
Miss Maria Casey
Miss Mary Anne Collins
Miss Catharine Callaghan

D
M. R. Dr. Delany, Kildare, 25 books
Mr. William Deveaux
Mr. Thomas Dunbar
Mrs. Ellen Denahy
Miss Mary Donovan

F
Mr. James Ferrall, Haymarket
Mr. Michael Flynn
Mr. John Flynn
Mr. Thomas Fitzmorris
Mr. Jeremiah Forrister
Mr. Dennis Forrister
Mrs. Margaret Ferrall, New Church-street
Miss Anne Fullum

G
Mr. Thomas Gorman, Bookseller, Clonmel, 25 books
Mrs. Eliza Galway

H
Mr. Bartholomew Hacket, Capel-street
Mr. Joseph Hayes, Cork
Master Patrick Hayes
Mrs. Catharine Hoare, Cork
Mrs. Mary Hayes
Miss Eliza Hayes, Cork
Miss Mary Hacket, Capel-street
Miss Ellen Hacket, Capel-street

Laurence

K

Laurence Kenny, Esq; Queen-street
Mr. John Kelly, Corn-market
Mr. Kelly
Mrs. Eleanor Kelly, College-green
Miss Mary Kenny
Miss Teresa Keating

L

Rev. Dennis Lane
Mr. Matt. Lynch, 14 books
Mr. Patrick Lennan, Armagh, 14 books
Mr. John Lordon
Mr. John Leahy
Mrs. Anne Lenargan

M

M. R. Dr. Moylan, Cork, 13 books
Rev. Bernard Mac Mahon, 6 books
Mr. Isaac Mann, Castle-street
Mr. Martin Mahony
Mr. Francis Mahony
Mr. Timothy Mahony
Mr. Jeremiah Mahony
Mr. Michael Mahony
Mr. Michael Murphy
Mr. James M'Allister
Mrs. Mary M'Carthy
Mrs. Ellen Mahony
Miss Martha Mehain
Miss Catharine Moylan
Miss Eleanor Mahony
Miss Anne Meade, 2 books
Miss Mary Moynehan

N
James Nangle, Esq; Kildalky, 2 books
Mr. James Neenan

P
Mr. John Potterton, Church-street.
Mr. Matthew Perry, Strand-street
Mrs Ellen Pendergast
Miss Margretta Pendergast
Miss Marg. Pendergast

R
Robert Richardson, Esq;
Mr. John Reardon
Mr. John Roache
Mrs. Eliza Richardson

S
Mr. Luke Shea, 2 books
Mr. John Shea
Mr. Daniel Sheehan
Mr. Daniel Sullivan
Mrs. Catharine Staunton, 2 books
Mrs. Mary Sheehan
Miss Anne Slack, 2 books
Miss Anne Sullivan
Miss Alice Shea
Miss Honoria Slack

T
M. R. Dr. Troy, Dublin, 6 books

W
Rev. John Walsh, Cork
Mr. Edmond Woods
Mr. Michael Woods
Mrs. Margaret Walsh

CONTENTS

	Page
OF the zeal and fervour with which we ought to approach the Holy Mysteries	13
Of the care with which we ought to prepare ourselves for Communion, and of the dispositions we ought to be in to receive worthily	29
Of the benefits we ought to reap from this august Mystery	50
A method for approaching with advantage to the Holy Sacrament	65
A Preparatory Exercise for Sacramental Confession	75
An Act of Contrition for such as are conscious to themselves of the guilt of Mortal Sin	78
An Exercise for Communion	114
An Immediate Preparation for Communion	117

Spiritual Exercises for every day in the Week, for the Use of the Clergy, and such of the Laity as communicate often

For Sunday	148
Monday	161
Tuesday	174
Wednesday	186
Thursday	197
Friday	207
Saturday	216
I. A short method for hearing Mass	225
Elevations to Jesus Christ when the Blessed Sacrament is exposed	232

II. Ele-

CONTENTS.

II. *Elevation*	239
III. *Elevation*	248
IV. *Elevation*	254
V. *Elevation*	264
VI. *Elevation*	270
VII. *Elevation*	275
VIII. *Elevation*	281
An Elevation to the divine heart of *Jesus* in the Holy Sacrament of the Altar	287
Eight Subjects of Meditation before the Blessed Sacrament, whether exposed or not	295
Devotions to *Jesus Christ* when the Blessed Sacrament is carried in Procession	302
Devotions to *Jesus Christ* during the time of accompanying the Blessed Sacrament, when it is carried to the Sick	308
A Formulary of Atonement, or Act of making reparation for any injurious treatment of the most Holy Sacrament of the Altar	315
An Abstract of the foregoing for such as have less leisure	322
Another Act of Reparation	324
A Morning Oblation of the actions of the day	326
An Act of Adoration of the Blessed Sacrament for the Morning.	331
Adoration at Noon and at Night	334
Elevation to *Jesus Christ* in the Blessed Sacrament, to implore his assistance on different occasions	336
A Preparation for Death	342
Manner of adoring the Blessed Sacrament	349
The Litany of the Blessed Sacrament	353

Feasts and Fasts of the Year.

THE following feasts only are to be strictly kept, that is, with the obligation of hearing Mass, and resting from servile works: (the whole obligation on the other holidays formerly observed being taken off, by a late regulation of his Holiness Pope Pius VI. and extended to Ireland, March the 29th, 1778.)

All Sundays.
The Circumcision of our Lord, or New-Year's Day. - - Jan. 1
The Epiphany, or Twelfth-Day. Jan. 6
Easter Monday, moveable.
Whit. Monday, moveable.
Ascension Thursday, moveable.
Corpus Christi, or solemnity of the most Holy Sacrament, moveable.
St. Patrick, Patron of the whole kingdom of Ireland. - March 17
The Annunciation of the blessed Virgin Mary. - - March 25
The Nativity of St. John Baptist. June 24
The Feast of St. Peter and St. Paul. June 29
The Assumption of the Blessed Virgin Mary. - - August 15
The feast of All Saints. Nov. 1
The Nativity of our Lord, or Christmas Day. - - Dec. 25

Fasting Days on one Meal.

All the Days in Lent, except Sundays.
The Eve of Whitsuntide.
Ember-Days, four times a year, being the Wednesdays, Fridays, and Saturdays next fol-
lowing

lowing the firſt Sunday of Lent ; Whitſunday ; the Exaltation of the Holy Croſs, and the third Sunday of Advent.

The vigils, or eves of the feaſts of St. John Baptiſt, of St. Peter and St. Paul ; of the Aſſumption of the Bleſſed Virgin Mary ; of All Saints, and of Chriſtmas Day.

All Wedneſdays and Fridays in Advent.

N. B. If a Vigil (being a faſting day) fall on Sunday, the faſt is kept on the Saturday before.—That fiſh is abſolutely forbid thoſe, who are diſpenſed with in eating fleſh on the ſame meal. When a faſt falls on Friday, eggs are forbid.

Days of abſtinence from fleſh meat.

All Sundays in Lent.

All Fridays and Saturdays throughout the year, except that on which the feaſt of the Nativity of our Lord falls.

Rogation-days, being the three days before Aſcenſion.

St. Mark's-day, unleſs it happen in Eaſter week, or on Sunday.

PIOUS SENTIMENTS

ON THE

HOLY COMMUNION.

CHAP. I.

Of the zeal and fervour with which we ought to approach the Holy Mysteries.

I. THERE is nothing in the world we ought to desire with a greater degree of zeal and fervour, than a worthy sacramental participation of the Blessed Eucharist; because nothing in the world contributes more to the honour of God, or draws down upon us more abundant graces.

II. It is the property of goodness to attract, and excite our heart to seek after the possession of it; and the more excellence there is in a thing, the more deserving it is of our earnest and ardent endeavours in the pursuit of it. Now as He, who is presented to us on

that we should exert, if it were possible, an infinite ardour and earnestness for obtaining the possession of him. As he is properly the only good we possess on earth, the only desire of our hearts should be to enjoy him by the means of Communion. As in fine, he is a good which comprehends all others; and as God, though infinitely perfect, can give nothing beyond himself; as, moreover, by possessing him, we possess the only thing necessary: hence the desire of enjoying him ought to comprehend all desires, and reduce us to the inability of desiring any thing else.

III. How little are you acquainted, O worldings! with the value of what is presented to you on our altars, and how great is your loss by keeping off from Communion! Which of you would not think his greatest diligence well bestowed in quest of an immense treasure, if you knew where it could be found? Which of you, having a favourable prospect of being advanced to a post of exalted dignity, would not strain every nerve to obtain it? Which of you, in fine, having had the honour of being invited to the marriage-feast of a powerful monarch, where he could not fail of being regaled with every thing highly sumptuous and exquisitely delicious, would not be extremely fond of accepting the invitation? And, are not you here presented with a treasure containing all that is rich and valuable, both in heaven and earth? are not you offered a dignity which infinitely transcends that of kings and emperours? one single Communion worthily performed, being sufficient to raise you to a
higher

higher degree of honour and glory, than it is in the power of all the potentates of the earth to bestow upon you In a word, have not you the honour of being invited to the marriage-feast of the King of kings, who exerts his omnipotent power in order to the magnificent entertainment of his friends? And shall not all this be capable of inspiring you with ardour for an object so worthy of your desires? If not, how great and grievous is your stupidity and blindness!

IV. Though to purchase the happiness of communicating but once, nothing less should be required than to relinquish all your worldly possessions, to undergo immense labours and sufferings, to submit to the most ignominious treatment possible, to undertake a long voyage and retire to the remotest part of the world; yet so great is the benefit of being admitted to the holy Communion, that to obtain it we should submit with pleasure to every thing of this kind, if required, and be persuaded, that even upon these terms we should not purchase it at too dear a rate.

V. History records of St. Gertrude, St. Catherine of Sienna, St Catherine of Genoa, and several other Saints, that to enjoy the happiness of communicating, they would have ventured through flames, and run the risk of being burnt alive. This great ardour was the effect and consequence of their light, and their right apprehensions of the matter, and of their love for their heavenly spouse. Penetrated with a due sense of the great advantages to be reaped by receiving worthily the Blessed Eucharist, they set so high

high a value on it, as to think it a happiness to be admitted to it, though at the expence of their lives.

VI. Souls, not exempt from lesser stains, are condemned, after separation from their bodies, to the flames of purgatory; that being purged from their sins, they may be in a condition to see God face to face. Though it were left to their option to be delivered out of their suffering condition, they would choose rather to continue in it, than to be delivered out of it without being admitted to see God. So it is, that we ought to be disposed to embrace with joy the most grievous sufferings, when necessary to qualify us for possessing God upon earth by the means of the holy Communion; he being no less deserving of our seeking after him on the holy altar, than in the mansions of the blessed above.

VII. Here is a terrestrial Paradise, planted with God's own hand with the view of affording us in this life a foretaste of the joys of heaven. Here is the Tree of Life, the fruit whereof bestows immortality on those that feed on it as they ought. What a folly must it be to banish ourselves from this garden of delight, by keeping at too great a distance from the holy table; and to deprive ourselves thereby of the fruit of this Tree of Life, the only thing that can preserve us from death! The death of sin is unavoidable if we approach not to this source of true life; whereas by coming to it with suitable dispositions, we shall be possessed of the life of grace here, and of that of glory hereafter. " If, says St. Ambrose, you keep
" at

"at a distance, you will perish; but if you approach to him, you will live."

VIII. To decline coming to the holy table out of contempt, is a mark of reprobation; because 'tis a proof that we love not Jesus Christ, that we will have no fellowship with him, and in some degree incur the guilt of what St Paul calls *saying Anathema to Jesus*, or calling him an accursed thing. It is a commencement, and kind of anticipation even here, of that dreadful and eternal separation between him and the reprobate which is to take place at the day of judgment. It is to pronounce beforehand the sentence of our condemnation; it being the same thing as to condemn ourselves to a separation from him. This great mystery, which is a precious pledge of life and felicity for those who worthily approach it, becomes a presage of reprobation and eternal death for those who criminally absent themselves.

IX. What man in his senses, being reduced to the lowest ebb of misery, would not embrace with pleasure the means offered him to be delivered from it? yet can there be a more wretched condition than that of one who sinfully forbears coming to the holy Communion? He is dying of hunger and thirst; he is poor, naked, sick, persecuted and helpless. Our altars afford him an expedient no less easy than sure, whereby to rid himself of all his ills: a divine aliment is offered him to appease his hunger; a heavenly drink to quench his thirst; rich apparel to cover his nakedness; sovereign remedies to cure his infirmities; immense wealth to relieve his poverty, and to change it into

into affluence; an all-powerful protector to rescue him from tyranny and oppression: must he not have lost his senses if he do not avail himself of expedients so salutary and advantageous?

X. We cannot pretend to enter heaven without partaking of Christ's bitter cup. To every one that aspires to this happiness, he puts the same question he once did to the sons of Zebedee, James and John; *Can you drink of the cup which I am to drink of?* a cup of bitterness and sufferings. Faint-hearted and base cowards, as we are, we want courage and resolution to partake of this cup, though our blessed Lord drank it to the very dregs. But if the cup of his sufferings be so disagreeable, that we cannot prevail upon ourselves to drink of it on that account, can we form a like excuse or exception to the partaking of the cup of his love, as St. Augustin calls it, which he holds out to us at the holy table? If we want resolution to die *for* him, let it be our choice to die *with* him at least by means of the holy Communion; let us die to the world, to sin, to concupiscence.

XI. To communicate, is to enter into a covenant, and to contract a very close union with Jesus Christ; it is to be admitted to the privilege of having him for father, friend, spouse, portion and inheritance. It is to receive, as a gratuitous donation or free gift, the merits of his death and passion in order to their being presented to his eternal Father in satisfaction for our sins, and as a valuable consideration for the kingdom of heaven; it is acquiring

ing a fresh title to his kingdom, and receiving a new pledge of the promise of it already made to us. It is, in fine, procuring for us, in order to the being possessed of it, the most powerful succours God has ever bestowed on man. Can any one seriously consider this, and continue cold and indifferent to the holy Communion, without renouncing faith and christianity?

XII. What a monstrous shame it is to see men so eager after corruptible food, which can only afford an animal and sensual satisfaction, and which can only serve to prolong a life full of afflictions and miseries? and at the same time to see them conceive such a distaste of that incorruptible food, which *contains all the delights of* heaven, and which procures those that partake of it a life of happy immortality? If the sensual man be so eager after corporal food, as often to value life only for the sake of the gratification he experiences in the use of it, common to men and brutes; ought not the spiritual man, the christian, for a better reason, be supposed to be so taken up with, and so eager after this heavenly food, as to be able to relish nothing comparatively to it, and make it the sum and complement of all his desires.

XIII. It is said by our Saviour, that where *the body is, thither shall the eagles* (Mat. 24. 28.) *be gathered together,* to feed on it. If then you be an eagle, in the mystical sense of the word, implying an elevation of thoughts and desires, a fervent disposition, generosity and courage in the pursuit of virtue, ought you not to fly with impetuous ardour towards the body of our
Lord

Lord in the Eucharift, and cleave to him with the warmeft fentiments of piety and devotion; that you may be nourifhed by his facred flefh and blood?

XIV. The Saints in heaven are ever longing after this heavenly food which is ferved up to them as well as to us, though after a different manner. They conftantly feed upon it with an ever-growing appetite, and place their greateft happinefs in partaking of it. The Saints upon earth hunger alike after this food, partaking of it daily at the holy table, if not facramentally, at leaft by means of a fpiritual communion; and they alfo place their greateft happinefs in feeding on it.

XV. With what rapidity does a torrent fwelled with heavy rains, make its way to join other waters? With what fwiftnefs does a fhip under fail, glide along the waves before a brifk gale of wind, and bear away to its deftined port? With what violence does the fragment of a rock, breaking loofe from the fummit of a high mountain, make its way to the bottom of the adjacent valley? With what impetuofity does fire, pent up in fubterraneous cavities, break its prifon to afcend to the place of that element? Thefe are but faint reprefentations of that eagernefs of defire, we ought to entertain for the facrament of our altars. For the ardency of defire we ought to have for being united to our Lord in it, fhould as much furpafs the celerity whereby natural bodies are carried towards their centre or element, as we furpafs them by the dignity of our nature; and

as

as much as the term we tend to, surpasses by its excellence and force of attraction that, to which they are carried.

XVI. Jesus Christ, says St. Fulgentius, is the sun which makes the day of eternity, feasting the heavenly spirits with contemplation of his glory. He is also the sun which makes the day of time upon earth, nourishing the faithful with his flesh and blood. The day therefore they do not feed upon him, at least spiritually, by a desire equally ardent and sincere of receiving him, is to them a day of darkness by the absence of this divine sun; a day in which whatever is formed in them by the inward man, becomes feeble and languishing; a day, in a word, deserving to be struck out of the number of their days, as being destitute for them of light, heat, joy and comfort.

XVII. Our Lord Jesus Christ gives us pressing invitations to come to his table; he expresses a vehement desire of our eating at it; he has been at an immense expence to feast us at it, and he there serves up to us a food which comprises in it all that is most rare and exquisite in the world. Can we slight his invitation without affronting him grievously? without obliging him like the king in the gospel (Mat. 23. 12.) to look upon our refusal as an outrageous contempt, and an injury provoking him to exclude us from partaking of his heavenly banquet.

XVIII. O Divine Jesus! the *desire* of the *eternal hills*, (Gen. 49. 26.) ever possessed, and

and ever longed for by the blessed inhabitants of heaven, thou dost verily and indeed descend on our altars to be there the bread of our desires. It is thy will that we should ever sigh and ever hunger after thee. This hunger thou dost require of us as the price with which thou would'st have us purchase in some measure this divine food. Yes, the breathings of my heart are after thee; its only desire is to have my spiritual hunger appeased by receiving thee in the Blessed Sacrament.

XIX. Thou cryest out, O dear Saviour, to the inward ear of every faithful soul, as thou didst to that of the spouse in the canticle of Solomon: *Open to me, my sister, my friend, my dove,* that I may *come in to* take entire possession of thy heart. Thou sayest to her, as in the Apocalypse: (Apoc. 3, 20.) *I stand at the door and knock, if any one opens to me I will come in, and will sup with him, and he with me.* Thou makest it known to this soul that thou actest the part as it were of a stranger in this sacrament, and that it is thy will that she should lodge thee in her bosom and in her heart. Who, O Lord, can shut the door upon thee and refuse thee admittance, without declaring himself thy enemy, and incurring thereby a sentence of perpetual exclusion from thy heavenly mansions?

XX. The religious zeal which urges us to partake of this mystery, glorifies the adorable Trinity, honours the sacred humanity of Jesus Christ, gives joy to the saints in heaven, relieves the suffering souls in purgatory, draws down

down fresh graces and blessings on the church, and merits for the worthy receivers new favours. Why then have we recourse to frivolous pretexts and subterfuges for stopping the current of all these blessings? If our dispositions for receiving, are none of the most perfect at all times, cannot we in virtue of the command of Jesus Christ present ourselves notwithstanding our manifold imperfections, and say with an ancient doctor of the church: " He has given it to us in charge: it is our " duty to obey."

XXI. What a degree of power and splendour heretofore, among the Romans, did the dignity of Consul impart to the person elevated to that high office? It constituted him master of the world. Yet a man raised twice to the consulship, did not, in ancient Rome, so much surpass in glory another who had been raised only once to the dignity, as one of the faithful, who having communicated twice in Christian dispositions, would surpass in heavenly glory another who had received only once, as our blessed Saviour revealed it heretofore to one of his dearest spouses. Can more be said to inspire us with an ardent zeal for Communion? and must not that person be an enemy to his own glory, who is cold and remiss in this respect?

XXII. Personal unworthiness is often alledged as a reason for keeping at a distance from the holy table, when in fact the true cause is sloth and indevotion: we love not Jesus Christ, and this is what gives us so little concern about approach-

approaching to the holy Sacrament to unite ourſelves to him. It is this that puts us upon inventing ſpecious and frivolous reaſons to excuſe our abſenting ourſelves. We are unwilling to undergo the trouble of preparing ourſelves, in which ſelf-love does not find its account. This is the true cauſe of our remiſſneſs on this head. To be well prepared, we muſt renounce our pleaſures, mortify our paſſions, correct our faults, and practiſe chriſtian virtues. But we prefer living by humour, purſuing our pleaſures, gratifying our inclinations, favouring ſelf-love, to laying the leaſt reſtraint upon ourſelves, in order to lead a Chriſtian life, and thereby to communicate worthily. Behold the true reaſon, for the moſt part, of our keeping at a diſtance from the holy table!

XXIII. An unconquerable averſion to food, even the moſt delicious and moſt neceſſary for the ſupport of life, is a proof that a man is very dangerouſly ill and very near his end. In like manner it is a very bad ſign for a ſoul to loathe the euchariſtical food, of all others the moſt delicious and ſalutary, and when ſhe cannot prevail upon herſelf to make uſe of it; or if ſhe uſes it, it is without reliſh or benefit to herſelf. If ſuch a ſoul be not dead in ſin, it is but too evident that ſhe is in a dangerous way, on account of the weakneſs of her love for Jeſus Chriſt.

XXIV. There are ſome who content themſelves with communicating once a year. Alas! how will Chriſtians of this claſs, be in a condition

dition to preserve the life of their soul? Their body must have a more copious supply of the food necessary for its subsistence, or it will decay and perish. Has the soul less need of spiritual sustenance to preserve the life of grace, than the body of material food to preserve animal life? Ought not therefore the soul to be daily fed, spiritually or sacramentally, with its proper food, the Blessed Eucharist?

XXV. *I have seen an evil under the sun*, says the wise man, *and it is this: God has given a man wealth, honour*, in a word, every thing that can make life comfortable and agreeable, *but has not given him the power to make use of them*, because his extreme attachment to those objects will not permit him. This evil is, in the opinion of St Bernardin of Sienna, a lively figure of that which we remark in Christians, on whom God has bestowed in the Sacrament of the Altar immense riches, sovereign honour, and all that can contribute to make them happy even upon earth, so far as this mortal state will allow of; but alas! their eager desires after things temporal, and the neglect of their salvation, debar them of the power of making use of them to their advantage.

XXVI. This great mystery is that precious talent which includes nothing less within itself, than the riches of the whole world, and of its maker, God himself. He has given it to us to put out to interest, and to return him what it gains. Can we bury this talent entrusted to us on these conditions, without incurring his just indignation? If the unprofitable servant

[Mat.

(Mat. 23. 30.) mentioned in the gospel, was for the like offence *cast into outward darkness, where there is weeping and gnashing of teeth*; what may not those justly expect, who, led aside by the inordinate love they bear to the things of this world, bury in some measure this talent, by keeping at too great a distance from the holy table?

XXVII. The dispositions required for a worthy Communion only once in the year, differ but little from those required for communicating often; since to communicate worthily but once, an ardent love of God is required, together with a profound humility, a great purity of soul, an utter abhorrence and detestation of sin, and a stedfast resolution of living entirely to God. Now these dispositions, if sincere, ought to be uninterrupted and permanent; and in supposition that they are so, what should hinder the person in whom they subsist, from communicating if not daily, at least very often?

XXVIII. Those who forbear going to Communion out of real respect, and those who approach on the motive of holy love, equally honour Jesus Christ; as the centurion, who, *conscious to himself* of his unworthiness, excused his acceptance of our Lord's intended visit for curing his sick servant: and Zachæus, who joyfully embraced the offer our Lord made of eating at his house. But the latter seems to enter the more perfectly of the two, into our Lord's designs, as also to second his intentions better than the former, the manner of his instituting

tuting this facrament being a very ftrong proof of it; for by inftituting it under the form of bread, he intimates that, as eating bread is one of the moft ufual actions in life, fo his defire is that our participation of this facrament fhould be frequent and familiar to us, yet with all the veneration that is due to it. It may likewife be alledged in favour of frequent communion, that as Zachæus derived more advantage from receiving Jefus Chrift into his houfe, than the Centurion did by excufing his receiving him; and we being withal not apprifed of any alteration for the better made in the conduct of the Centurion, nor of his giving fo large a portion of his fubftance to the poor, as was the cafe of the publican; we may thence infer a much greater advantage on the fide of communicating out of love, than of keeping at a diftance through fear and refpect.

XXIX. Where is now that refpect, that zealous ardour of the primitive Chriftians, for approaching the holy myfteries, which would not fuffer them to pafs a day without feeding on this heavenly bread? where is now that love which engaged their affections fo powerfully to this divine facrament, that nothing could feparate them from it? They crowded to it, as a holy doctor expreffes himfelf on this fubject, like bees to the hive. "We cannot live "without eating the bread of the Lord," was the anfwer a holy martyr made to a perfecutor, upon enquiring whether he had not partook of the myfteries of the Chriftians; hence, no queftion, fprung that commendable con-

defcenfion

descension of the Church to the fervour of Christians in the primitive times, of allowing the faithful to take the holy Eucharist, under the form of bread, to their respective habitations, and to carry it about them wherever they travelled. Alas! how far short of their devotion to this divine Sacrament do we fall! and at the same time how much colder are we in our love for Jesus Christ! The more we love this divine Saviour, the more eager is our desire to partake of his body and blood in the Blessed Eucharist; and the oftener we receive this divine Sacrament, the more does our love for him increase in us and advance to maturity.

XXX. The grace we receive in this sacrament is proportionate to the fervency of our desires; and the more vehement our desires are, the greater grace we receive: we ought on this account to let no bounds to these, that grace may flow into our souls with the greatest abundance, even to infinity itself, were it possible. Lord, *what is there besides thee that I expect in heaven, and what else can I desire upon earth?* thou art in this sacrament the only object of my desires, as thou art in heaven the only object of my hopes. It is thou alone whom I long for with my whole heart; thee only do I wait and hope for.

CHAP.

CHAP. II.

Of the care with which we ought to prepare ourselves for Communion, and of the dispositions we ought to be in to receive worthily.

1. THERE are some, whose devotion consists in often approaching to the table of our Lord, but who give themselves little or no concern about approaching in a worthy manner. This proceeds from their leading a life, influenced by desires and views meerly human; being moreover strangers to recollection, averse to mortification, sensual, full of themselves, inordinately attached to earthly things, swayed by their passions, slaves to their self-love, faithless to grace. No resemblance can suit them better than that of a man, who being invited to the king's table, should be so insolent as to appear at it in rags, filth and nastiness; must not such a behaviour offend the prince to a high degree, and excite his just anger and indignation? The rashness of such persons in like manner must needs be highly offensive and displeasing to our Lord, and cannot fail of drawing down upon their guilty heads the dreadful effects of his just and grievous resentment. If it be sinful to neglect going at proper times and seasons to Communion, it is still more so to receive improperly disposed, or un-

provided with suitable dispositions. Hence it was, that the person that offered himself a guest at the nuptial feast without a nuptial garment, was treated with greater severity than those who refused to go; for he was ordered to be bound hand and foot and cast into outward darkness, (Matt. 22: 13.) a punishment not inflicted on those who only absented themselves from the banquet.

II. What is your notion, what are your sentiments of communicating? in what light do you consider it? Are you not convinced and persuaded that it is the most noble, the most holy, and the most important action not only of the whole life, but of the whole Christian religion? It certainly is of all others the most *noble*, as a man cannot be more honoured and distinguished than by being united to, and incorporated with Jesus Christ's happiness bestowed upon him in this sacrament; it is the most *holy*, there being none by which he receives more grace; it is the most *important*, because life and death eternal depend on the manner of its being done. Whence you ought to conclude that no action requires a more ample and diligent preparation than this.

III. The world was 4000 years in preparing itself for the reception of the Son of God, in the flesh. For all the longing desires of the ancient patriarchs, all the oracles delivered by the prophets, all the sacrifices offered by the priests, all the ceremonies of the old law, all the actions of just men tended to no other end, and had no other view than to obtain of heaven

ven the *defired of all nations*, and to be prepared for receiving the effects of that grace, which he was to bring down with him upon the earth. Even all the creatures of the univerfe had received being on no other account, than to be employed in his fervice. Now what the world did with refpect to the incarnation, ought to be done by every Chriftian in regard to Communion. Their whole conduct ought to be levelled at no other end, than worthily receiving their Saviour in this adorable facrament, and reaping the fruits of a worthy Communion. To this alone ought all their thoughts, defires and actions to tend. Neither 4000 years, nor even millions, would fuffice to difpofe us for receiving Jefus Chrift in this facrament in a manner fuitable to his excellence. But though it be out of our power to fpend a long feries of years upon our preparation, let us at leaft confecrate to it the fhort time we have to live.

IV. Jefus Chrift in this myftery exhaufts his treafures, and exerts his power and wifdom, to feed and enrich us. Though he was to beftow upon us all created nature, nay, thoufands of fuch worlds, the donation would fall infinitely fhort of what he gives us by once receiving him in the Bleffed Euchariſt. Can we in return do lefs, than with all our might and utmoft care, correfpond with this his generous and difinterefted love; omitting nothing in our power that may enable us to receive him in the moft perfect manner?

V. What

V. What magnificent preparation do subjects make for receiving their prince into any of his cities which he choofes to honour with his prefence? with what care is every thing removed out of his way, that it is thought may prove offenfive? The ftreets are made clean and neat, the houfes are embellifhed in the moft elegant manner. If fo, what ought we not to do, for receiving in a fuitable manner the fovereign monarch of the whole world, whofe majefty infinitely furpaffes that of all the kings and potentates of the earth, and from whom we have already received, and hope to receive hereafter infinitely greater bleffings, than it is in the power of the greateft monarch upon earth to beftow upon his fubjects? Omit nothing then, O my foul, forget nothing which can qualify and difpofe thee in a manner worthy of him.

VI. When we receive a great perfonage into our houfe, and find ourfelves unprovided of furniture fuitable to his rank or dignity, we endeavour to borrow the beft and richeft that can be found. In like manner, falling infinitely fhort as we do, of the difpofitions, that are requifite for the worthy reception and entertainment of the Son of God in our hearts, let us have recourfe to the faints, to the holy angels, to the Bleffed Virgin and mother, even to Jefus Chrift himfelf, intreating him, with all humility and favour, to clothe us with their merits; and let us then offer them to that divine Saviour, to fupply for what we are deficient in.

VII. If

Chap. II. *on the Holy Communion.* 33

VII. If you have any love for the divine Jesus, and are animated with zeal for his glory, it is chiefly by preparing yourself for Communion that these pious dispositions ought to shew themselves. If you had received him into your house as a guest during his mortal life, consider what manner of entertainment you would have afforded him on the occasion. You ought not to be less solicitous for giving him a good reception, as often as he vouchsafes to visit you by Communion; since he is no less worthy of it under the veil of the Sacrament, than when visible in his human form. You receive him not in the Blessed Eucharist, as you do in the persons of the poor or any other of his representatives, but in his own person. You ought then to omit nothing within the reach of your power, which may any way contribute to your receiving of him in a manner worthy of his excellence.

VIII. The holy scripture very justly reproves the Jews for not having received and acknowledged the Son of God as their Messiah, on his appearance in the flesh, notwithstanding they professed themselves the people of God, and had expected his coming some thousands of years past. What manner of reception do you afford him, whom you own to be your Saviour, visiting you in the Blessed Eucharist? Do you make him a faithful tender of all the respect, love, zeal and submission, which are justly due to him, and are expected from you? Has he not a just charge against you, that notwithstanding all your professions of being his and wholly devoted to his service, you are so far from giving him a proper reception by reason of your lukewarmness and indifference, that you even load him with injuries, and crucify him anew, by the criminal dispositions in which you receive him.

IX. We are here presented with the new wine which flowed from the press of the cross; but new wine requires to be put into new vessels, because it would burst old ones. We ought in like manner to be renewed in spirit, and to put on the new man, to partake worthily of this venerable myftery. If the old man be still alive in us, he will not fail of becoming the inftrument of our ruin.

X. The Bleffed Euchariſt is a Viaticum, or the provifion for our journey in paffing from the preſent life to the next. We ought therefore never to receive this facrament, but in fuch difpofitions as we could wifh to leave the world in, that is, in a like difengagement of our affections from earthly objects, a like compunction for fin, and humiliation before God on that account, a like confidence in God's mercies, love of his adorable perfections and defire of poffeffing him in heaven; in a word, as often as we communicate, we ought to be thoroughly difpofed for dying, and fay, when we prefent ourfelves at the holy table, that we are going as Mofes (Deut. 34. 5.) to expire in the peace of the Lord.

XI. Jefus Chriſt places himſelf on our altars as our judge on his tribunal, and there pronounces fentence on all that come to receive;
a fen-

a sentence of life in behalf of every worthy communicant, but a sentence of death upon all those that approach in a criminal state. You ought then to approach to this mystery in no other condition than that which you wish to be found in, when you shall be presented before the judgment-seat of Christ; that is, clothed with the same purity, innocence and charity, which you desire to be possessed of, when summoned before him to receive the definitive sentence on your eternal lot.

XII. Open thy eyes, O my soul, open thy eyes, I say, to consider the wonderful excellencies and advantages of this divine food, before thou eatest of it. Reflect that thou presentest thyself a guest at the table of the sovereign Lord of the universe.

XIII. Jesus Christ comes forth from the bosom of his Father, to exhibit himself on our altars, and to pass from thence into our hearts; where, by means of holy Communion, he proposes to take up his abode in us. Our souls then ought to make the nearest approaches possible to that infinite purity of the adorable bosom of the Father from whence he comes; of that of his own person, which comes into us; and of that of the womb of the Blessed Virgin, into which he entered by becoming incarnate, if we desire to provide him a suitable habitation. What ray of the sun should yield in purity to a heart which hath the happiness of receiving Jesus Christ, since the purity of this heart ought to bear some resemblance to the purity of the Eternal Father, to that of his
Son

Son Jesus Christ, and to that of his divine Mother?

XIV. Jesus Christ, as the royal prophet observes, has pitched his tent in the sun. A soul that receives him by Communion, becomes in some manner his tent. She ought therefore to be a sun by the lustre of her virtues, by the ardency of her love, by the elevation of her mind raised above all earthly objects, by a punctual exactness in the discharge of all her duties, by her fervent and zealous progress in the ways of grace, by her love in doing all the good she is able, and by a steady perseverance in the practice of all christian virtues.

XV. It is only among the *lilies* of purity, that the divine spouse of our souls delights to dwell; he enters none but *inclosed* gardens, he drinks of no springs but such as are *sealed*. The meaning of all which in the mystical expressions is, that to make our souls an agreeable habitation to him, and to engage him willingly to abide with us, we ought to observe an inviolable purity of heart, shut out all created things, and preserve it from all the stains and blemishes usually occasioned by our disorderly affections and attachments to creatures.

XVI. Man had it in his power to eat of the fruit of life, so long as he lived in innocence. He was deprived of this fruit, and expelled paradise upon his falling into sin. The Blessed Eucharist contains the true fruit of life, none but spotless souls are worthy to partake of it. The defiled must not presume to approach; so long

long as they continue such, they must live in a state of banishment from the holy table. Make it thy study then to imitate, as near as thou canst, the innocence of our first parents before their expulsion, that thou mayest be admitted to eat of this divine and life-giving fruit.

XVII. Jesus Christ celebrated his passover with none but his disciples, and before he allowed them to partake of it, washed their feet from the dust that stuck to them. This was to inform us, that to be qualified to partake of this christian passover, a man must be a disciple, not in name only, but in truth and reality; and must have cleansed his soul, not only from gross sins and corruptions, but others less offensive, figured by the dust that cleaves to their feet.

XVIII. To be qualified to partake of the paschal lamb in the old law, it was required of the Jews to be free from all legal uncleanness. This prefigured that to feed on the lamb of God at the holy table, we ought to be as exempt as possible from all sinful stains, how light soever they may appear to our eye, and to have purged away the old leaven of sin. There is no receiving worthily without the unleavened bread (Expurgate vetus fermentum. 1 Cor. 5. 8.) of innocence, or as St. Paul calls it, of *sincerity and truth.*

XIX. The Blessed Eucharist is the bread of angels; no wonder then that angelical dispositions should be required of the partakers of it. Those who live not like angels with regard to the purity of their manners, the perfection of their love for God and their neighbour, a constant separation from the world, at least in affection, and the sanctity of their actions, are unworthy to partake of this bread of angels.

XX. This mystery makes a heaven of earth: now as nothing defiled can enter heaven, and as it is necessary for whatever is defiled to pass through a state of purgation before it come to be admitted there, no unclean person, while he continue such, must presume to approach the holy table; he must first have washed off his sinful stains by the severities of penance.

XXI. Manna was not given to the Israelites, till they had quitted Ægypt, and had consumed the meal they had brought with them out of that land. In like manner, the participation of this mystery ought to be allowed only to those souls which have quitted the bondage of sin, withdrawn all affection to it, and detest its fatal sweets.

XXII. Manna was preserved, by God's command, in a vessel of gold, and placed within the ark of the covenant; the shewbread was in like manner offered to God on a table of massy gold: both served to point out that those who partake of the eucharistical bread, represented by both these figures, should be all of gold, by the purity and eminent charities that ought to appear in their lives.

XXIII. The bridegroom, in Solomon's Canticle, praises his spouse for being completely beautiful, and having not the least blemish in her.

her. The soul which approaches the holy mysteries, has the honour of being united in and through them to Jesus Christ, her adorable bridegroom: but then in order to render this union acceptable to him, she ought to be so pure and beautiful, that upon seeing her, he may be able to say with secret complacence and satisfaction, she is without blemish, and that he is highly delighted with the innocency of her life and purity of her manners.

XXIV. But it is not sufficient for a soul to preserve herself without blemish, to be well pleasing in the eyes of this divine bridegroom, she must also be clothed and decked with those graces and ornaments which she knows have the attractive charm to draw down his favourable regards upon her. Hence it is that this sacred bridegroom so often mentions with applause the rich attire and precious ornaments of his spouse. He extolls, by the mouth of the royal Psalmist, the beauty of the robe of *cloth of gold* with which she is arrayed, the beauty and the admirable variety of the *jewels* she is adorned with. And in the Canticles he highly commends *her necklace of pearl*, her *chains of gold variegated with silver*, and her rich *hose*. All this imports that the pious soul, in order to render herself agreeable to her heavenly bridegroom, when she approaches him in this mystery, ought to add the practice of the most eminent virtues to her purity and innocency of life.

XXV. You ought never to appear in the presence of this divine bridegroom, when you are

are going to receive him in the sacrament of the Eucharist, without bringing him out of the garden of the soul some newly gathered fruit which he is most fond of. By this I mean, that you ought ever to present him on this occasion with some fresh heroic actions of charity, humility, patience, mortification, obedience and other virtues.

XXVI. God heretofore forbad his people to appear before him at any time with empty (Exod. 23. 19.) hands: he accordingly required that on all these occasions something should be offered him by way of present: intimating thereby, that as often as we approach the holy altar, we should not fail of bringing with us some new act of virtue which had been practised by us since we last appeared there.

XXVII. The holy women mentioned in the Gospel, (Mark 16. 2.) brought with them ointments for anointing the body of their divine master, when they went to visit his tomb. The holy Eucharist, in the language of the holy Fathers, is the tomb of Jesus Christ, and we in some measure perform his funeral obsequies as often as Mass is celebrated: but we ought never to assist at it without bringing along with us the mystical spices of alms, prayers and mortification, whereof we have made a fresh compound for anointing spiritually the body of our Lord.

XXVIII. None but the victorious ought to be admitted to partake of the eucharistical manna: *I will give*, says our *Saviour* in the

Apoca-

Apocalypse, (Apoc. 2: 15.) *a hidden manna to him that conquereth.* This bread of the true Melchisedech, ought to be imparted to none but those who like Abraham (Gen. 14. 18.) have born away the rich spoils of their enemies. If you do not conquer the world, the flesh and the devil, if you do not bear away a rich booty from these enemies of your salvation to consecrate it to the altar, you do not deserve to have this divine manna dispensed to you; which for this reason is deservedly called the *bread of the strong,* because none but the strong and courageous, who by their noble and heroick actions have conquered their enemies, are worthy to partake of it.

XXIX. The Blessed Eucharist is a forerunner and antepast of heaven, which is bestowed only in consideration of good works performed on earth. Those that perform none, are no less unworthy of participating in the happiness commenced here below in this mystery, than in that consummate happiness which is enjoyed in heaven. *If any man,* says the apostle (2. Thes. 3. 10.) *refuse to work, neither let him eat.* He who does not labour for the glory and service of his divine master, deserves no share in his bread at the holy table.

XXX. Before the prodigal son (Luke 15. 22.) was permitted to eat of the fatted calf, he was not only to abandon the swine he had tended, but was also to be clothed with the *best robe,* receive a *ring* to his finger, and *shoes* to his feet. This intimates that to feast upon the precious flesh of Jesus Christ, in the Blesfed Euchariſt, we muſt not only have forſakèn all immediate occaſions of ſin, but be clothed likewiſe with the virtues of faith, hope, and charity, of which the *beſt robe*, the *ſhoes*, and the *ring*, beſtowed on the prodigal ſon, were emblems.

XXXI. How many were the ceremonies (Exod. 12. from ver. 3. to ver. 12.) the Jews were commanded to obſerve in the eating of the paſchal lamb ? It was to be eaten not only with *unleavened bread*, the ſymbol of purity, but likewiſe, with *bitter herbs*, the ſymbol of penance; with their *loins girded*, the ſymbol of mortification; with *ſtaves* in their hands, the ſymbol of correction, or reformation of manners; *ſhoes* to their feet, the ſymbol of hope: it was to be eat *about the evening*, the ſymbol of faith; and *in great haſte*, the ſymbol of fervent charity; in fine, *all* in a *ſtanding* poſture like people ready to ſet out upon a journey, the ſymbol of preparation for death. All this was ordained to point out to us that we muſt enter into all theſe diſpoſitions and poſſeſs all theſe virtues, in ſome degreee, to partake worthily of the euchariſtical Lamb.

XXXII. The angel in the Apocalypſe (Apoc. 19. 17,) invites only thoſe birds *to the ſupper of the great God, that fly in the midſt of heaven*, as it is there expreſſed. The Bleſſed Euchariſt is alſo the Lord's great ſupper, where the nuptials of the lamb are celebrated, Jeſus Chriſt being there united to his ſpouſe, the church. But none deſerve to be admitted to this banquet, except thoſe ſouls, which like myſtical

Chap. II. *on the Holy Communion.* 43

myftical birds rife with courage and refolution above all earthly things, foaring aloft *in the midft of heaven,* by a converfation altogether heavenly, and by the ardour of affection with which they feek after eternal good things. If you ftill grovel on the earth, or if you lofe not fight of it in your intentions and defigns, you are unworthy of being received as a gueft. Whence, St. John Chryfoftom fays, that this divine table is for eagles which foar and mount aloft, but not for fmall birds which rife but to a fmall diftance above the furface of the earth.

XXXIII. Who would fuffer a limb to remain tied or faftened to his body, I do not fay a dead or putrify'd limb, but one ulcerated, unfeemly and deformed ? how then can it be prefumed that Jefus Chrift will fuffer an union like this with his adorable body in this auguft facrament ? This, notwithftanding, is what you attempt as often as you approach it, I don't fay in a criminal ftate, the ftate of mortal fin, but under the guilt of and a ftrong attachment to many venial fins ; for then it may be truly faid of you, that you attempt to unite to the precious body of Jefus Chrift, an ulcerated, fhocking and notably deformed limb ; thefe forts of fins being, in the fpiritual fenfe, fo many ulcers, ftains, and frightful disfigurements : judge now how grievoufly you difhonour Jefus Chrift. Study therefore to clothe yourfelf with purity, grace and inward beauty, by copying after his divine virtues, that you may not difhonour him when you feek for an

union

union with him by a participation of the holy myſteries.

XXXIV. Thou hadſt juſt reaſon, O my Saviour, to complain by the mouth of holy Job, that men had no more regard for thee than the very dirt, (Comparatus ſum leto. Job 30. 19.) which appears from nothing ſo much as their extreme negligence in approaching to thee in this adorable myſtery. But none more properly incur this imputation, than thoſe who communicate in the ſtate of mortal ſin, becauſe they caſt thee forth when they receive thee, into a ſink of filth and infection; I mean into a conſcience polluted with ſins and enormous crimes.

XXXV. Where doſt thou lodge, O my ſoul, where doſt thou lodge this adorable Saviour on thy receiving him into thy houſe? Is it, as indeed it ought to be, on a throne of light and flames, in a conſcience purer than a beam of the ſun, in a heart more intenſely glowing with heat than fire itſelf? Alas! I rather fear he will have reaſon to complain, that after he has entered under my roof, he will find himſelf plunged into an abyſs of mud and filth, (Pſ. 68. 2.) through the vicious affections he ſhall diſcover in thee. Let no endeavours therefore henceforward be wanting in thee, to purify thy heart and affections; and to render them a fit abode for him; where ſo far from ſuffering indignities, and being treated with coldneſs and contempt, he may find a fit habitation.

XXXVI. May

XXXVI. May we not apply to this divine myftery what the Wife man fays, that the mouth deftroys more than the fword? I mean that more Chriftians are loft by unworthy communions, than by any other fin. And indeed the fuppofition feems very probable; firft, becaufe as this fin which is very frequent, is the moft enormous, forafmuch as it immediately attacks the facred perfon of Jefus Chrift himfelf, whom it caufes to fuffer a new death in our fouls; fo likewife it draws down on the perfon guilty of it, a more dreadful dereliction on the part of God, and a more fatal withdrawing of his grace than any other. Secondly, becaufe this fin being lefs obferved than others, through want of attention to the difpofitions of one's own heart at the time of approaching to the holy table, repentance for it is the lefs thought of. In fine, becaufe the blood of Jefus Chrift, being the only remedy of our fpiritual difeafes, a finner that has, as it were, annihilated the virtue of it in regard to himfelf has no further refource left for recovery. The Apoftle St. Paul complained heretofore, that the faithful in his time were deficient in the duty of approving themfelves, he therefore affured them that on this account many of them *flept the fleep of death.* (1 Cor. 11. 30.) With how much more reafon may we not make the like complaint of the Chriftians of our unhappy days, and juftly fear that they are but too many, who in punifhment of their unworthy Communions, are fuffered to fall into the

fatal

fatal lethargy of the death of sin out of which they never more awake?

XXXVII. O that we did but reflect on the great injury we do ourselves, in being so indifferently disposed for receiving this great sacrament as we ought; thereby defeating its virtue, and obstructing its salutary effects f Jesus Christ who vouchsafes to visit us with a love that surpasses all human understanding, and by unheard of prodigies, would fain operate in us prodigies of grace, and raise us to an high degree of sanctity, were it not that we ourselves opposed this design, though so much in our favour. A single Communion performed as it ought to be, might transform us into Seraphims, if the want of proper dispositions to it and the obstacles we throw in the way of it, did not prevent its good effects. Yet alas! how often hitherto have we received the holy sacrament, without our observing any change in us for the better? How great then must be our opposition to divine grace! Call forth, O my soul, thy powers, and exert thyself in removing whatever opposition of this kind may justly be laid to thy charge. Give thy redeemer full liberty to act within thee according to his good pleasure: beg of him to remove this opposition, by the strength of his almighty arm, and to accomplish in thee his merciful designs.

XXXVIII. Is it not astonishing, that we so indolently and without sentiment approach such a tremendous mystery? All heaven trembles with a religious awe, in the presence of of Him whom we receive within us. One look from him makes the whole universe to quake for fear; yet we receive him with the same coldness and insensibility, as if he had nothing in him to induce us to fear him, or to excite us to love him, nor do we seem to make the least motion towards entertaining him in a manner suitable to his greatness. The generality of christians, it is to be feared, go to this sacrament like beasts to their food, with little or no thought of what they are about, without shewing any mark of their respect and gratitude to their divine Saviour. They resemble, says a holy Father, swine feeding under an oak, which never lift up their eyes to behold what it is that supplies them with the food they eat. O stupidity, O blindness inconceivable! Be not so thoughtless, O my soul; rather light up the lamp of faith within thee, as often as thou approachest the holy Sacrament to weigh with care all its surprising excellencies. Let it be the employment of thy whole life to prepare thyself for a worthy reception of Jesus Christ in this holy mystery; and omit nothing on thy side, to testify to him thy gratitude for so signal a benefit.

XXXIX. The hungry multitudes that followed our blessed Lord into the wilderness, were not fed the first day of their attending. The five barley loves miraculously multiplied in their behalf, were not distributed to them till the third day: the Son of God, intending, no doubt, by this trial and delay, to dispose them to partake worthily of this bread, which

was

was the figure of the Blessed Eucharist. In like manner, it is not, strictly speaking, proper to admit those to partake of this divine bread, of which the other was only a figure, who are yet but raw and uninstructed beginners, and have but just taken up the yoke of Christ. Like the multitudes that followed our Lord, they must have undergone some labour and fatigue in his service. The master of a family does not make his hired servants begin the day's labour with eating, but employs them some time at work: so is it expected that we should have been employed for some time in the service of the Gospel-housholder (Matt. 20. 1.) before we presume to sit down at his holy table to eat of his bread: for we ought in some measure to have earned our bread before we eat it. *In the sweat of thy face* (Gen. 3. 19.) *shalt thou eat thy bread.*

XL. In former times the deacon that officiated at the consecration of the Eucharist, used to proclaim aloud before the distribution of it, *Sancta sanctis*, Holy things for holy persons: intimating thereby, that things so holy as the Blessed Eucharist, were for none but the holy. It must however be granted, that absolute perfection is not a necessary qualification for a worthy communicant, it being sufficient to be free from the actual guilt of mortal sin, and that the party sincerely tends to christian perfection in obedience to the command of Jesus Christ: Be *ye perfect* (Mat. 5. 48.) *as your heavenly Father is perfect.* This sacrament is no less a remedy for the sick, than a deli-

Chap. II.   *on the Holy Communion.*   49

a delicious food for the found; and as much a *milk* (Heb. 5. 12.) for children as *strong meat* for the robuft. But then it muft not be denied, that in order not to defeat its efficacy, and incur the danger of changing a remedy into poifon? endeavours muft be ufed to recover out of this languid ftate, and to advance in a fpiritual life; this being the proper effect of the Bleffed Eucharift. If a perfon be not completely holy and perfect before receiving, there is at leaft an obligation after having been admitted to the holy table to tend with all the might and powers of the foul to perfection, becaufe we are bound to correfpond with the impreffions of that grace which excites and leads us to it.

XLI. The principal difpofitions we ought to bring with us to Communion, are thefe in fubftance; great purity of foul; a fervent practice of chriftian virtues; an utter abhorrence of fin, how light foever it may appear; a lively forrow for having offended God; a ftedfaft refolution to avoid whatever is difpleafing to him; the devoting ourfelves wholely to his fervice; a firm faith, which implies an entire conviction of the mind of the real prefence of his body and blood in the Bleffed Eucharift; exalted fentiments of efteem, veneration and refpect for the adorable perfon of him that is contained in the facrament; a profound humility, giving us a quick fenfe of our own unworthinefs, and conftantly exciting us to repute ourfelves as nothing in his prefence; a moft ardent love for this divine Saviour; an

E   extreme

extreme longing after this celestial food; a great desire of being united to Christ, of being transformed into him and reaping the fruits of his passion, in this adorable sacrament; a perfect confidence in God's mercy; a profound recollection that may blot out of our mind the remembrance of creatures, and employ us wholly on God; a great fervour in the performance of the *spiritual* excercife before and after communion; an angelical modesty, perfectly composing our whole exterior. These are the dispositions all ought to endeavour to enter into whenever they communicate.

CHAP. III.

Of the benefits we ought to reap from this august mystery.

1. WHAT are we going to do, when we present ourselves at the holy table? We are going to die with Jesus Christ, and make a sacrifice of ourselves together with him to the majesty of God. We declare and shew forth his death, as St. Paul says, by dying with him and like him, to the old man and to all creatures. If after receiving this Sacrament our affections carry us as much as ever towards the world; if we experience in our soul the same love of pleasure, vanity and riches, it is a plain indication

indication that we are not dead with Christ, that we have not as yet crucified with him the old man, that our Communion has been fruitless: it is a sign indeed, that we have received the Sacrament: but not the effect of the Sacrament, which makes us partakers of his death. Let us then die to all that is not God; let us lead a life conformable to the nature of a victim consecrated to the divine Majesty, as we hope to share in that grace which this Sacrament bestows on the worthy receivers.

II. By Communion we are *incorporated* with Jesus Christ; we ought therefore in consequence of it to live by his spirit, because the members ought to live by the life and by the spirit of their head; we must live by him as he lives by his Father. In every particular of our conduct, we ought to act in so strict a conformity to the will of this divine Saviour, as to be influenced and directed by him in every thing, like the members of the natural body, which neither move nor act but as influenced by the head to which they are united. A member not subject to its head, and not receiving from it its motion, would be monstrous: we are in like manner monstrous members, if after having been united to Jesus Christ in this mystery, we are not entirely subject to him, if we are not animated by his spirit, live not by his life, and are not influenced by him in all our actions.

III. A Christian that has been united to Jesus Christ by the means of this divine mystery, ought always to consider to what head he belongs,

belongs, and be careful not to dishonour it by an unworthy and criminal life. He ought never to forget the dignity, the sanctity and the perfection of this head; but to use his best endeavours to maintain its glory by a life conformable to the life of Christ; that is, holy, perfect, and divine.

IV. In the holy Communion we give ourselves to Jesus Christ, and he gives himself to us. We devote ourselves to him to abide in him, and to serve him as instruments in the execution of his will and the accomplishment of his designs. He give himself to us to abide in us and to be the centre of all our affections and desires, the source of our spiritual life, and the spring and governing principal of all our actions. Wherefore after Communion we are no longer at liberty to apply ourselves to any thing but the execution of the designs of the divine Jesus, co operating with him to promote his Father's glory. We are not to perform any actions but such as derive their origin from him, because we have received him within us to be the only principle of our life and of all that is done in us.

V. It being the property of this divine food to transform us into Jesus Christ, we must not therefore return from the holy table, without being wholly changed and transformed into him. To return the same, is a certain proof that we have received the Sacrament without the effect, or without the grace of the Sacrament. If we had received this grace, Jesus Christ would have visibly shone forth in our conduct,

conduct, and we should have been his living images by a lively and faithful imitation of his virtues. What just grounds have we not to fear and tremble on this account? because whatever is an argument of our continuing unchanged, is also an argument of our not having received the grace of the Sacrament, and rendering our Communion suspected of sacriledge. After such a number of Communions shall there not appear in us at least some sketch of the virtues and excellencies of Jesus Christ? not the least visible change, not the least reformation of conduct? Would it be so, if the Sacrament had produced its effect? and if it has not, have we not reason to fear that our Communions have have been so many sacrileges? Who can help being seized with dread, at the very thought of this truth?

VI. Communion being, according to the holy fathers, an extension of the Incarnation or hypostatical union, it must also be an extension of the graces with which the sacred humanity of Jesus Christ was endowed in the Incarnation; and as this was replenished thereby with a superabundance of those, which is in some degree infinite; we must also by Communion be in a condition of receiving graces in some measure infinite. How then comes it to pass that after Communion we find ourselves so void of graces? Alas! it is greatly to be feared as this is owing to our supposed union with Jesus Christ that it is only such in outward show and not in truth and reality.

VII. The

VII. The sacred humanity of Christ by its union with the divine Word or second person in the Godhead, was always impeccable; for the members of Jesus Christ contribute in no wise to iniquity. (Rom. 6. 13.) The union we contract with him in this august sacrament, ought also to make us in some degree impeccable, that is, it ought to prevent our making our members the instruments of sin. If then we still observe in ourselves certain remains of the *body* (Rom. 7. 24.) *of sin*, which are certain weaknesses and frailties we cannot entirely rid ourselves of, at least let there be nothing in them of the *spirit* of sin, which is an affection or voluntary attachment to these faults; let us never more commit them deliberately, how immaterial soever they may appear.

VIII. In this august sacrament we eat and receive into us life, and we there make an eternal alliance with life; but he that hath done this ought to die no more. How shall he die, says, St. Ambrose, whose very food is life? He that has consecrated his heart to life to be its eternal mansion, ought never more to return to the death of sin. We wash, says St. Ambrose, at Communion the inner garments of the soul in the blood of the lamb; but he that has done this should be aware how he fouls them afresh by committing new sins.

IX. The Israelites heretofore (Exod. 12. 15.) were enjoined not only to eat the paschal lamb with unleavened bread, and not to suffer any leaven to remain in their houses while they were eating it; but were also ordered to eat the

the same unleavened bread, and to admit no leaven into their houses on any consideration during the seven days that immediately followed the eating of the paschal lamb. This was a figure that the worthy communicant ought to be pure and free from the guilt of sin, not only in the actual receiving the Sacrament, but that he should also preserve the same purity after receiving, and abstain from sin the whole term of this life, intimated by the seven days of the week upon which the circle of our lives turn.

X. This mystery is the christian Passover, that is, our passage to a heavenly and immortal life, such an one as Jesus Christ entered upon at his resurrection. We ought not, in consequence, to continue any longer in our former life after having partaken of this passover, but must enter upon a new life, a life altogether heavenly and divine; and we incur the guilt of a kind of sacrilege when we act otherwise, as we thereby render the signification of this sacrament false, and its virtue barren.

XI. This great mystery according to St. Chrysostom, raises us from the earth and translates us to heaven. It furnishes us with wings for taking our flight into the bosom of the Divinity, that we may be united to, and absorpt in God. We are in some degree even deified by it. If after having partaken of it we continue the same imperfect christians, and still lie groveling upon the earth by our attachment

its virtue. Let us then amuse ourselves no longer with earthly things, after having partaken so often of this heavenly sacrament; let us take wing like mystical eagles, and direct our flight to heaven where our future abode and conversation (Phil. 3. 20.) are to be: let us lead a life quite heavenly and divine.

XII. The virtues are so many mystical plants that grow admirably, and produce plenty of exquisite fruit by being sprinkled with the blood of Jesus Christ. As therefore we are sprinkled with this blood in the adorable Sacrament of the altar, which contains him really and substantially, all virtues should flourish by it, and become wonderfully fruitful in good works.

XIII. The Israelites, by means of the manna became possessed of a kind of immortality because it preserved life in them without the use of terrestrial food, and because they neither wore out their garments nor their shoes during the whole time of its being their food. But it was no more than a bare figure of what this divine manna operates in us. It translates us in some measure, even before our final dissolution, into a kind of eternity, by giving us here below a foretaste of the joys of blessed above. We are no longer beholden to earthly food for our sustenance, while we partake in the manner we ought of this divine nourishment, because we feed no longer on worldly vanities, nor continue fond of a voluptuous and worldly life. On the contrary, we are sustained by the bread of heaven, as it is in partaking of

that

that food that we seek our comfort, and lead the life of the blessed in heaven. The garments of the inward man, I mean our virtues, are no longer liable to decay, because we never desist from the practice of them, during the whole remaining course of our life.

XIV. The holy scripture observes, (Pf. 104. 37.) that from the time the Israelites eat the paschal lamb, till their leaving Egypt, they were not afflicted with any disease. They were all endued with sufficient health and vigour, to quit Pharoah's dominions, to pass through the Red Sea, and to offer sacrifice to God in the wilderness. In like manner, there ought to be no distempers nor languors among the faithful, after having had the happiness of feeding on this divine lamb. They ought all to be sufficiently healthy and robust, for shaking off the tyrannical yoke of Satan, for passing through the red sea of toils and difficulties, which they experience in consequence of their late change of life, and for withdrawing into solitude, in order to a total application of their minds to God.

XV. On part of the character of the virtuous woman (described Prov. 30.) consisted in her not eating the *bread* (Prov. 3. 27.) *of idleness*. After eating what was *sufficient* for the support of nature, she applied herself with diligence to her houshold affairs, and the several duties of her station. Thus ought every Cristian, after partaking of the eucharistical bread, to apply himself to the affairs of his salvation, and acquit himself in the best manner of his
several

several duties and obligations. We contract much guilt by indulging idleness; and what excuse can be alleged in our behalf, when nothing is done by us, though aided by so powerful a succour as the Blessed Eucharist.

XVI. One of these reasons why the most strengthening food is of no service, but turns to corruption in the stomach, is a defect of natural heat, and not using proper exercise to concoct and digest it. The reason also why we reap no benefit from partaking the Blessed Eucharist, is, that charity is cold within us, and that we do not sufficiently apply ourselves to the practice of good works. A great degree of love, and an assidious and vigorous application to labour are very necessary to prevent this divine food from lying heavy and turning into corruption in our stomach, especially when frequently partaken of.

XVII. In the holy Eucharist we have a free access to an ocean of graces; yet when we leave the holy table we hardly bring back with us a small drop for quenching our thirst. Whence comes this, but because the vessel we bring with us is already full, or contains but very little? It is already full, being filled up with sinful desires, and irregular affections for the things of this world. Its capaciousness is very small, because we have no relish, no longing for heavenly things. Ah! let us empty this vessel in order to its being filled, as St. Augustine says. Let us banish from our hearts all our attachments to the world, and make place for heavenly graces. Let us dilate and expand them

them still more, by a profound humility, which may make us sensible how unworthy we are of them; and by assiduous and fervent prayer, render our hearts capable of receiving them in greater abundance.

XVIII. One of the greatest, and most just reasons of fear for the salvation of our souls, is the small advantage we reap from the use of this divine sacrament, and of such efficacy for our sanctification as is that of the altar. It is not to be questioned, but that as often as it is worthily received, it in some degree increases grace, charity, and the other virtues that are the inseparable attendants of charity. A thousand Communions ought in consequence to increase by a thousand degrees all those qualities, and make us possess them in an eminent degree of perfection. But since we can discover no such proportionate increase in our souls, we have but too just reason to fear that our Communions have not been attended with suitable dispositions. I tremble, O my God, when I reflect on the number of my Communions, and that I have profited so little by them; and have I not just grounds for my apprehensions on this score? For if the unprofitable servant had a righteous sentence of condemnation passed upon him, for having not embezzled, but only buried his master's talent, what will become of me, who have so often lost and squandered it away, by my abusing the grace of this same sacrament?

XIX. What are those engaging charms of thine, O deceitful world, for captivating a
soul

soul which has been feasted with the spiritual delights this divine sacrament abounds with? How tasteless and insipid, are thy pleasures, when compared with the heavenly delights vouchsafed by it to the worthy communicant? Thy false riches put in balance with the invaluable treasures he there acquires? thy fading honours with the incomparable glory to which he is raised? Ah! how criminal should I be, if having had so great a treasure bestowed upon me, I still sought after possessions of any other kind? This mystery lays me under the strictest obligation to renounce every thing foreign to it, and I do it a very signal injury, if I still cherish any inordinate desire or inclination.

XX. How great do you think your obligations would have been to the Son of God, had he become incarnate, and died for none but yourself! what demonstrations of gratitude would not you have thought incumbent on you for so immense a favour? But, in the opinion of a great Saint, you are not less obliged to Jesus Christ for partaking of his blood in the Blessed Sacrament, than if he had shed it on the cross for you alone. And as he has so very often made you partaker of that same blood, at the holy table, you are no less obliged to him for it, than if he had made a sacrifice of himself for you alone, on the altar of the cross. You may see by this what obligations this sacrament lays you under, and what heroic actions of virtue it justly challenges at you hands, that you may avoid the odious sin of ingratitude.

XXI. Jesus

XXI. Jesus Christ in this sacrament, gives us his body for our food, with no other view than to communicate to us his spirit, and so inspire us with a holy zeal for acquiring the most perfect virtues. Though a man had received this sacrament but once in his whole life, he would be obliged by this single Communion to labour with all his might for acquiring every Christian virtue, in the highest degree; what then, what must be said of those who have communicated very often! How shall we sufficiently set forth the extent and greatness of this obligation?

XXII. What a high degree of sanctity, what sublime perfection does not this wonderful sacrament require of us? There is nothing in this world that should induce us more effectually to aspire to perfection, than this adorable sacrament, and for these reasons: First, it being the greatest benefit that divine love ever bestowed upon us, we ought to strive to make the best return in our power for it, by our respect and services. For as God in some measure bestows himself to enrich and raise us up, we ought, in like manner, to exhaust ourselves, by exerting every power and faculty to serve and honour him, in leading a holy and divine life. Secondly, having Jesus Christ before our eyes, in this sacrament, who there sets us an example of all virtues in a sovereign degree of perfection, and invites us to tread in his steps; can any one think himself excused from following and imitating him, and consequently from aspiring to the highest virtues. Thirdly, we here

here receive the moſt powerful ſuccours for our advancement in the ways of grace; and it is the property of this great ſacrament, to raiſe us to the higheſt perfection, and to the moſt conſummate ſanctity. Laſtly, we take upon ourſelves the obligation of tending to perfection by league and covenant with Jeſus Chriſt which we renew with him as often as we communicate; for the participation of his body in the Bleſſed Euchariſt, obliges us not only to a participation of his ſpirit, to prevent a monſtrous ſeparation of the one from the other, but alſo of his ſentiments, his fervour, his deſires, his actions, his ſufferings and his perfections; we are obliged to a participation of all theſe things, and conſequently to be holy and perfect as he is.

XXIII. St. Chryſoſtom does not heſitate to ſay, that the exceeding great liberality and magnificent treatment Jeſus Chriſt honours us with in this divine ſacrament, impoſes on us the obligation of ſurpaſſing, even the angels and archangels in virtue and holineſs, becauſe he therein heaps more honour upon us, and beſtows upon us more graces than he ever granted to thoſe bleſſed ſpirits, becauſe he never communicated himſelf to the angels in a manner ſo glorious to them, or which exalts ſo much their nature. I affirm that he therein beſtows more graces upon us; firſt becauſe the grace of Jeſus Chriſt, which is the grace of the redeemer, is more powerful and perfect than that which is not the fruit of his blood, ſuch as was, in the opinion of moſt divines,

that

that grace beſtowed upon the firſt man and upon the angels. Grace by paſſing through Jeſus Chriſt, aſſumed in him certain characters of excellence and efficacy which are peculiar to it. Secondly, becauſe the angels received but a part, and as it were a rivulet of grace, whereas man receives here the entire ſource; ſo that finding himſelf raiſed by means of this divine myſtery above the angels, he is alſo under an obligation of ſurpaſſing thoſe bleſſed ſpirits, by the eminence and perfection of his virtue and ſanctity.

XXIV. The faithful, in the legal phraſe, ought to be *clean animals*, chewing eternally the cud of the celeſtial paſture on which they feed: but that which they ought to chew the cud of with the greateſt reliſh, is that euchariſtical meat, particularly on the day they ſacramentally fed upon it at the holy table. It is therefore their duty on that day frequently to recall this to remembrance, that by ruminating upon it they may taſte over again its ſweetneſs, extract the virtue of it, retain its ſpirit, and clothe themſelves with its ſtrength. The more the worthy receiver ruminates upon it, the more nouriſhment it affords him, the more it ſtrengthens his ſoul, enlightens his underſtanding, inflames his heart, purifies his body, and ſanctifies both the inward and outward man. It will not be amiſs too for a man ſometimes to call to mind all his paſt Communions, that by reflecting on them all at once, they may all with united power communicate to him greater virtue, fill him with greater ſtrength,

F 2   inflame

inflame him with greater charity, inspire him with a more lively ardour and more generous courage for making a more rapid progress in the ways of grace.

XXV. Where our treasure (Mat. 6. 21.) is, there our heart is also. It is on our altars and in our tabernacles, that our treasure lies concealed: so that whatever we are, we ought to turn all the affections of our hearts towards this treasure, and make it the subject of our most respectful and submissive homage and adoration. The blessed Jesus himself has the eyes of his mind ever fixed upon us; he has us always present to him to make an offering of us to his eternal Father, for drawing down his graces upon us. In that great number of parts of the habitable earth, in which he has as it were multiplied by the real presence of his body and blood, there is not one in which his thoughts are not continually employed about every one of us, and in which he does not interest himself with his Father for promoting the great affair of our salvation. Ought we to do less for him than he has the charity to do for us? and is it not therefore reasonable that he should be the subject and entertainment of our thoughts, and that we should in some measure multiply ourselves, by desire and in spirit, to present ourselves before him in every part of the earth, which he honours with his sacramental presence, and to pay him every where the most perfect adoration we are able, and perform to him the most religious worship, which is in our power?

· CHAP.

CHAP. IV.

A method for approaching with advantage to the Holy Sacrament.

I. THE method for worthily receiving the blessed Eucharist comprehends two parts: the first is the Preparation, the second is the Thanksgiving: both which are subdivided; so that there is a *remote*, as well as an *immediate* exercise of both kinds.

The Remote Preparation is that which takes place at some distance of time before Communion, and answers to the preparation made for the reception of a king in one of his cities, before the ceremony which accompanies his entrance. This preparation consists in three particulars:

The first is a great purity of heart, whereby a strict guard is kept, not only against mortal sins, for which we conceive an utter abhorrence, but even against venial sins which we earnestly endeavour to avoid. For it is quite unseemly and shameful, that a person who approaches frequently to the source of all purity, in the sacrament of the Eucharist, should wilfully and deliberately defile himself with venial sins; such as officious lies, slight detractions, spurts of anger, some transient motions of aversion, contempt of our neighbour and the like.

Because

Because though venial sins do not kill Christ in our heart, they are notwithstanding like so many wounds given him: they bring not death on our souls, but they are filthy mud which stains and fouls the nuptial garment; or like ulcers which tarnish the beauty and disfigure the face of the soul, and so displease Jesus Christ. For this reason a soul that frequents this sacrament ought to avoid, with the utmost caution, all sins of this kind, committed with full consent and deliberation; those especially against the virtues of charity, chastity, humility, and obedience, which are of all others the most opposite to the grace of this sacrament. Whoever therefore has contracted the guilt of such sins, should not fail to have recourse to the sacrament of penance, to be washed clean from them (a duty of strict obligation in the case of mortal sin): he should also break off entirely all attachment to them before he presents himself at the holy table.

The second thing required by remote preparation, is the constant practice of all virtues: for it is not sufficient to clear that house of the filth of sin into which Jesus Christ is to be received, it must also be embellished with the ornaments of virtue. The life of those that frequent this sacrament, ought to be one continued exercise of good works. But those who waste their time in idleness and frivolous amusements, or, who do not spend it in the service of the evangelical housholder; (Matt 20. 1.) deserve not to eat of his bread, intended only for the support of those labourers who work in his

his vineyard. Those, therefore, who approach frequently to the holy table, ought, in the first place, to have stated hours for prayer, meditation, spiritual reading, examination of conscience, &c. In the second place they ought to be no less diligent and regular in the distribution of their alms, in their fasts and mortifications. In the third place, they ought to acquit themselves punctually, and with a christian spirit, of the duties peculiar to their condition and state of life; performing all their actions with a sincere desire of pleasing God, and practising with fervour christian virtues, those especially which shine forth so eminently in this sacrament, namely, charity, humility, obedience and meekness: and for some days before Communion, but especially on the day itself, they should make an offering to God of all their actions by way of preparation for the worthy receiving of this sacrament. And as to such as communicate daily, or several times in the week, they ought to make a daily offering of all their actions, both by way of thanksgiving for past Communions, and of preparation for those that are to follow.

The third thing included in the remote preparation, is prayer and recollection. It is proper that for several days before we purpose to communicate, we should make frequent and serious reflections on the dignity of this august sacrament; and the consummate dispositions required in those that approach to it, the wonderful effects it produces in those that receive it worthily, and the dreadful judgments those

draw

draw upon themselves who receive it unworthily: God is moreover to be intreated by many short, but fervent prayers, of the ejaculatory kind, that he would vouchsafe to infuse into our souls those dispositions, which may qualify us to receive him to our advantage. Certain elevations, or forms of prayer, are here set down for the help of those that stand in need of such a succour. They may make use of them, repeating with fervour, sometimes one, sometimes another, as they find themselves most affected; or, at least, in the morning of the day they are to communicate, they may spend a little time at home in devoutly repeating them altogether.

What has been hitherto said on this subject relates to the distant or remote preparation for Communion, that which is called proximate, or immediate, consists in a series of pious thoughts and affections, which immediately precede the holy Communion, and is of a similar nature to the actual pomp and ceremony with which a king is received into some city of his dominions. It is of great moment to acquit ourselves well of this exercise, because, if performed with fervour and devotion, it disposes us to draw from this sacrament extraordinary succours and graces, which we forfeit by a superficial and negligent performance of it. We ought on this account to set a guard upon our exteriour senses, and stir up all the powers of our soul to perform this part in a proper manner. Those who are blest with a

relish

Chap. IV. *on the Holy Communion.* 69

relish and facility for mental prayer, may consider.

1. With a lively faith, on one side, the excellence and perfections of him that comes to them, concealed under the sacramental veils, and on the other, their own baseness and unworthiness. They may also continue for some time in sentiments of the most profound humility at the feet of this adorable majesty, taken up entirely with paying him their most respectful homage, and acknowledging their miseries and nothingness.

2. They may admire the excess of goodness which Jesus Christ testifies for them, by crowning all his other mercies with this the greatest of them all; detesting at the same time their own malice, bewailing with sighs and groans the multitude and enormity of their sins; and humbly asking him pardon for them with a sincere and lively sorrow.

3. They may enter in spirit into the divine heart of Jesus, to consider the ardent love he bears them, which induces him to desire an intimate union with them; and they may hereby excite themselves to a return of love for so much goodness, and to produce the most fervent acts of love they are capable of forming.

4. They may weigh in their minds the wonderful advantages which will accrue to them from the possession of so great a good; excite themselves to the most ardent desires of possessing it, and hope by this means to be supplied with all the helps they may have occasion for.

5. They may reflect on the sublime sanctity
which

which so great a sacrament requires in the receiver, and be thence covered with shame to see themselves at so great a distance from it; for which reason they should beg of Jesus Christ to clothe them with his sanctity and that of his saints and holy angels, and offer it up to supply what is wanting on their part.

6. They may pass in review the mysteries of Christ's passion, of which this sacrament is a memorial; thank him for having suffered so much for them; sympathize with his sufferings; beg pardon for having been the cause of them, and beseech him to apply to their souls the benefits of them in this sacrament.

7. They may consider the excellency of that unbloody sacrifice which Jesus Christ offers on the altar, the glory which this sacrifice procures to God, and the graces it draws down upon men: offering it conjointly with Jesus Christ, and with the same intentions he offers it; offering also themselves in quality of victim.

8. They may purpose going to Communion with the design of uniting themselves with Jesus Christ, and entering into a strict league and covenant with him, by eating his flesh; with the design also of making him reign in their hearts, of being transformed into him, and of dying with him to the world, to sin and to all creatures.

9. They may invite him, with the most earnest and affectionate desires, to take entire possession of their hearts.

10. They

10. They may also make the gospel of the day the subject of their meditation, by applying it to the purposes of Communion. But all these meditations must be performed, not in a cold and languid manner, but earnest, animated and fervent, such as may make a deep impression on their souls of the sentiments above recited. Such as have neither the same relish for this sort of prayer, nor are so ready at it, ought, towards preparing themselves, to produce divers acts of faith, hope and charity, contrition, humility, petition, desire and the like.

It would be of greater service, and attended with better effect, if every one was to form them himself, instead of borrowing them from books, as thus they would be more fervent and spirited. But as few are capable of this, and as even those who are, do not always find themselves in a situation of mind that will permit them; those acts are drawn out here to a full length together with the Elevations, which are intended to serve for the remote preparation. Devout Entertainments have been also formed for each day of the week, in behalf of priests and others that communicate often. Those whom they suit, may make use of them: others will find at least in them sufficient matter for the purposes they require.

The immediate thanksgiving consists in the devotions which immediately follow Communion, and is so called, because the giving of thanks constitutes its principal part, in which the rest are in some measure included.

It

It is of the highest importance to perform this part well. For as we have Christ at that time actually residing within us, and as he pours forth his graces in great abundance on those that ask them, and endeavour by their respectful behaviour to qualify themselves for them, it is the most precious time, and the most favourable opportunity of our whole life, for obtaining from him extraordinary favours.

We should therefore be exceeding careful to avail ourselves of these happy moments. Those whom God has favoured with the gift of prayer may on this occasion endeavour:

1. To thank Jesus Christ with sentiments of the most profound gratitude, for having vouchsafed to give himself to them in the way of food: admiring the greatness of the benefit, with that excess of love, which induced this divine Saviour to bestow it; and inviting all the creatures of the universe to join with them in a due return of thanks.

2. To adore him as their king, and as their God, with all the sentiments of the greatest respect and veneration they are capable of; and to join the holy angels and the blessed in heaven in adoring him with them.

3. To render homage for their being, for their life, for all that they are, and for all that they possess; to consecrate themselves entirely to him, to protest that they will henceforward employ themselves wholly in his service, and to ask him pardon over again for the offences they have committed against him.

4. To

4. To offer this adorable victim to the Eternal Father as an acknowledgment of his supreme power and greatness, as a thanksgiving for his benefits, as a satisfaction for the sins they have committed, and to obtain from his bounty the graces they stand in need of.

5. To offer also themselves as joint victims with Jesus Christ, together with the Church, both militant and triumphant, to the glory of the adorable Trinity; to the honour of the sacred Humanity of Jesus Christ; to the honour of the Blessed Virgin and all the saints, and holy angels, and for all the necessities of the Catholic church and her children.

6. To join in all the acts of adoration, love, praise and others performed by Jesus Christ, for honouring his Father through him; and with him.

7. To lay before this divine Saviour their own miseries and necessities; those of the public, and of such private persons as have been recommended to them, or with whom they have any connection; and to entreat him earnestly to relieve them.

8. To renew their good resolutions in general, and to purpose to themselves in particular the conquering of some vice or of some singularly dangerous passion; and the confirming themselves in the practice of some most necessary virtue.

As to such persons as have received of God the gift of passive prayer, they need not put themselves to the trouble of going over all the points here specified, either by way of thanksgiving, or preparation for Communion : they may be guided by what their devotion suggests, or dwell only on the principal points, or on whatever it shall please God to employ their minds. There are some who have a particular liking for making the passion of Christ the subject of their devotions on this occasion, and they find therein great consolation; they may accordingly meditate on its mysteries, either in the preparation or in the thanksgiving, by applying to this mystery, which is the representation, and in some sort the renewal of the death of their redeemer.

Acts are here made on all the heads just now recited, for the use of those who cannot so easily form them themselves. They may repeat them after Communion, but this must be done with great fervour and devotion.

The Remote thanksgiving is that which is performed during the remaining part of the day of Communion, or even for several days after; for it is of great use and advantage to employ several days in thanking Jesus Christ for so great a benefit, and the same may be said of our preparation for receiving him. This remote thanksgiving consists in three things: first, In preserving our whole heart for Jesus Christ, taking care not to suffer creatures to rob him of the least part of it, or permit its purity to be stained with the least sin. Secondly, In corresponding faithfully with the grace of this sacrament, by doing all our actions with perfection, and in a spirit of love and gratitude,

titude, and carefully practising virtue as occasions offer during the course of the day. Thirdly, In raising our hearts frequently to Jesus Christ in thanksgiving to him for the favours received, and inviting all the creatures of the universe to join us in thanking him, and in beseeching him to operate in them effects worthy of his greatness. Elevations have been formed for this purpose, and they succeed the acts which are calculated for the immediate thanksgiving.

A Preparatory Exercise for Sacramental Confession.

Elevation before the examination of conscience, to beg of God that he would make our sins known to us.

ETERNAL source of light who searchest the reins and the heart of man, and to whom nothing is hidden, I am come to entreat thee to enlighten my mind, that by the help of thy divine light I may discern the true state of my conscience, and know the sins I am guilty of before thee. Say then, Lord, as heretofore, *fiat lux*, let there be light: send forth thy light into my soul that it may dispel the thick darkness that surrounds me; shew me to myself such as I am in thy sight, that fully conscious to myself of the number and enormity of my sins, I may be able to accuse myself of them at the tribunal of confession, and obtain pardon for them. Enlighten me with a ray of that divine light which thou wilt shed on my soul at the moment of her separation from the body, when upon the point of appearing at thy dreadful tribunal; that sensible of the deformity of my sins, I may make some attonement for them in the sacrament of penance. Shew them to me in such a light as is most proper to fill me with horror and confusion, and inspire me with a hearty sorrow for them. Pour forth into my heart the sentiments of a true and sincere contrition, that I may deplore and detest them, so as to obtain the remission of them. Suffer me not to impose upon myself by a false repentance, which would serve only to aggravate my guilt. I beg this grace of thee, O Lord, with the greater earnestness, it being very difficult to conceive in the heart all the sorrow that is necessary for being benefited by this sacrament, and the more so, as this sorrow is rarely met with.

* The penitent in the next place is to examine himself upon the commandments of God, and of the church; on the seven capital sins; the duties of his station in life; the business he has transacted, and the occasions he has been in. A competent time must be allowed for this examination, that the penitent may become acquainted with the state of his conscience, and the sins he has committed. Those that live regularly, and lead a christian life,

life, will find in the sequel a form of confession, comprehending a pretty extensive enumeration of such sins as they usually fall into, and this will be a great help to them for discovering these sins. The penitent, after having acquired a competent knowledge of the state of his soul with regard to the sins he has committed, must excite himself to a sincere sorrow for them from the most cogent motives, and must form a true and sincere resolution of amendment. It is to be feared that the greater part of the confessions of those people especially who are much engaged in the world, are no better than so many sacrileges, through the want of a sincere sorrow for their sins and a firm purpose of amendment. This appears but too plainly from their constant relapses into mortal sin, from as strong an attachment as ever to the things of this world, and a kind of contempt for those of heaven. We ought therefore to be particularly careful in exciting ourselves to a true contrition for our sins. It would be proper for this purpose to reflect seriously on this for some days before we confess, that we may raise compunction in our hearts by considering the enormity and multitude of our sins, and by animated and fervent ejaculations towards almighty God. The act of contrition here set forth, may serve for asking God pardon for our sins; but they must be recited in such manner, that what the mouth utters the heart may feel and be warmly affected by.

An act of Contrition for such as are conscious to themselves of the guilt of Mortal Sin.

O God of infinite majesty, I am so full of confusion for the ingratitude, perfidiousness, and malice I acknowledge myself guilty of, and particularly for the sins I have committed since my last confession, that I dare not appear in thy presence. I confess O great God, I confess that I have deserved to be a thousand times struck dead by thy thunder, and sunk as often into the abyss of hell for the multitude and enormity of my offences. Ah! wretch that I am, how have I had the rashness to offend thee, thou art greatness, power, goodness, wisdom, and beauty itself, and infinite in all perfections! thou who art my God, my creator, my beginning and last end, my happiness, and my all! thou from whom I have received being, life, and all that I am; and who hast created heaven and earth with all they contain, for the love of me? Thou who hast constantly sustained and preserved me, provided for me, protected and cherished me under the shadow of thy wings? thou, in fine, who hast adopted me for thy child, made me the heir of thy kingdom, and of all thy wealth; hast given me thy only Son in the mystery of the incarnation, and admitted me so often to a participation of his sacred flesh and blood in that of the Blessed Eucharist. But notwithstanding so many, and such great benefits, I have offended thee,

thee, O my God, numberless ways; I have deserted thee to take part with thy enemies against thee; I have forsaken thee for a vain honour, a frivolous pleasure, a trivial interest. I have preferred to thee the meanest of thy creatures, and chosen rather the pleasure of enjoying them for a moment, than the eternal fruition of thee and all thy riches, Oh ingratitude! Oh infatuation! Oh madness! What was become of my judgment and understanding when I give myself up to such prodigious excesses of malice? Oh! how I detest my ingratitude, how I abhor my crimes, and how sensibly I am afflicted for my sinful behaviour? Oh! that I could deplore it as it deserves? How I could wish that my heart might burst this instant with grief for having offended its God! that all the veins of my body might empty themselves, by my eyes in tears of blood to form an inundation wherein I might drown all my iniquities! that all the marrow of my bones might dry up through the greatness of my affliction! that all my flesh might melt away through the excess of my sorrow; and that I might finally die with grief for having offended so good and gracious a God!

But thou, O Lord, whose goodness and mercy know no bounds, wilt thou not cast an eye of pity on me, and grant me pardon for my crimes? I acknowledge myself unworthy of it in all respects, more especially on account of my faithless promises and frequent relapses. So great notwithstanding is thy mercy and charity for poor sinners, that I dare hope thou wilt
grant

grant me the pardon I now humbly crave. Yes, pardon, Lord, pardon: I earnestly beg it of thee through the merits of the blood of Jesus Christ, and by the labours, afflictions and sorrows of all thy penitent saints, which I offer unto thee to supply whatever is deficient in my repentance. Forget all my iniquities, blot them out of thy remembrance; I am resolved, by the help of thy divine grace, never to fall again into them; no, there is an end put to them, from this moment I renounce forever the world, the flesh, the devil, and sin; this very moment in good earnest I return to thee never to forsake thee more. Neither honour, interest, pleasure, human respects, nor any thing else shall ever hereafter prevail with me to transgress thy divine commandments; I will keep them inviolably, tho' it should cost me a thousand times my life, and every thing that is dearest to me in the world; It is with the hopes, Lord, of thy granting me pardon, that I am going to present myself in the tribunal of penance; that the sentence of absolution the priest shall pronounce upon me in thy name, may save me from the rigours of thy justice at the last day Amen.

A Prayer to JESUS CHRIST.

DIVINE Redeemer, whose love I have unhappily slighted, whose blood I have trampled upon, whose wounds I have caused to bleed afresh,

afresh, and whose death I have renewed as often as I abandoned myself to sin; how dare I appear in thy presence after such excesses of ingratitude and malice? I am so filled with confusion for them, that I dare not lift up my eyes to heaven; and all creatures seem to me to rise up continually against me to upbraid me with them. Amiable Saviour, what hadst thou done to me to deserve at my hands such unworthy treatment, thou who hadst always loved me with such unparalled tenderness? Didst thou not suffer sufficiently for my salvation during thy mortal life? was it possible that I should be guilty of fresh outrages against thee even in thy state of immortality? could I be capable of extending my madness so far as to add new wounds to the former? What affliction, what uneasiness have I not given to thy loving heart by robbing thee of the fruit of thy blood, by depriving myself of all the advantages thou didst procure for me by shedding it for me on the cross? Thou didst reconcile me with thy Father by thy death, and yet by my crimes I have drawn down a new upon myself his just anger and indignation; thou didst rescue me from the bondage of the devil, and yet I am again entangled in his chains. Thou didst heal my wounds; and yet I have given myself new ones; thou didst deliver me from the flames of hell to which I had been condemned for my sins, and yet I gave headlong again into the same misery. Thou didst, in fine, merit heaven for me, and yet I sold the right which thou hadst acquired for me at the price of thy blood

blood for a trifling pleasure, for a sordid interest. What folly, stupidity, or malice can be imagined equal to mine? Ah! I acknowledge it, Lord, here before thee, I detest it from the bottom of my heart, my sorrow for it exceeds all sorrows, and I beg thy pardon a thousand times; resolved to do penance for it the remainder of my days, and to die a thousand deaths rather than return again to my former course of sin. Wilt thou, then my Saviour, reject a contrite and humble sinner, thou who camest from heaven to call sinners to repentance? Wilt thou shut the door of thy mercy against a poor wretch that knocks at it, thou who hast commanded him to knock? Wilt thou turn away this lost sheep which comes back to thee after going astray, thou who hast been so long in quest of it to bring it back? Wilt thou cast off from thee this prodigal child, who comes to throw himself at thy feet, thou who hast so much bewailed his destruction? Wilt thou suffer me to groan longer under the insupportable weight of sin, thou who hast invited with so much tenderness those that are laden with it to come to thee and lay down their burthens at thy feet? In a word, wilt thou refuse me pardon for having so often abused thy goodness and relapsed into my sins, thou who hast commanded us to pardon all that do us wrong, without limitation of number, or degree of injuries? Thou didst absolve the sinful woman when she came to throw herself at thy feet: thou didst forgive the publican his sins on his humbling himself for them:

thou

thou didſt ſhew mercy to the thief crucified with thee upon his repentance and ſincere converſion; and we do not find that thou didſt ever reject any ſinner that had recourſe to thy clemency by ſincere repentance. Shall I be the only one to whom thou wilt refuſe pardon? No, merciful Saviour, no: I hope that how unworthy of pardon ſoever I have made myſelf, thou wilt be ſo gracious as to grant it me, and reinſtate me in favour with thy Father. O Jeſus Saviour, I have no hopes but in thee: thou art my only refuge and reſource. I have no other protector, mediator, advocate with thy Father but thee; nothing leſs than thy precious blood can appeaſe his wrath which is kindled againſt me, and blot out the ſtains of my ſins. Offer it therefore to him I beſeech thee in my behalf, and apply to my ſoul the ſaving efficacy of it ſo perfectly in the ſacrament of penance, that I may be interiorly purified by that *fountain open for waſhing of the ſinner and the unclean*: (Zach. 13. 1.) that when I come to appear at thy tribunal I may be qualified to enter thoſe manſions where nothing defiled ſhall ever find admittance.

Upon Mortal Sin.

MORTAL ſin, thou furious monſter, that doſt riſe up againſt God himſelf, that attackeſt all his adorable perfections, that tendeſt to deſtroy and annihilate them. Oh! how I abhor

and

and detest thee? A thousand deaths, and a thousand torments do not appear to me afflicted with so many terrors as thou art. I had rather suffer them, than ever admit thee again into my soul. Alas! how great has been my folly, nay, my madness, to fly in the face of my God, my heavenly Father, and to be guilty of such horrid outrages against him, as I have been! Wretch that I am, to have crucified anew my loving Saviour, and have put him to death in my soul as often as I have incurred the guilt of mortal sin!

What ingratitude, what malice ever equalled mine? The very moment I was receiving with one hand the most signal graces and favours from that affectionate Father, I plunged a poignard with the other into his bosom; I crucified him a second time within myself. To what greater lengths could ingratitude and barbarity be carried? Oh! weep, weep my eyes, to drown in your tears so horrible a parricide.

Miserable creature that I am! I have bartered away my soul to the devil for a trifling gratification; I have given up all right to the kingdom of heaven, for a frivolous amusement; I have ratified the sentence of my eternal damnation, by consenting to a brutal passion; I have incurred eternal punishment in devouring flames, for the sake of a sordid interest. What blindness and stupidity can be imagined equal to mine? It is, however, what now I acknowledge myself guilty of; O Lord, before thee, and I most humbly crave thy pardon for it.

Thou

Thou hardened heart of mine! thou, that notwithstanding the many grievous injuries thou haft been guilty of against thy God, and the moſt dreadful misfortunes thou haſt brought upon thyſelf, art ſo little ſenſible of the iniquity of thy meaſures, and beholdeſt with ſuch coldneſs and unconcern thy ill conduct, how long wilt thou perſiſt in thy obduracy? Pardon, O God, pardon not only my ſins, but ſtill more my impenitence and the inſenſibility of my heart. Smite, O God, ſmite this rock, ſoften its hardneſs, make torrents of tears to flow from it; inſpire me with ſentiments of a ſincere compunction, of a lively ſorrow, of a perfect repentance. Make me to know, and ſo ſenſibly to feel the malice and enormity of my ſins, that I may die here at thy feet of grief, for having offended thee.

Could I think of no other way of ſpending my life than making it one continued ſeries of crimes, than ſinking deeper and deeper into the mire of ſin, than falling from one precipice into another; devoting myſelf now to one vicious paſſion, and now to another, and thus becoming a baſe ſlave to all? Could I form the leaſt pretenſions to heaven, while I lived at this abominable rate? Do not I know that none but thoſe whoſe life is without blemiſh, can have any hopes of entering there? Shall my whole life then be nothing but one continued ſucceſſion of riſing and falling? Can I be ignorant that theſe diſmal alternatives are the ſtrongeſt proof of the falſhood of my repentance, and an almoſt certain ſign and forerunner

runner of my eternal reprobation; since dogs, that is, thofe who by relapfing into fin, return to their vomit, (2. Peter. 2. 22.) ftand excluded from the holy City? There is no moral affurance of falvation, but for fouls that are fettled and fixed for a long time in the good habit of leading a pure and innocent life, free from all mortal fin.

It is this pure, this innocent life, O Lord, that I am now entering upon; determined, with the help of thy grace, to acquire the habit of never committing any mortal fin. For this purpofe, I will lead as retired a life as my ftation will allow of. I will fhun all wicked and dangerous company, and other like occafions of fin. I will not engage in the commerce of the world, nor in affairs that may prejudice the intereft of my foul. I will have ftated hours for prayer and recollection, for pious reading, and other fpiritual exercifes; I will keep a watchful eye over my felf; and if at any time I am folicited to break thy commandments, I will keep my felf fteady to my duty. Ah! what can be dearer to me than my falvation? Shall I for a foolifh pleafure, for a trifling intereft, irrecoverably lofe my foul? No; I heartily defire to be faved; I will fpare no pains, nor coft for that purpofe.

An Act of Contrition.

PRoſtrate at thy feet, O Lord, I moſt humbly beg pardon for all the failings and negligences which I daily commit through ignorance, frailty, or malice; for thoſe in a more particular manner, which I have been guilty of ſince my laſt confeſſion. I am utterly confounded when I reflect on their number, and conſider how much I have diſpleaſed and offended thee by committing them. O fountain of all good, how little have I loved thee? How little charity have I had for my neighbour? How ſluggiſh and luke-warm have I been in thy ſervice? On the other hand, how full of ſelf-love, and how warm and eager in the purſuit of things temporal? My mind has been ſo taken up with worldly thoughts, that I have ſeldom entered into myſelf to think ſeriouſly of thee. What a number of diſtractions have I not given admiſſion to in my prayers, in my meditations, whilſt I aſſiſted at the holy ſacrifice of the Maſs, and in my other exerciſes of piety? How ſelfiſh and earthly-minded have I been in all my actions! How much attached to my pleaſures, to my eaſe, to my conveniencies! How fretful, impatient and prone to anger on the leaſt diſappointment and contradiction! What a multitude of thoughts have I entertained contrary to charity, humility, purity, and other chriſtian virtues! How unruly and uncontrouled have been my paffions! In what liberties have I indulged my fenfes and inclinations! In a word, how faulty in every refpect has been my conduct! All this I have fuch a thorough conviction of, that I fee myfelf funk into an abyfs of filth and uncleannefs. Draw me out of this abyfs of mifery, I befeech thee, O Lord, cleanfe me from my numberlefs fins: and though, through thy mercy towards me, I do not know any of them to be mortal, they are yet very grievous in thy fight, as being contrary to thy divine precepts, injurious to thy infinite fanctity, derogatory to thy glory, difhonourable to thy holy name, in fhort, difpleafing and offenfive to thee. On all thefe accounts I deteft them with my whole foul, and am forry from the bottom of my heart that I committed them. I am confounded, and do humble myfelf before thee for them, earneftly begging pardon and grace to amend my life, refolved to labour for this purpofe with my whole might. I may hope, from thy infinite mercy, that thou wilt be pleafed to pardon them; and it is with this hope, that I am now going to declare them to the prieft, who is thy vicegerent in the tribunal of confeffion.

Sentiments on Venial Sins.

CANST thou, my soul, bear the thoughts of remaining so indolent, as not to make the least effort for recovering out of thy infirmities and miseries? Is it after this manner that a God of infinite majesty is to be served? Is this what thou hast so often promised him, and what the sanctity of thy baptism, and the profession of the christian religion which thou madest at the font, engaged thee to perform? Thou mayest fancy that because thy sins appear not to thee to be mortal, that they are therefore of small consequence, and may be overlooked: but thou art mistaken; for knowest thou not, unless thou art blind, that the least venial sin, inasmuch as it offends the infinite majesty of God, contains in it a malice in some sort infinite? that it being an evil which dishonours and injures the Creator, all the evils of creatures are not comparable to it. And that it would have been much better if the whole world was annihilated, than one venial sin had been committed? It is thy blindness which occasions thy imagining venial sin to be but a slight evil. Alas! if thou knewest what it is,

opinion, and prefer laying down a thousand lives, if thou hadst them, to the polluting thyself with one venial sin.

Thou findest it difficult to conceive a true sorrow for thy ordinary failings, because they are only venial, but this is owing to thy want of judgment in spiritual matters: for if thou didst but see all the deformity, and comprehended all the heinousness of venial sin, it would not have been in thy power to dry up thy tears, but that instant thou wouldst even die of sorrow and confusion for having incurred the guilt of it, and though thy body were as hard and durable as adamant, it would crumble into dust, says St. Catherine of Sienna, at the sight of so frightful an object. The saints, whom God had favoured with right notions in this respect, wept most bitterly for their faults, though less grievous than those which thou makest no scruple of committing hourly. If thou hadst viewed them in the light they did, thou couldst not sufficiently punish thyself; and thou wouldst be inconsolable for having committed any, if thou wast thoroughly acquainted with their degree of malignity.

How light then and pardonable soever these sins may appear to me, it is enough that they displease thee, O Lord, to make me deplore them extremely, and to oblige me to use my utmost efforts to avoid them hereafter. The love I bear thee, O God of love, the reverence I have for thee, O God of infinite majesty, will not suffer me to offend and displease thee again, by faults committed with full deliberation.

beration. As I neither love nor revere any thing in this world, so much as I love and revere thee, no care shall equal mine hereafter, for guarding against these faults; and in particular, I will avoid such a one, *N*, which I believe displeases thee, most. O purity of heart that dost not admit of any affection or voluntary attachment to the least venial sin, or the slightest imperfection, how amiable art thou, and how happy is the soul that possesses thee! since thou makest us the favourites of God, our soul the temple of the Holy Ghost, and dost besides draw down upon us the manifold graces and blessings of heaven. No care shall be wanting henceforward, on my side, to possess thee. But it is from thee, O Lord, and from thy mercy alone, that I can hope for this great happiness; I am too weak to entertain the least hope of being able to acquire it by my most strenuous endeavours, thou alone canst enrich me with so precious a gift; grant it I beseech thee, by the merits of thy Son Jesus Christ. *Amen.*

Elevation to be used immediately, before we go to present ourselves to the Priest in the Tribunal of Confession.

I AM going, O Lord, my heart pierced with sorrow, my face covered with confusion, my eyes bathed in tears, to cast myself at the feet of the priest, who is thy representative in the tribunal

tribunal of penance; it is to thee, in his person, that I am going to make a full and sincere declaration of my sins. My first view in this action is to make some amends, by my humiliation and sorrow, for my very injurious treatment of thee by my sins. In the next place, I propose thereby to obtain in thy mercy, to clear me of the guilt of my sins, and grant me a release of the punishment due to them. Lastly, I propose to obtain of thee grace to amend my past life, and to begin a new one. Grant me, I beseech thee, all the dispositions that are necessary for reaping all these benefits from this sacrament; and do not suffer, that instead of obtaining by it the pardon of my sins, I commit a new crime by a sacrilegious confession.

Come then, my soul, come let us go and cast ourselves at the feet of our divine Redeemer, there to disburthen ourselves of the heavy load of our sins and to obtain grace and mercy. Let us go to be washed and purified in the precious bath of his blood, which he has prepared for us in this sacrament. Come, let us go before his face, and let us confess our transgressions to the Lord, that he may forgive us the iniquity of our sin by the ministry of the priest, his representative.

An Examen of Conscience preparatory to Sacramental Confession, for such as lead a Christian Life.

Sins against God.

SINCE my last confession, which was at such a time, I accuse myself of not having had for God, all the love, reverence and zeal which I ought: Of having had, in some measure, more solicitude about creatures than his love: of having been cold, slothful and negligent in his service: Of not having been careful to please him, and procure his glory, as I was obliged, and of having neglected the opportunities of so doing: Of not having had a due sense of his benefits, nor been thankful for them: Of having had thoughts against him, against his saints and against faith, to which, however, I cannot charge myself with any wilful and deliberate consent: Of having wanted confidence in his goodness: Of not having had recourse to him in my necessities: Of having been diffident and mistrustful of relief from him in my corporal and spiritual wants: Of having had thoughts of despair of his mercy, which I did not dwell upon: Of not having accepted with submission the crosses and adversities he was pleased to permit me to be tried by,
having

having been troubled and uneasy under them, and even had some thoughts of murmuring against him, which however, I rejected; Of having sworn unnecessarily: Of not having kept Sundays, or the festivals of the church, holy, having spent a considerable part of them in idle amusements, thinking but very little on spiritual things: Of not having been faithful in following the inspirations of God, nor in performing the promises and the good resolutions I made in his presence: Of having approached the last time the sacrament of penance and the Blessed Eucharist with little preparation, devotion or sorrow for my sins; Of having carelesly performed the penance enjoined me: Not kept my attention on our Lord the day I received him in the Blessed Eucharist; profited very little by the use of this sacrament; assisted at Mass with little or no devotion, even on days of obligation; had frequent distractions which I rejected, indeed, but very remisly; been also subject to these distractions during the publick service of the church, in my private devotions, in my meditations, in my spiritual lectures, in hearing the word of God and other exercises of piety; all which I feebly resisted, having besides giving occasion to them by my inapplication and neglect of watching over my eyes and my other senses: Of having suffered sleep to steal upon me in the times of prayer, sermon, publick offices and spiritual lectures: Of having talked, laughed, and committed several irreverences in the church, and before the Blessed
Sacrament,

Sacrament, even in the time of Mass, whereby I might have given scandal to those that saw me: Of not having kept myself recollected in the day time, but suffered myself to be drawn away by dissipation and unprofitable thoughts: Of having spent several hours successively without calling God to mind, or raising my heart to him: Of having omitted, through negligence, my morning and evening prayer, and other pious exercises, intirely or in part: Of having been deficient in purity of intention in my actions, sought myself and my own ends to a great degree in all I did: Omitted often the offering up of my actions to God; performing them without that spirit, attention, fervour and perfection which ought to have accompanied them, and for the most part out of custom, humour, self-love, inclination, passion; besides being guilty of an infinity of other negligences and imperfections in the performance of them. Of not having profited as I ought, of the graces of God, and the means of salvation and sanctification, which he had favoured me with; and of not having corresponded with his merciful designs over me, nor laboured in acquiring the perfection he expects from me.

Sins against our Neighbour.

I ACCUSE myself of having been deficient in point of charity towards my neighbour; in
having

having loved him only on human motives, and not for God's fake: Of not having had that efteem for him I ought to have had, nor confidered Jefus Chrift in his perfon: Of having had thoughts of contempt for him, judged rafhly of him, though not in matters of moment; fufpected evil of him without fufficient grounds, which I did not reject fo readily as I might have done: Of having conceived alfo againſt him thoughts of hatred, averfion, rancour, coldnefs, and antipathy: was not fufficiently careful to divert my mind from them, and I believe I might have fuffered feveral of them to have paffed unnoticed, though as foon as I perceived them, I renounced them: envied him his merit, reputation, fortune, employments: fpoke of his faults, and thefe not trifling, before fuch a number of perfons who were ftrangers to them, out of levity, and fo often, and alfo fometimes not without fome degree of envy and malice; being befides pleafed to hear others fpeak of him in the fame manner, and having given credit to what was faid on thofe occafions to his difadvantage, and even added fomething thereto of my own, relating what I knew of it, but the whole regarded a matter of no great confequence: Of not having taken his part when he was ill fpoken of, when his faults were exaggerated, and falfe things laid to his charge, and having faid nothing in his vindication or defence though in my power; fo many times. Of having reported things which have chagrined him, given him difturbance *for Sacramental Confeſſion.*

diſturbance and excited animoſities, hatred and diſſenſions among three or more perſons, &c.

I accuſe myſelf of not having helped, ſuccoured, comforted and aſſiſted him in neceſſity; of having been hard-hearted, without any feeling or compaſſion for him in affliction; of having even done him ill offices, wronged him, but in trifling matters; of having been uncivil and diſreſpectful to him, troubleſome, and out of humour with him; of having ſpoken harſhly to him, given him abuſive language with the view to vex and teaze him, and make him uneaſy, ſo often: Of having had ſome difference with him, and wherein I uſed him ill; had warm diſputes with him, was out of patience with him, railed at him, miſcalled him, and was the occaſion, by my haſtineſs of temper, of his loſing patience and flying into a paſſion againſt me; and to theſe ſucceeded my tardineſs in ſeeking to be reconciled with him, wilfully entertaining for ſome hours a coldneſs and reſentment againſt him, endeavouring on this account to avoid meeting him, declining to ſpeak to him, and conceiving deſires of revenge againſt him, and wiſhes that harm might befall him, even death; but as ſoon as I perceived theſe motions, I ſuppreſſed them: Of having felt in myſelf a ſecret pleaſure and ſatisfaction when any diſgrace happened to him; and on the other hand, diſcontent on ſeeing him thrive and flouriſh: Of having neither excuſed, nor patiently borne with his faults: Of having cenſured his conduct, found fault with every thing he did, pryed into his actions in

I   order

order to discover exceptions against them, put wrong constructions upon them, mocked and ridiculed him, exposed him to scorn, expressed my contempt of him, and affronted him: Of having likewise sometimes indiscreetly flattered and commended him, exposing him thereby to vanity and self-conceit; advised him ill, given him bad example, entertained him with idle discourse, instilled bad or dangerous principles into him, and thereby occasioned his falling into some sin, great or small: neglected to admonish him when I saw him do amiss, though I had authority over him; applauded him for acting contrary to his duty: Of having neglected to inspect into the behaviour of such as were under my care, being also little solicitous to instruct and correct them, and to induce them to do their duty.

Sins against Ones self.

I Accuse myself of having inordinately loved and flattered myself; Of having been too solicitous about my life and health; too fond of the pleasures, comforts and conveniencies of life; too much wedded to my own opinions and inclinations, which I have almost always followed; much addicted to the gratifying of my senses, humour, passions, and self-love, and too much attached to creatures; Of having indulged too freely the emotions of vain joy: Of having followed diversions on no
other

other motive than the pleasure and satisfaction I found in them: Of having been guilty of sensuality in eating and drinking, by seeking my pleasure more than satisfying the demands of nature: Of having exceeded the bounds prescribed by temperance, sought after the nicest bits, eat with greediness and indecency; eat between meals out of mere gluttony and for the pleasure of eating; not observed the fasts of the church with due exactness; exceeded the quantity which is usually allowed at collation: Of having spent too much time in bed, and neglected to rise at the time prescribed me by superiours, Of having entertained too great an intercourse with the world; going too much abroad, leading a life of idleness, voluptuousness and dissipation; been fond of company, exposing myself thereby to many occasions of offending God: Of having been too sensibly affected by the troubles, inconveniencies, sickness, fatigues, and crosses which befel me; having fretted inwardly, and murmured outwardly on that account, and suffered myself to give way to dejection, grief, melancholy and impatience, which appeared too visibly in my words and behaviour; and this so many times; not having withal used any violence against myself to repress these commotions: Of having overmuch declined trouble, labour and crosses: Of having entertained thoughts of pride and self-esteem; cherished in my mind desires of honours and places of trust, with the view of being esteemed, loved, honoured, praised and applauded; having felt a singular pleasure wherever any thing of that kind fell to my lot; and having been as much chagrined on the other hand, when frustrated of my pleasures, and when others were more caressed and respected, praised and honoured than myself: Of having also been influenced in what I did by human respects for obtaining the esteem of men, having spared no pains for that purpose: Of having affected to please, been vain in my discourse, in my air, in my manner, saying several things in my own commendations: Of having been too nice and finical in my dress in my furniture: Of having wished for qualifications and talents for shining and making myself more distinguished, admired and spoken of than others, and having been full of impatience in finding myself destitute of them: Of having been too sensible of the contempt and reproaches I met with among men, and as little moved and affected by the just rebukes my ill conduct and behaviour have occasioned, though guilty of the fault laid to my charge, which instead of owning and begging pardon for, I had recourse to excuses and lies to clear myself of the blame; not even scrupling to palm it upon others to exculpate myself. In fine, instead of being humble of heart I have cherished pride, haughtiness and excessive vanity. I have had thoughts and imaginations contrary to purity, sometimes troublesome and violent which I was remiss in rejecting, having dwelt on them a little, but I am not sensible that I yielded or consented to them; however, my negligence in this respect

was

was considerable, and so often: I perceived at the same time some irregular motions of the flesh, which, though I know not that I consented to, I might have more vigorously checked; I have not also been circumspect enough in regard to my body, having been guilty of an indecent look or touch, yet without any evil or impure design; neither have I been reserved enough in regard to others, those especially of the other sex, in looks, words, behaviour, which might have given the enemy an occasion to disquiet me with temptations, and perhaps caused them in others: I have besides sung some songs which was not modest enough, looked at indecent pictures, and read books capable of exciting in me bad thoughts; I have also had an impure dream, but don't know that I dwelt upon it, or gave occasion to it.

I have had too great an attachment to, and placed too much confidence in the goods of this life, having coveted more than that portion of them which providence was pleased to allot me: I have been too solicitous in acquiring, increasing and keeping those I possess, which has been attended with great disquiets of mind, anxieties and troubles, fretting and pining when unsuccessful, or when it has pleased God to deprive me of any thing: I did my neighbour some small wrong, and had so often the intention of doing so: Have not inviolably observed the laws of justice in the dealings I have had with him in buying, selling, making payments, ordering work. I have not
paid

paid my juft debts though in a condition to do it. I have been backward in giving alms, gave them morofely, with repugnance and almoft againft my will: fquandered away in gaming, or in vain and foolifh expences the fubftance that providence had given me: I have been too curious to know things that did not in the leaft concern me, and learn news: I have alfo held a number of vain and unneceffary difcourfes, fpoken many idle words, told lies, in matters of no confequence, have played the buffoon, exaggerated things, and fpoke words of a double meaning.

I have lived by humour, without rule, and followed the bent of my inclinations and paffions: I have been flothful, pufillanimous, and neglected to be inftructed in, and to perform the duties of my condition, particularly fuch and fuch a one; having alfo trifled away a confiderable deal of time and fpent it in ufelefs and unprofitable things; not availed myfelf of certain occafions that fell in my way of doing good and performing good works; being befides backward in my endeavours to correct my failings, to improve in virtue, mortify my fenfes, check my paffions, vices, and bad habits, and make a proficiency in the ways of grace: I have been too eafily difcouraged from the profecution of what is commendable, on meeting with difficulties and the leaft oppofition: I have refifted temptations very faintly, I have been wanting in vigilance and attention to myfelf, which has been the occafion of my having paffed by unregarded and unrefifted a great

for Sacramental Confession. 103

great number of irregular thoughts, desires, affections, words and actions.

I accuse myself of all these sins and of many others which I have committed, and which I do not remember; as also of all those of my life past, and in particular of such a one: And I am sorry for all of them from the bottom of my heart for the love of God of whom I humbly ask pardon; and I purpose now to confess them and perform the penance that shall be enjoined me.

To this detail those sins are to be added by each penitent which more particularly regard his state and condition, together with all others not comprised in this list which he knows himself to be guilty of. Persons under religious vows for instance, are to accuse themselves of the sins they have committed against their superiours through the want of love, respect and submission to them: Against their religious institute by giving but indifferent example, causing disturbances among their brethren and neglecting their duty: Against their vows, by not observing them with that exactness and perfection to which they are obliged: Against their rules and observances, by violating them through levity, self-love, even against the voice and testimony of their own conscience, and by making a habit of these transgressions.

It is unnecessary for those that confess often to examine themselves each time of every sin set down in this table, it being sufficient to mention the most considerable faults they are guilty of. What they know themselves guilty

guilty of them, they may excuse themselves of it in the extraordinary confessions which are sometimes made within the year, wherein the penitent descends to a larger detail.

For the conveniency of those that are inclined to make use of this work I shall give an abridgement of the examen which may be made use of for ordinary confessions.

An Abridged Examen of Conscience for Ordinary Confessions.

SINCE my last confession, which was on such a day, I accuse myself of having had little love for God: Of having communicated the last time with little respect and devotion, having been lukewarm and negligent in my preparation and thanksgiving, and of having reaped but little benefit therefrom.

I accuse myself of having had many distractions in hearing Mass, during other parts of divine service, in my meditations, prayers, spiritual reading, examinations, and other practices of piety, and of having been negligent in resisting them, three or four times in particular, when they were longer than ordinary; and of having given occasion to them by carelessly looking about me, and by suffering my mind and my heart to be too much taken up with temporal things: Of having fallen asleep during my meditation, another time curtailed it, and culpably omitted a spiritual reading. I accuse myself of not having kept myself recollected

lected in the day of time: Of having passed whole hours without the least motion of my heart towards God: Of not having sufficiently purified my intention in my actions, but sought myself too much in them, being almost always byassed in performing them by motives of self-love: been remiss in animating them with all the fervour, zeal and attention which I ought, doing them merely through custom, and as a task: Of having sometimes been wanting in offering them to God: Of having been idle, and so long: Of having mispent so much time in trifles and useless occupations; Of having neglected to follow pious inspirations which suggested the performance of a certain work: Of not having taken care to avail myself of opportunities of practising virtue, several of which escaped me through my own fault.

I accuse myself of little charity for my neighbour, of having had many thoughts to his prejudice, in the nature of suspicion, rash judgment, contempt, aversion, rancour, revenge, envy, and the like; and of having been very negligent in rejecting them, particularly that I dwelt a little on a passionate thought: Of having spoken to him in a blunt rough manner, and spoken also of his faults behind his back, but in matters of no moment: Of taking pleasure in hearing disadvantageous things said of him, and such as did him some prejudice; censuring withal his conduct, bearing his faults with impatience, giving him some trouble, and being the occasion of his flying into a passion.

I accuse

I accuse myself of senfuality in my meals, having been too intent on pleafing my palate: alfo of having eaten with greedinefs and indecency, and exceeded a little the bounds of neceffity, which brought upon me a flight indifpofition: Of having eaten between meals without neceffity: Of having been too fond of diverfions, and fpent too much time in them: Of having indulged to excefs, on a certain occafion, fome fentiments of vain joy.

I accuse myfelf of having had thoughts of pride, felf-efteem, and complacency in my own merit, which I dwelt upon a little: Of having taken pleafure in being commended or honoured: Of having fought to pleafe men in my actions, and of having acted merely out of human refpect.

I accuse myfelf of having had thoughts and imaginations contrary to chaftity: Of having finned through remiffnefs in checking them; but I don't remember any thing voluntary, or deliberately confented to on thofe occafions: Of having felt an irregular motion in the body; and of having looked with too much curiofity or freedom on perfons of the other fex, which might have given occafion to thefe thoughts and motions.

I accuse myfelf of not having been refigned to the difpenfations of divine providence; been uneafy and difturbed thereat. Of having told a lie once or twice, (*If oftener mention the number*) but not of any confequence: Of having held idle talk, and on feveral occafions difedified.

disedified my neighbour. Of thefe and many other fins, which I cannot now call to remembrance, I accufe myfelf; as alfo of all thofe of my life paft, particularly of giving way feveral times to heat and paffion; all and every one of which I deteft and am heartily forry for, for the love of God, of whom I humbly afk pardon, and I purpofe to confefs them to my ghoftly father.

We are never to accufe ourfelves of any venial fins which we are not truly forry for, but difpofed to commit again upon the firft opportunity; becaufe without contrition they cannot be the matter of the facrament of penance, and becaufe it would be finful to affign as matter to it that which cannot be fuch. If a penitent mention thefe faults in confeffion, it is with a view of humbling himfelf for them, and to receive advice from his confeffor, and for acquiring more ftrength to amend them.

As to fuch penitents as have feldom any thing elfe to accufe themfelves of befides habitual venial fins of the lighteft kind, they would do well to mention fome fin they have formerly confeffed, and do fincerely repent of, and are thoroughly refolved to fall no more into; that thus there may be always a certain and fufficient matter for abfolution, and the danger of profaning the facrament, by confeffing without true repentance, prevented.

A Prayer

A Prayer to be said while the Priest recites the Form of Absolution.

I Once more cry aloud to thee, O Jesus, for mercy and pardon for these and all my other sins. Grant me, I beseech thee, O divine redeemer. I am sorry from the very bottom of my heart, for the love of thee, that I have offended thee, and am sincerely resolved, by the assistance of thy grace, to reform my life. I offer to thee all the grief and sorrow of holy penitents, for supplying the dificiencies of mine. Flow then, precious blood of my Saviour nailed on the cross, at the foot of which I represent myself! flow down upon me to cleanse me from the filth of my sins: flow, sacred balsam! to heal me of my wounds: flow, divine oil! to anoint and fortify me, that I may be enabled for the future to resist all the attempts of hell, and never more relapse again into sin.

After Confession.

MAY immortal thanks be rendered unto thee, O God! for the unspeakable goodness thou hast had in waiting my return to thee by repentance, and for pronouncing upon me, by the mouth of thy minister, the sentence of absolution from my sins. Confirm in heaven, I beseech thee, that which thy vicar has done

upon

upon earth, and pardon me whatever sins I have committed against thee: cleanse my soul from the stains of my sins; blot them in such manner out of thy remembrance, that they may not be laid to my charge when thou shalt summon me to judgment. I once more crave pardon for them, with extreme sorrow for having committed them; it is my firm purpose and resolution to make satisfaction, and to punish myself for them; not only by a faithful performance of the sacramental penance enjoined by the priest, which I am very sensible falls far short of what my sins have deserved; but also by mortifications; self-denials, fasts, and the like penitential exercises, and particularly by patience, humility and resignation under all the pains and crosses it shall please thy divine providence to send me, together with those which are inseparably from my station in life. I also renew the promise I have made to thee of amending my life, and especially of avoiding such a sin, by which I believe thou art more grievously offended. Thou that knowest my weakness and inability, O Lord, take pity of me, and vouchsafe to grant me such a powerful and victorious grace as may effectually prevent my relapsing any more into sin. *Amen.*

A Preparatory Exercife

Pious Sentiments after Confeffion.

How wonderful, O Lord, are thy mercies towards me, in pardoning me my fins, after fo many relapfes? I am now more fenfible than ever of the injuftice I was guilty of in offending fo good and gracious a God. Thou couldft, no doubt, have deftroyed me a thoufand times, and thrown me headlong into eternal fire, and thy juftice feemed to require it; but thou hadft compaffion on me. Since therefore my foul has been fo precious in thy fight, though no damage could accrue to thee from my deftruction, thy honour fhall for the future be infinitely dear to me, and I fhall be ready to lay down my life rather than offend thee again. An now, my foul, as thou art purified from all thy fins, by the power and efficacy of the blood of Chrift, do him no more the injury of defiling thyfelf again by new crimes, but keep thyfelf pure and fpotlefs in the midft of this depraved world. Deteft henceforth every fin; for evermore caft off all inordinate attachments, and all eagernefs after and violent inclination to things here below. Thou alone, O my God! fhalt be henceforward the object of my inclinations and defires. I will no longer fuffer myfelf to be tyrannized over by my paffions; thy love alone fhall bear fway in my heart. I will no more fuffer myfelf to be carried away by anger, vanity, avarice; I will never more give envy, hatred, rancour admittance

for Sacramental Confession.

thnce into my heart; I will no more open my mouth in defamatory speeches, in murmurings, in lies; neither will I more indulge myself in indolence, remissness, or the love of softness. On the contrary, I will acquit myself with inviolable fidelity, of all my duties, and serve thee to the best of my power, with a fervour and attention, which I hope may be worthy of thee.

O my soul! God has hitherto waited for thee, out of a mercy thou hast rendered thyself a thousand times unworthy of, while others less guilty than thyself have been cast headlong into hell; but he that has hitherto waited thy return, does not promise thee the like forbearance for the time to come. Do not therefore, any longer abuse his goodness; force him not to avenge, by destroying thee, thy base and ungrateful contempt of his graces; avail thyself carefully of the grace of reconciliation he has just now bestowed upon thee, it may perhaps be the last he has allotted thee; perhaps there will be no further pardon for thee if thou art again so unfortunate as to relapse into thy sins.

The Lord has now broken thy chains, and rescued thee from the grievous slavery of Satan: but be exceeding careful not to suffer thyself to be entangled again in the yoke of the former bondage: Remember that the cruel tyrant, out of whose his hands thou hast been delivered, encreases the weight of his yoke on those who fall again under his power, and plunges them into new and more enormous crimes than those which they had forsaken by repentance. Doubt not, but that thou wilt become worse than thou hast ever been, if he can once more subject thee to his tyrannical dominion.

Every sin God in his goodness has pardoned thee, ought to be a powerful and pressing motive for exciting thee to love him with fresh ardour; and as these sins have been little less than infinite, both in number and enormity, thy love of him, were it possible, ought also to be infinite. Let it therefore be thy earnest endeavour to surpass others henceforward as much in love, as thou hast heretofore surpassed them in iniquity.

Reflect that the divine justice will not be at any loss, and think effectually of paying whatever thou remainest indebted to it. Thou canst now clear away large debts for a small matter. Embrace therefore the opportunity, and for that purpose, turn to good account every minute of thy time, that not one may slip from thee without being employed in something available to the expiation of thy sins. Not content with offering to God in this view thy usual prayers, and the troubles inseparable from thy station in life, do every day some work of supererogation, some act of piety, charity, humility, mortification, self-denial, or sacrifice of what thy inclination may prompt thee to.

But thou art not to consider thy actions, and thy good works, howsoever numerous and excellent they may be, as the just payment of
thy

for Sacramental Confession. 113

thy debts, but as dispositions to the end that the merits of the death and blood of Jesus Christ may be applied to thee, by which alone the divine justice can receive an adequate satisfaction for thy offences; Place therefore all thy hopes in the death and in the blood of thy Saviour; pray unto him without ceasing to apply to thee the merits of them. Having already cleared thee of the guilt of sin in the sacrament of penance, say to him with the royal prophet: *Wash me still more from my iniquity, vouchsafe still* farther *to purify me*, by acquitting me of the debt of temporal punishment. His Father has loaded him with the sins of mankind, intreat him to take thine also upon him in order to their expiation. Beseech his Father at the same time *to look upon the face of his anointed*, and to hearken to the prayer he puts up to him for pardoning thee, as one *not knowing what he did* when he offended him. He speaks to him in a still more affecting and tender strain than his apostle did to the master of a fugitive slave. *If he has wronged thee in any thing, or is in thy debt, put it to my account.* Place, Father, to the account of thy beloved Son, all the injury this man has done thee, and whatever he is still indebted to thy justice; I charge myself therewith for his sake, and take the whole upon myself.

AN EXERCISE FOR COMMUNION.

Elevation for the Remote Preparation.

GREAT, my foul! muft be the bufinefs thou art charged this day with the execution of, fince thou art to prepare within thee *a lodging, not for man but for a God* of infinite majefty. But this preparation muft be thy work O Lord, for what can I do, weak and miferable creature as I am, that may be worthy of thee?

Holinefs, O Lord! ought to be the ornament *of thy houfe*: glory and magnificence fhould every where fparkle in it. Fill my heart then with holinefs I befeech thee, difplay in it the wonders of thy magnificence, that it may become a fit habitation for fo noble a gueft.

Sun of juftice! that vouchfafeft this day to vifit me, prepare, I befeech thee, thy abode in my heart. The sun prepares its throne in the heavens by the resplendency of the rays of light he shoots forth before his entrance, or visible appearance; do thou in like manner prepare thyself a throne for thee in my soul before thou comest into her, by dissipating her darkness with the lustre of thy rays.

Come, Holy Ghost, come I entreat thee, and prepare my heart for receiving the blessed Jesus; come and purify this heart, come and sanctify it, come and inflame it with the sacred fire of thy divine love.

Divine Jesus! thou didst send heretofore thy Holy Spirit to prepare the womb of the blessed Virgin Mary for receiving thee in the mystery of the incarnation; vouchsafe, I pray thee, to send the same Spirit to prepare my heart for receiving thee in the mystery of the Eucharist.

Adorable blood of my Jesus! purify me, cleanse me from all my filth, that I may worthily receive my divine Redeemer.

I bathe myself in the laver of his precious blood, and there I wash and purify myself from all my filth; there it is that I get thoroughly cleansed from all my remaining corruptions, that I may no more be defiled therewith.

I offer to thee, O Jesus, all thy merits and all thy sanctity; all the merits and sanctity of thy blessed mother and of all thy saints and angels: accept of them, I beseech thee, O Lord, to supply for my want of those dispositions which are required to approach worthily to this great mystery.

O God,

O God, whose sanctity strikes terror into the highest Seraphims, and whose purity makes, as it were, stains to appear in the purest spirits, how shall I dare to present myself before thee, who am but filth and sin! Oh! with what justice and truth do I here acknowledge myself unworthy of such a favour! How is it possible, O great God, that thou shouldst condescend to come into so mean and wretched a place as my heart, thou who art so jealous of thy own glory! O how exceeding great are thy goodness and thy mercy!

God of glory! I tremble for fear when I reflect how unworthy I am to receive thee; but since it is thou thyself that requirest it, impute it not to me, I beseech thee, as sinful. It is my most humble request to thee, O Lord, not to permit that my approaching this day to the Blessed Sacrament may be the cause of my condemnation at thy tribunal; grant rather that it may become, in regard to me, a source of grace and every kind of blessing.

O my soul! what a glorious day is this for thee, thou being on this day to receive within thee the creator of the universe and the God of all nature? Fail not to avail thyself of so great a happiness.

Prepare, O my soul, prepare the ways of the Lord before he comes to meet thee; make straight whatever is crooked, bring low whatever is too high, raise whatever is too low, cleanse whatever is impure, and plant it with the flowers of all virtues.

I offer

I offer to thee, O Lord, all my actions, thoughts desires and sufferings during the course of this day, that they may tend to dispose me to receive in a suitable and worthy manner this great mystery. Great indeed will be my happiness to lodge in my bosom the God of the universe?

Come, thou beloved of my heart, come thou object of all my wishes and ambition, come thou my glory my treasure, and my delight!

O! who will give me to satiate myself with the sacred viand of thy flesh, and with the cup of thy precious blood!

Dilate, my soul, dilate, my heart, to receive that abundance of graces and favours thy Saviour designs this day to bestow upon thee. He requires only a spacious heart capable of containing them. Banish from thine all inordinate love of creatures, that it may be disposed for receiving his divine effusions.

An Immediate Preparation for Communion.

An Act of Faith.

THOU hast declared, O Saviour Jesus Christ, that this sacrament is thy body and thy blood; I firmly believe it upon thy word, persuaded that it is infallibly true, and that heaven and earth shall sooner pass away than it
should

should fail of producing its effect. Yes, I verily believe that in the Blessed Eucharist is that adorable body which was born of the blessed Virgin Mary, which was nailed to the cross for the salvation of mankind, and which now shines in heaven brighter than the sun; and that there also is the precious blood which flowed out of thy divine side, and out of all thy sacred limbs on mount Calvary. I believe that thy most holy soul, thy divine person, thy divinity are there likewise, as being united to thy body and to thy blood; and that the adorable persons of the Father and of the Holy Ghost are there besides equally present, as being inseparable from thine. I believe that thy body, being a living body, is accompanied with the blood, and that both of them are really present under each kind. I believe, in fine, that upon the priest's pronouncing the words of consecration, the substance of the bread and wine is changed into that of thy body and thy blood, which continue hidden under the appearances of those elements; and though my eyes, my taste, my feeling and my other senses contradict this admirable change, and would fain persuade me that there is nothing more than bread and wine on the altar as before, I reject notwithstanding, all their testimonies, convinced that they can be no competent judges in supernatural things, and that they ought not to be believed against the testimony of thy word. I acquiesce with the profoundest submission and unconquerable steadfastness in whatever thou hast.

hast revealed, and thy church teacheth us concerning this great myftery. I am not forry to find myfelf at a lofs for comprehending what is here performed, that I may be able thereby to give thee the more fignal proof of my fubmiffion and refpect. I believe the real prefence with all the faith of thy faints, and I fhould be ready, if neceffary, to feal my belief and confeffion of it with my blood; I believe it with greater certainty than if I beheld with my eyes, and felt with my hands the facred body of my Saviour.

O my foul! have a full conviction of the truth of all thefe fentiments; let this truth fink deep into thy mind, entertain a lively and perfect faith of it; pierce by the light of faith the darknefs of this myftery, and behold with a fixed and fteady eye under the veil of the facrament that divine body which fills heaven with the fplendour of its glory. This is a myftery of faith which requires a great fhare of that virtue in thofe who partake of it. Faith is one of the moft excellent difpofitions for a worthy Communion. Strengthen thyfelf therefore ftill more and more in the firm and full perfuafion of whatever faith teaches concerning this myftery.

An Act of Humility.

O LORD of glory! before whom the pillars of heaven fhake with a religious dread, and whofe whose majesty the highest Seraphims dare not through respect look upon; how shall I dare present myself before thee to partake of these tremendous mysteries, I who am nothing but a vessel of rottenness and corruption? I sincerely acknowledge myself infinitely unworthy of the inestimable favour which thou this day art pleased to grant me, in giving thyself to me to be the nourishment of my soul. For what am I, Lord, what am I, to deserve so singular a grace, I who am but a compound of ignorance, sin and misery; and who on account of my grievous transgressions have so many times deserved to be struck dead by thy thunder, and cast headlong into hell? I confess myself to the last degree unworthy, and that there is nothing in me, but should have obliged thee to refuse me this immense favour. I bow down and cast myself at the feet of all thy creatures, as the vilest and most wretched of them all: I bury myself a thousand times in the abyss of my nothingness; and if I dare appear before thee, O Lord, to partake of this mystery, it is entirely in obedience to the command which thou hast laid on me, to display, no doubt, thy infinite mercy in bestowing, by this living bread, life on him who has so often deserved death, and in heaping thy benefits on the most unworthy, and the most wretched of all thy creatures.

Act of Adoration.

THOUGH no visible sign of thy greatness appears on our altars, O God of majesty, and though thy infinite love for men has placed thee there in the most abject state imaginable, in order to condescend to their weakness which could not have borne the splendour of thy glory, I there acknowledge thee, notwithstanding for my Lord and my God; I there adore thee as the sovereign Lord of all things, as the God of all nature, and the creator of the universe; grant that I may there pay thee all the veneration a mere creature is capable of. I there do thee homage with my being, my life, with all that I am, and all that I possess, which I acknowledge to have received from thy liberal hand. I have a sense and belief of thy infinite greatness, and of all thy other perfections, which transcend every idea and expression I can form of created excellence. I consider this great universe, with all that it contains, as less than an atom, compared with thee; and not being able to find within myself, and the compass of my own being, wherewithal to honour thee, in a manner suitable to thy divine majesty, I join with all thy saints and angels in heaven, and with all thy just upon earth, with the blessed Virgin, thy holy mother, and in particular, with thy most sacred humanity subsisting in the divine Word or second Person of the blessed Trinity; to honour thee by them,

them, and with them, and to offer unto thee all that honour and glory which they are continually giving thee during time, and will never cease giving thee to all eternity. Hereto I also join all that glory which thou possessest within thy divine essence, and which thou acquirest from thy divine perfections. In all which, I join as much as is possible for a feeble creature, and make an offering of it to thee in the spirit of homage and adoration.

Act of Contrition.

I WILL confess my injustice to the Lord, I will confess unto him that my *iniquities are gone over my head*, and, as a *grievous burthen, are become heavy upon me*. I will acknowledge in his presence, that my whole life has been one continued series of crimes and disorders, and that there is no ingratitude, no malice I have not been guilty of: since even after he had given me the grace of entering into myself, and of returning to him to spend the remainder of my days in his service, I notwithstanding neglected all my duties, and followed only the suggestions of passions and self-love. But how much do I grieve for all my disorders! how sincerely do I now detest and deplore my past conduct! My heart is pierced with sorrow for having so often, and so grievously offended thee. I am sorry from the bottom of my heart,

heart, for the love of thee, for having been so base and disloyal. I ask pardon thousands of times with tears in my eyes. I promise faithfully, by the assistance of thy holy grace, which I beg thou wouldst grant me, never to offend thee more, and to serve thee with unshaken fidelity to the end of my life. But what a vile wretch must I have been, in having offended a God so good, who all my life long has not ceased heaping benefits upon me! who gave me a being when I was not; who adopted me for his child, and made me his heir after having given me a being: who always protected, favoured, showered down his graces upon me, and to whom in fine, I am indebted for all that I am, and all I possess! Was there ever ingratitude and malice equal to mine? Weep, my eyes, weep, melt into tears; flow like two springs of living water, without ever drying up, to wash away stains of so deep a dye as those I have been polluted with. And thou, O lamb of God, who takest away the sins of the world, blot out mine, I beseech thee, by the virtue of thy most precious blood; wash, cleanse and sanctify me: clothe me with the white robe of innocence and charity, that I may be found worthy to have a share in the feast thou hast prepared for us in this august sacrament. *Amen.*

Act of Hope.

INEXHAUSTIBLE source of all goodness and mercy! how great soever the multitude, and enormity of my offences may be, and how unworthy soever I may have made myself of thy graces by my ingratitude and my crimes, I hope nevertheless, to obtain of thee relief in my distress, and pardon for my transgressions. Thy gospel affords no instance of any one in misery having had recourse to thee, without being succoured; shall I be the first that thou wilt reject? Thou speakest aloud to us from thy altars, and invitest all *that labour and are heavy laden* to come to thee for refreshment, assuring them that they shall not be disappointed, but find rest to their souls; wilt thou reject me when I come to claim a share in this thy gracious promise? Thou dost there sacrifice thyself anew to thy Father for me, thou dost there give me thy precious flesh for nourishment, and dost work an infinity of unheard-of prodigies, to make thyself there present that I may there receive thee; but wouldst thou do all this to no purpose? No, my divine Saviour, thou meanest thereby to alleviate my miseries, to heap benefits upon me, and enrich me with all thy treasures. I hope, therefore, that by the merits of thy bitter death and passion, I shall be reconciled to my offended Father, and shall obtain the forgiveness of all my sins, I hope that thy precious
flesh

flesh will cure me of all my spiritual infirmities; that it will communicate to me its sanctity, that it will be unto me a source of grace, spiritual knowledge, love and strenght; that it will serve me as a buckler and safeguard against all my enemies, and that it finally will conduct me prosperoufly to the haven of salvation. Chear up, my soul, chear up in the firm hopes of receiving from thy divine Saviour all the succours and advantages thou canst wish for. From that infinite love, of which he gives thee such signal proofs in this facrament, expect nothing short of infinite graces and blessings; and prepare thyself for receiving them by the firmness of thy hope, the fervency of thy love, and a thorough disengagement of thy affections from all created beings. *Amen.*

Act of the Love of God.

THOUGH my heart were as insensible as that of a favage beast, could I, O Jesus! refrain from loving thee? since, on one side thou art infinitely amiable by the assemblage of all those beauties and excellencies which are happily united in thy divine person as in their centre; and on the other, hast always loved me and dost still love with an inexplicable love and tenderness, notwithstanding my extreme baseness and the many sins I have committed and do constantly commit against thee? Ever since I had a being thou hast loaded me with thy benefits,

nefits, how unworthy foever I have made myfelf of them by my ingratitude and rapeated rebellions againft thee: and thou art now about giving me thy adorable body and precious blood to be the food of my foul, the remedy of all my ills, and an affured earneft of that happinefs which thou haft prepared for me in thy heavenly kingdom. How is it poffible after all this that I fhould refufe thee my heart? No, I give it to thee, O Jefus! and do confecrate it to thee intire, with all its love, affections and defires; I love thee with all the ardour and ability of this heart, and with all the fincerity and tendernefs it is capable of; I break from henceforth for ever with all creatures, and renounce all the delufive fweets of life to love thee, and thee only. All that grieves me is not to be poffeffed of a heart fufficiently inflamed and comprehenfive for loving thee in a manner more worthy of thee. To fupply this deficiency I have recourfe to the interceffion of thy holy Mother, to that of all the Saints, and to thy great mercy I join with them in loving thee by them and with them, both in time and eternity.

An Elevation on the Paffion of Jefus Chrift.

SINCE thou haft inftituted, O Jefus, this great facrament to be the memorial of thy death and paffion, I am fenfible I ought not to approach to it without calling to mind what thou

thou haft endured for the love of me. O! how great was thy love, O divine redeemer! which induced thee to undergo, for the falvation of this vile creature, the cruel agony thou didft fuffer in the garden of Gethfemani, when every part of thy facred body was covered with a fweat of blood, trickling down to the ground: The unworthy treatment of the foldiers, who having pinioned thee and bound thee with cords, led thee like a thief through the ftreets of Jerufalem: The confufion thou waft expofed to, when they dragged thee from one tribunal to another to be examined and tried by wicked judges: The pain thou didft endure, and the infult oftered thee, when thy adorable body was ftript naked, bound to a pillar and torn with fcourges, when thy facred head was pierced with fharp thorns, and the foldiers feemed to vie with each other in putting thee to ignominy and fhame by their feint homage of bending the knee before thee, and by buffeting thee and fpitting in thy face; and at length by the infamous and cruel death thou didft fuffer on the crofs between two thieves? Bleffed for ever be that unfpeakable love, which caufed thee to undergo fo much for my fake. For all which I return thee the moft fincere and moft fervent thanks my heart is capable of, humbly begging pardon of thee at the fame time for having by my fins been the occafion of thy fuffering and even of thy death. I earneftly entreat thee by the fame love that made thee fuffer them, to apply to my foul the merits of them in this divine facrament,

in

in making me die to sin and iniquity, that I may live henceforward to justice and to grace. Amen.

Act of Oblation.

SINCE thou dost me the favour, O Jesus, not only to invite me to thy banquet, there to feed and nourish my soul with thy precious body, but even layest thy commands upon me to become a guest at thy table, I am here come to obey them, and with the same views and intentions which thou hadst in commanding me. I come to honour the supreme majesty of God, and to do homage to his infinite greatness by this divine holocaust; to thank him for all his benefits by this victim of thanksgiving; to make atonement for my sins by this victim of expiation; and to obtain of his goodness the succours I want, by this peace-offering. I come, O my most amiable sovereign! to honour thee by establishing thy reign in my heart; by being transformed entirely into thee, incorporated with thee, washed, purified, and sanctified by the virtue of thy blood. I come to be animated with thy spirit, filled with thy grace, and enriched with thy virtues. I come to honour, and give joy to the whole court of heaven by the precious gift I offer in their honour, for succouring the church in her necessities, and procuring relief for the suffering souls in purgatory. I come, for

for obtaining fresh supplies of grace for the just, that they may persevere in justice, and make a continual progress in the ways of grace and sanctity; also for obtaining new helps for sinners to enable them to forsake their sins; new comforts for the afflicted, that they may bear their sufferings with resignation and fortitude. I come, in fine, to beg of thee to relieve the public and private necessities of thy faithful, particularly of such, and such a person, and to accomplish all the secret designs thou hast in regard to thy creatures, for whom it is thy will I should offer it.

Invocation.

I CANNOT reflect on the favour thou dost me this day, O divine Saviour! in admitting me as a guest at thy table, without trembling at the thoughts of my unworthiness. I tremble, and with good reason, lest this Communion, instead of drawing down upon me new favours, as did the ark on the house and family of Obededom on its being received into it, may rather call down a new judgment on my guilty head, as the same ark did upon the Philistines, while it continued in a kind of captivity among them; I fear its drawing on me a curse instead of a blessing. But do thou, O God! who vouchsafed me this happiness; prepare me, I beseech thee, for receiving worthily so singular a favour. Impart to me all the dispositions that

are

are necessary for receiving this august sacrament in such a manner as may give glory to thy name, and at the same time promote my salvation. Replenish me with thy spirit before thou feedest me with thy body; clothe me with the nuptial robe of charity before I am admitted to thy marriage-feast; purify me before I presume to partake of thy sacred flesh; wean my affections from creatures before I attempt to incorporate myself with thee who art my Creator, blessed for evermore. I could wish, my Saviour, to possess the merits and perfections of all thy saints and angels to receive thee in a manner more worthy of thee. I offer them up to thee, to make amends for my exceeding great poverty and wretchedness. With the same view, and in a more particular manner, do I offer to thee all that eminent sanctity with which thou didst replenish thy ever blessed Mother to qualify her for receiving thee in the mystery of the incarnation, and all those perfections with which thy sacred humanity was adorned at the instant of its being united to thy divine person.

Most holy and most adorable Trinity, whose temple I am to have the happiness to become this day by receiving my Saviour in the Blessed Eucharist, look down upon me, I beseech thee, with an eye of pity, to cleanse and sanctify me, that I may become an abode worthy of thee. My heart has been indeed hitherto the receptacle of venomous and unclean beasts; banish from it these monsters, cleanse it from all the infections and all the filth they may have left
behind

behind them; change it into a holy sanctuary; enrich it with thy gifts and thy graces, that there may, if possible, be some proportion between the infinite greatness of thy majesty, and the place of thy intended abode.

Holy Virgin, who bearest so great a part in whatever concerns the honour of thy dear Son, thou knowest how unworthy I am to receive him; obtain for me, I most earnestly entreat thee, by thy intercession, those christian and holy dispositions that are requisite for receiving him in a worthy manner.

Angels of the Lord, who, as ministering spirits most zealous for his glory, are careful to prepare the lodging where he is to take up his abode, use your endeavours, I pray you, to prepare my soul for receiving him. Obtain of him in my behalf, those precious gifts and that rich furniture wherewith to adorn and beautify it for his reception. Join them, ye saints in heaven and ye just on earth, and jointly entreat my divine redeemer, that he would endow me with whatever is necessary for receiving to my spiritual advantage so great a sacrament.

Joy ; Desire.

WHAT a subject of joy and happiness it is to me to receive this day within me the God of glory! to be feasted with the body and blood of my redeemer! to be so united to his body as to be incorporated together, and to partake,

take, in some measure, of its glory and its felicity!

The God of majesty comes to dwell within my breast to enrich me with the treasures of his grace and mercy, to admit me to a participation of his divine nature, to transform me in some measure into himself by clothing me with his divine excellencies, and by enabling me to lead a holy life.

He is a God whose power is infinite, and who delights in working prodigies. He comes to me to make my soul a theatre of wonders, to display there the magnificence of his love, and to work there miracles of grace, sanctity and perfection. What a source of consolation and advantages must it be for me to receive him!

No thirsty Hart pants after a fountain of living water with more eagerness, no dry ground stands more in need of rain, no famished person more earnestly longs for food, no patient is more desirous of a remedy by which he hopes to be restored to health, than my soul is for receiving thee, my God and my Saviour.

Upon the point of receiving.

MAY then this sovereign good, this God of love come unto me; may he come, the sole object of my desires and of all my hopes. O! who will be the means of my possessing him in the midst of my heart! Come, come, my my only love! my only treasure! my only good! that thou mayest possess me, and I thee. Come, O God, of majesty! and change my soul into a mansion resplendent with the lustre of thy sanctity; come and make it the temple of thy Holy Spirit, and establish in it a seat fit for thy residence.

Act of Faith after receiving.

IS it thou then, O God of glory! is it thou that art hidden under the sacramental veils, whom I have just now received and who dost reside at this instant within me? Is it thou, O sovereign majesty, who with a word created the universe, who with another canst annihilate, and who according to the expression of a prophet (Isai. 40. 12.) bearest this great fabrick with *three fingers* which are thy power, thy wisdom and thy goodness. Is it thou in fine, O divine redeemer! who hast ransomed the world by thy precious blood, and art now seated at the right hand of thy Father in heaven? Yes, it is thou thyself that art here really present; I firmly believe it, because thou thyself hast said it.

Act of Adoration.

I THEREFORE adore thee, O great God! I adore thee with sentiments of the most profound respect, and the most perfect veneration a mere creature is capable of. I repute myself as nothing in thy presence, to testify to thee my respect and to do homage to thy infinite perfections. I acknowledge thee for my God, my king, my redeemer and my all. I confess that thou art the sovereign Lord of all things; that thou art the only God that reigns in the heavens, and throughout the whole world; that all things belong to thee, depend on thee, and have received their being from thee, and subsist only by thee and for thee. I exalt, praise and glorify for ever thy most holy and adorable name. I join with all the saints and angels in heaven, and with all the just on earth in adoring, praising and glorifying this thy holy name for them, and with them for ever and ever. Amen.

Act of Admiration.

BUT what could induce thee, O Saviour of the world! to visit this thy wretched creature, thou who art the Being of beings, the infinite abyss of perfections, and the immense ocean of all good? How is it possible that thy incompre-

after Communion.

incomprehensible greatness should stoop so low as to bestow thyself upon so despicable, ungrateful and perfidious a wretch as myself, whose sole employment has been to provoke thy wrath by my sins? O ineffable goodness! O boundless love! O unparalleled generosity, never sufficiently to be admired! *Come and hearken all ye that fear the Lord* (Ps. 65. 16.) *and I will declare unto you what he hath done for my soul.* He came down from heaven to visit her, he made a sacrifice of himself to redeem her, and has given her his own flesh as food to nourish; to heal and to strengthen her.

Lift up, O my soul, lift up the eyes of thy mind to heaven, and there contemplate thy divine Saviour sitting at the right-hand of his Father, receiving homage from the whole court of heaven. Afterwards cast them down on thyself, and behold that same Saviour in thy breast, where all his glory appears eclipsed, his greatness annihilated, his power destroyed as it were and reduced to nothing. Is it possible that thou shouldst not be struck with astonishment at the sight of such a change?

Consider again with what eyes all the saints and blessed spirits in heaven behold the divine Jesus in thy breast; and what their sentiments must be in seeing him humbling himself to such a condition for the love of thee.

Act of Thanksgiving.

BUT what return shall I make unto thee, O Lord, for this ineſtimable benefit? what tokens shall I give thee of my gratitude? What more can I do, feeble and miſerable creature as I am, than to bleſs and thank thee; than to proclaim thy goodneſs and ſing forth thy mercies? Bleſs therefore, *O my ſoul, bleſs the Lord* (Pſ. 102. 1.) *and let all within me praiſe his holy name: Let all my bones* (Pſ. 34. 10.) *ſay, Lord, who is like unto thee,* who haſt done ſuch wonderful things in my behalf; who haſt bowed (Pſ. 17. 8.) the heavens to come down to me, and who in beſtowing thyſelf upon me haſt given me every thing. Ye creatures of heaven and earth which are the work of his hands, bleſs him with me, celebrate his praiſes, proclaim his glory and goodneſs, and aſſiſt me in giving him proofs of my perfect gratitude. Lord, who would ever been ſo bold as to hope that thou wouldſt have extended thy magnificence to ſuch a length in favour of ſo unworthy a creature? At the very thought of it my hear melts away with love and gratitude, and I can never ceaſe from thanking thee.

Act of Love

AND how can I refuse to love a God so abounding with goodness, and who has shewn so tender, so ardent and so generous a love for me? I love thee therefore, O God of love, God of goodness, God of mercy! I love thee with my whole heart, with all the powers and faculties of my soul, and with all the abilities my nature is capable of exerting. In desire, at least, I love thee with an immense love, with an infinite love, with an eternal love, and with a love comprehensive of all love whatsoever. O that I had a million of hearts burning to an infinite degree of intense heat, and infinitely perfect to love thee with infinite might, ardour and perfection! Ye angels and saints of heaven lend me, I pray, your hearts that I may love perfectly my God; or at least infuse into mine all the fire and flames your hearts burn with, that I may love so amiable an object with a greater ardency of affection. Ah! if my wishes could be obtained and my desires accomplished, my heart would burn with the most ardent, tender, and perfect love, which the omnipotence of God can kindle in the heart of a creature, that I might in some measure compensate the excess of love which my Jesus has for me in this mystery. But as all those sentiments are only desires and ideas the execution of which is impracticable, I make a sacrifice unto thee, O Jesus! of this heart itself

self which thou hast given me, even a holocaust or whole burnt offering, I consecrate unto thee all its affections, inclinations and desires, as some amends for its inabilities.

Act of enjoyment.

SINCE thy divine Jesus, O my soul, has given himself to thee, enjoy him in peace; *See and taste* (Ps. 33. 9.) *how sweet and amiable is the Lord*, and what a happiness it is to possess him. Replenish thyself therefore with his spirit, and lay in a large stock of his virtues. I possess thee then, O divine object, yes I possess thee in the very centre of my heart. There thou residest, happily for me; there thou art wholly mine as my substance, my treasure, my joy, my crown, my felicity. O how great is my happiness! for all my happiness is to have thee with me, and to keep myself united to thee. I may say with thy apostle on mount Thabor, *It is good* (Matt. 17. 4.) *for me to be here*. Yes, it is good to be with Jesus whom I have the happiness to possess. I enjoy here in his person the same object that constitutes the happiness of the saints in heaven; I drink at the same fountain-head, I am inebriated with the same delicious beverage, I am encompassed on all sides by the same torrent of delight: and if I have not an equal relish for these sweets, it is the weakness of my nature that blunts

blunts the edge of sensibility. O my Jesus, whom I have within me, make, I beseech thee, a paradise of my soul, that satiated with thy ineffable pleasures I may no more go after the fatal allurements of vice, nor court the insipid consolations of creatures.

Pour forth into my soul thy joy, peace, light, purity, love and justice; make them abide in my heart. Communicate unto me thy divine spirit, that for the future I may live only in thee, by thee and for thee. *Amen.*

Act of Oblation.

ETERNAL Father, thou hast this day made me a present of thy only Son. I possess him within me as a gift which thou and himself have bestowed on me, and as a bounty which in consequence of this gift, is my real property. I make a return of it and offer it unto thee in quality of victim, to acquit myself of all my duties to thee. This then, O great God! this is my Holocaust for honouring the infinite greatness of thy majesty, and the sovereignty of thy dominion on which all things depend. This my Eucharistical offering to thank thee for all thy benefits. This is my victim of Expiation to make satisfaction to thee for all my sins. This is my Peace-offering, to obtain from thee all the graces that are necessary for me in order to my salvation and perfection. I unite myself to this divine victim,

tim, and with it do offer myself up unto thee. I join in that infinite glory which it procures thee, in that immense love which it bears thee, in that excellence of praise which it gives thee, in that perfection of sacrifice which it offers thee, in all the sanctity of the duties it pays thee.

I offer thee his love to make amends for my coldness, and lukewarmness; his humility to make amends for my pride and vanity; his meekness to make amends for my anger and passion; his patience to make amends for my impatient and fretful humours; his purity to make amends for my uncleanness and filth; his obedience in satisfaction for my disobedience and rebellion: his poverty and disengagement from all created things, as an atonement for all my vices and defects: begging of thee, to grant me, by the virtue of his merits, all those graces I have occasion for. I not only offer up this divine victim for myself, but also for the whole church triumphant, I mean in honour of the blessed Virgin Mary and all the saints and angels; and in a more particular manner in honour of the sacred humanity of my Saviour; to thank thee for all the blessings and all the graces which thou hast ever bestowed upon them, and to pay thee every homage due to thee from them. I offer it up to thee for the whole church militant, that thou wouldst be pleased to guide her by thy holy Spirit, fill her with knowledge, love and strength; preserve her amidst the manifold dangers and temptations she is constantly exposed

posed to, and multiply her children, and propagate her faith throughout the world. I offer it up to thee for the whole suffering church, that thou wouldst in thy mercy be pleased, to deliver from Purgatory the souls detained there for the expiation of their sins, and to grant them admittance into heaven. I lastly offer it up to thee by way of atonement for the failures of all those who do not render all they owe to thy adorable majesty. I love thee in and through this victim for all those who do not love thee; I adore thee for all those who adore thee not; and I praise and glorify thee for all those, who either make flight of, or quite neglect thy praise and glory.

I likewise offer and consecrate myself unto thee, O divine Jesus to be, in my turn, thy victim. I consecrate unto thee my body, my soul, my powers, my life, my thoughts, my desires, my actions and whatever belongs to me, to be employed intirely to thy glory. Dispose of me in what manner soever it shall please thee; I resign myself entirely to thy will. I place myself in thy hands; form and fashion in me thy work, accomplish in me thy designs, and execute in me all the purposes of thy adorable will.

Act of Petition.

ADORABLE Jesus! who by an incomprehensible effect of thy love, hast vouchsafed to visit this thy wretched and unworthy creature, and

and to give thyself to it for food; operate in it, I beseech thee, the effects of this admirable sacrament. Wash and purify my soul from all its corruptions, by virtue of thy most precious blood; destroy in me the usurped power of sin, establish in me thy kingdom, plant in my heart thy divine virtues of charity, obedience, humility, patience, meekness, the love of the cross, and all others; make my life conformable to thine; enlighten my darkness, strengthen my weakness, root out my malice and evil dispositions; establish me in thy ways, draw me after thee that I may follow thee; deliver me from the dangers I am constantly exposed to; protect me against my enemies, and permit me not to become their prey. O my Saviour! thou art my sole resource, my refuge, my only hope. I expect no succour but from thee; do not abandon me, I beseech thee. The tokens of affection and goodness, which thou hast given me so lately by feeding me with thy flesh and blood, give me a full assurance of thy protection. Let me not then be frustrated I entreat thee, of my expectations of experiencing its happy effects.

Another Act of Petition.

DEAREST redeemer! whom I now possess within me, thou seest thyself the unfathomable depth of my miseries; have pity on me, I beseech thee, and relieve me. Behold, Lord,

the

the multitude of the sins I stand guilty of before thee, the little sorrow I have for them, and the little violence I use against myself to make satisfaction for them by penitential exercises, and to relinquish them by leading a new life. See, how many different passions I am subject to; to how many vices my inclinations lead me; what a propensity I have to pleasures, and for seeking my ease and conveniencies; and how destitute I am of faith, hope, and charity and all other christian virtues. See how wrong my understanding, how cold my will, how treacherous my memory have been in regard to thy service, and my own salvation: also how volatile and wandering has been my imagination, how violent my appetite, how licentious my senses; how easily I have suffered myself to be drawn into all sorts of vice, and how obstinately I have persisted in them. Consider in fine the rage and unrelenting malice of my enemies bent upon my destruction, and what risks I run of perishing every moment of my life. Now, Lord, shall not this my miserable condition move thee to compassion? Wilt thou leave me without help when I so much stand in need of it? Remedy therefore, I beseech thee, all my woes, grant me the true spirit of penance which may excite in me such a sincere and effectual sorrow for all my sins, as may make me expiate them by self-denials and mortifications, and which may enable me to *walk in the newness of life*, and become a new creature. In order to this, make me victorious over all my passions, and

root

root out my bad habits, and perverse inclinations; break off all my vicious attachment to myself and to creatures; grant me a lively faith, a stedfast hope, an ardent charity, and all other virtues in an eminent degree; open the inward eyes of my soul that they may see the truths of heaven; banish from my heart all lukewarmness and indolent dispositions; store my mind and memory with holy thoughts; put a stop to the wanderings of my imagination; subdue my rebellious appetite; restrain the licentiousness of my senses; check my unhappy propensity to sin; cover me with thy protection, as with a buckler, to shelter me against (Eph. 6. 16.) *the firey darts of the wicked one*; take me, in fine, upon thy shoulders, or into thy bosom, to carry me, as the eagle her young, into thy heavenly mansions; leave me not, I beseech thee, till thou hast placed me in that happy state, where I shall be no more exposed to any danger of being lost. *Amen.*

Resolutions.

GRANT, O my Saviour, that I may neglect nothing that may promote in me a faithful correspondence with thy grace and the accomplishment of thy adorable will. I promise by the assistance thereof, which I humbly implore, to reform my life, and to forsake whatever I perceive in myself to be displeasing to thee. I will

will use my earnest endeavours to amend those faults and failings, in particular which I know give thee most offence, as *N. N.* I promise also to apply myself with singular fervour, to the practice of virtue and good works, such a thing, *N. N.* in particular I will do for thy service. I will, in fine, for the future live for thee alone, and this shall be my motto, (Pf. 21. 31.) *My soul live to God.*

Remote Thanksgiving.

BE thou, O God of my heart! eternally blessed and thanked for the inestimable benefit thou hast this day bestowed upon me, in giving me nothing less than thyself to be the food and nourishment of my soul. May all the saints and angels, and all creatures both in heaven and earth, join in blessing and thanking thee for ever. Oh! how passionately I wish that I may not be ungrateful for the favour which I have this day received from thee, my divine redeemer? But whence shall I borrow a thanksgiving proportionable to the greatness of the benefit? Thou alone art worthy of thyself. Be thou therefore thyself, I pray thee, my thanksgiving. I thank thee by thyself. O devouring and consuming fire! which I have this day received within me, why dost thou not destroy there every thing that displeases thee? I desire no terms of composition: burn, devour, consume without reserve, whatever is there not agreeable to thee.

Make me sensible, O Jesus! of the effects of thy visit, by delivering me from my miseries, and transforming me into a new man. Alas! shall it be said that I continue the same, though thy main purpose in coming down from heaven was to work this change in me?

Accomplish it then in me, I beseech thee, and transform me entirely into thee.

Great and wonderful mystery! do thy work on me, I beseech thee; make me experience the effects of thy all powerful virtue, by recovering me from my weaknesses, and placing me in the situation where my God desires I should be.

Where, O Lord! are those immense stores of wealth, those precious gifts which thou gavest me hopes of being one day possessed of, and which I expected from thy liberality, when thou didst vouchsafe to visit me? wilt thou always leave me poor and miserable? Ah! enrich me, I beseech thee, with the treasures of thy grace and wisdom; and let not my past ingratitude, which I sincerely regret, cause an obstruction to this signal favour.

I have this day given thee my heart, O Jesus! I have consecrated my whole self to thee. I renew this my consecration, and do protest to thee again that thou art the sole object of my love and of all my affections.

And what other object is there in the world, O Jesus! which can be compared to thee in beauty, perfection, and excellence, and which bears me a love equal to thine? How then is it possible that I should withdraw my affections

from

from thee to place them upon any other object?

Withdraw, ye worthlefs creatures, withdraw far off from me, and leave unto my Jefus the full and undifturbed poffeffion of a heart I have fo often confecrated to him. You ftrive in vain to rob him of it, for I have refolved and promifed that he fhall be for ever the fole poffeffor of it.

Couldft thou dare, my foul, after having been fanctified this day by the prefence of the divine Jefus, to abandon thyfelf any more to fin? No, my Saviour, I would rather die a thoufand times than wilfully, and with full deliberation, commit any fin how inconfiderable foever it may be; and by the affiftance of thy grace, I will for the future, preferve myfelf pure and clean from all filth of fin whatever. Reflect ferioufly, my foul, on the obligation, the auguft facrament thou haft received this day, has impofed on thee of leading a virtuous life. It is the bread of heaven, and the bread of God; nothing lefs than a divine and holy life is expected from all who have partaken of it.

SPIRITUAL EXERCISES

For every Day in the Week, for the Use of the Clergy, and of such of the Laity as communicate often.

SUNDAY.

Consider Jesus Christ as a King; and in the Morning form the Resolution of making him that Day reign in thy Heart.

Divine Monarch come and reign in my Heart.

Remote Preparation.

THOU art this day come to me, O adorable sovereign! to ascertain thy conquest of my heart, and there to reign with absolute authority. Oh! how happy do I think myself to be under thy government? *Put on therefore thy armour,* (Ps. 44. 5.) *bend thy bow, march prosperously* against thy foes who have hitherto been in possession of this heart; and having expelled them, establish therein for ever thy empire.

O king

O king of nations, and object of all their desires! I groan under a most oppressive yoke, because, alas! *other* (Is. 26. 13.) *Lords beside thee have* hitherto *had dominion over me;* but come and break my bands, and set me at liberty.

Cheer up my soul; this day the Saviour of the world will begin to reign over us. We shall live no longer in slavish subjection to sin and satan, but under the mild government of our amiable redeemer. Ah! when shall I possess this gracious sovereign? when shall I have the happiness of seeing him reign in my heart?

If thou hadst, O my soul! a just idea of the inestimable favour done thee this day by the king of glory, in giving himself to thee, together with his kingdom and all his riches; *if thou understoodst the gift of God,* how great a value wouldst thou not set upon it? with what care and diligence, wouldst thou not strive to dispose thyself for it? Make me sensible, O Jesus! I beseech thee, of the greatness of this favour, and prepare my soul for receiving it.

Behold thy king cometh towards thee, O my soul! go forth to meet him by the ardour of thy desires, and a holy eagerness and impatience; and prepare for him a throne worthy of him in thy heart.

Come, O adorable sovereign, come and reign in my heart. *May thy kingdom come.* Every thing there longs for, and sighs after thy coming; every thing is eager for the establishment of thy kingdom; come, thou shalt be the Lord and master, thou shalt reign there with absolute power.

But wilt thou not, my soul, bring some offering to thy king, when thou presentest thyself before him? Thou must, as the wise men, offer him presents on thy going to adore him, if thou art desirous to meet with a favourable reception. The presents he most delights in are acts of humility, charity, obedience, mortification, patience and the duties of thy state done in his spirit and for the love of him. Canst thou then say with truth, as the spouse, *I consecrate all my actions to the king*; I consecrate all I do to my beloved sovereign, to dispose myself thereby to receive him worthily. Here is the royal feast which this great monarch gives to all his subjects, to display the glory and opulence of his empire; prepare thyself to taste of its delights, and in order to this renounce all insipid earthly pleasures.

Immediate Preparation.

HAST thou sufficiently considered, O my soul! who it is that comes to thee this day. Hast thou seriously reflected that it is the sovereign monarch of the universe who governs with absolute power in heaven, on earth, and in hell. His power is not confined to a small territory in a corner of the world, or to one particular nation; but he is the king of the whole creation, and of every nation in the world.

world. He is not a temporary king, a king for a limited space of time; he is the king of all (1 Tim. 1. 17.) ages, and of whose kingdom (Luke 1. 33.) there shall be no end. He is not a king indebted to his people for his glory and power; being all glorious of himself, he borrows nothing from creatures. He is not a king whose reign is liable to troubles and revolutions, for uninterrupted peace and tranquillity always flourish in it. He is a king, in fine, who gives his subjects whatsoever dignity or perfection they possess; being infinitely holy, infinitely wise, infinitely just, infinitely powerful, infinitely rich, infinitely munificent, infinitely beautiful, infinitely amiable, infinitely happy, in short, infinitely perfect in all and every kind of perfection. What a happiness it is for thee, O my soul! that so great a king should condescend to honour thee this day with his visit? One favourable look, a single word or mark of esteem from a king of the earth would transport thee with joy; how great then ought to be thy comfort this day, to receive a visit from the King of kings.

But why do I say a visit? his views are much more extensive: he comes to bestow himself upon thee to be equally thy king and thy kingdom. Thy king, because he is desirous to reign in thee; and thy kingdom, because he would have thee reign in him, and with him, and enter into a participation of all his excellencies, his riches and his glory.

See to what a degree he has carried his love for thee! Though thou art entirely unprofitable

ble to him, and though he be entirely rich, infinitely powerful, and infinitely happy in himself, yet he was willing to purchase that petty kingdom of thy heart at the expence of his life and blood. He was torn with scourges, crowned with thorns, besmeared with spittle, bruised with blows, and lastly fastened to the cross on which he died with pain and ignominy to rescue thee out of the hands of thy enemies and establish his kingdom within thee.

Reflect at the same time on the excess of thy ingratitude towards him. For though thou didst cost him so much, and though thy entire happiness consists in having him for thy sovereign, thou hast, notwithstanding, so far forgotten thyself, as shamefully to expel him thy heart, and to deliver up his kingdom to his most cruel enemies. Is it possible to carry ingratitude and perfidiousness to greater lengths? Be confounded, and beg pardon for so great an injury.

Ah! pardon my perfidiousness and rebellion, O august sovereign! pardon them I beseech thee. Oh! how hearty is my sorrow, how afflicted my soul on this account? Oh! how do I detest my wretched behaviour? my heart is pierced with grief for it. I promise thee, O my king and my God! by the assistance of thy grace, never to relapse into the like traiterous practices, though I were to suffer a thousand deaths I will for the future be as loyal and faithful to thee, as I have been hitherto rebellious. I will be as zealous in promoting thy interest, as I have been unhappy in in derogating from thy glory. Forget then, I pray thee, the trespasses I have committed against thee; I firmly hope for it from thy clemency and compassion.

I come this day, O divine monarch! to make reparation for the injustice I have done thee by delivering up thy kingdom into the hands of thy enemies. I come to replace it in thine, and to beg of thee to make thyself master of it, and to secure to thyself the possession of it for ever. In compliance with, and in perfect submission to the will of thy Father who has established thee King of all nations, I choose thee this day for my king: thou wast so already by inheritance and conquest, thou shalt be so for the future by election. Come then, my amiable sovereign, come and reign in me, and protect me against all my enemies.

O king of all the hearts of men and angels! I see plainly that notwithstanding thy immense wealth, thou dost desire the possession of my heart. Thou hast concealed thyself under the appearances of bread, with no other view than to enter there, and make thyself master of it. Come then and reign in it, it is intirely devoted to thee; it pants only after thee, and from this moment it consecrates to thee all its love and all its affections.

Be opened, ye gates of my heart! be opened, ye gates of iron, which have been so long shut against the divine Jesus, and let the king of glory enter. Yes, come in, O my Saviour! come in, all is open for thee, there is nothing to obstruct thy entrance: every thing in me owns thee for its fovereign, and fighs after the eftablifhment of thy kingdom within my foul. I here give up to thee the keys of my liberty. I furrender unto thee all the power which thou haft given me over my foul and body, over all their faculties, and over every thing elfe I poffefs; all is thine, and it is my defire that henceforward every thing within me may be entirely fubject to thee, and that nothing may be done in me but conformably to thy orders and commandments.

If I cannot give thee a reception fuitable to thy dignity, O divine monarch! I will receive thee at leaft with the deepeft fentiments I poffibly can of love, reverence, joy, adoration, humility, forrow for my fins and defire of being poffeffed by thee. I offer to thee to fupply what is deficient in my homages, all the acclamations, all the honour, and all the refpect with which the angels and bleffed fpirits received thee into heaven on the day of thy triumphant (Apoc. 3. 21.) afcenfion, and all the glory and magnificence with which thou waft received by thy Father, and placed at his righthand on a throne equal to his own. Come then, once more, O my king! come: I burn with the defire of feeing thee reign within me; come and take poffeffion of a kingdom which belongs to thee by fo many claims of juft right. Come and compel thy enemies to keep at a greater diftance from it than ever. Come and difplay thy glory in it; come and by thy prefence blefs it with peace, plenty, and happinefs!

ness! Yes, my beloved sovereign, my divine monarch, my king! I am thine, and thine indeed, without the least reserve.

Immediate Thanksgiving.

THOU art then within me, O King of glory! *My king and my God.* Yes it is my king and my God; I acknowledge and adore thee as such. What an excess of goodness must it be in thee, thus graciously to humble thy incomprehensible greatness to the lowliness of my condition? Ye heavens, stars, elements, and creatures of heaven and earth, bless this great king. Ye angels and saints of the Lord especially, sing to him a new song, for the new and incomparable favour he has just now conferred upon me. And do thou, O my soul! bless him also. May all my members, and all my powers cry out with holy David, *blessed be his glorious name for ever;* and with the apostle, *Unto the king eternal, immortal, and invisible, be honour and glory* given for ever and ever. Amen.

But since thou art within me, divine monarch, seat thyself, I beseech thee, in the midst of my heart, and make it thy throne. Thy throne is a throne of light and fire, a throne of justice and sanctity: illuminate my heart therefore with thy light, inflame it with the fire of thy love, clothe it with thy justice and
sanctity,

sanctity, that it may be a habitation worthy of thee.

Abide for ever in my heart, O amiable sovereign! may nothing ever obstruct thy reigning there with absolute authority. All rule and empire is thine; riches and glory belong to thee; thou possessest a sovereign and absolute power over all things: *strength* and authority are in thy hands. *Thine, O Lord, is the greatness and the power, and the glory; and thine is the kingdom, and thou art exalted as head above all.*

All ye powers of my soul and body, come and adore your king upon his new throne. Come my understanding and my will, my memory and all my senses, come and pay him homage and adoration. *Come, let us adore and fall down before him.* May every thing in me adore thee, O august sovereign! may every thing own thee for its king, and submit with the most profound veneration to thy power, authority and dominion.

Rule then upon this thy new throne *in the midst of thy enemies,* O divine monarch! Thou art there beset with a multitude of passions, vices, wicked inclinations that are within me, and stand up in opposition to thy divine laws: but do thou rule notwithstanding in the midst of them all; triumph over them by thy power; raise for thyself trophies upon their ruins; confound the devices, defeat the efforts of all thy adversaries; drive them out of all their strong holds and rule in their stead. Reign in my mind, in my memory, in my appetite, in all my senses: reign, in short, throughout my whole being.

Behold, O my king! to what a wretched condition thy enemies have reduced this little kingdom. They have plundered, burnt, and sacked every thing. Nothing more is seen but the melancholy remains of the ravages and desolations they have committed. Repair, I beseech thee, the damages they have caused in it; send into it powerful succours for its defence: make opulence and plenty to reign in it; display there thy glory and thy magnificence, and prevent thy enemies evermore becoming masters of it.

Proclaim, O sovereign king! thy laws in this thy little kingdom, engrave them so deep in my heart, that the impression may never be effaced; write them in characters that cannot be effaced; cause them to be observed by all my powers with an inviolable exactness. Thy laws are the dictates of love, meekness, patience, humility, obedience and mortification; make me therefore practise all these virtues; fill my soul with thy love; establish thy peace in it; make it humble, meek, patient, obedient and mortified.

Thou justly requirest of me, O divine monarch! fidelity and tribute, I promise thee both. I will for the future be inviolably faithful to thee; I will never hearken to any proposal contrary to thy service, though my refusal were to cost me my life a thousand times over. I will never engage in any enterprise which displeases thee, how much soever solicited, or even

even compelled thereto. All my thoughts, desires and actions shall be a kind of tribute that I will pay thee; for it is my firm purpose that every thing of this kind shall be wholly thine, and shall tend to no other end, shall have nothing else in view than to promote thy glory. In a more particular manner I consecrate unto thee whatever I am to do this day.

The only request I have to make, O my gracious sovereign! is, that thou wouldst always reign in me, and never leave this little kingdom to my own management, nor abandon it to my enemies. I will have no other king to reign in my heart but thee, because it is thou alone that I love, reverence and adore. Rule in me at all times; give ever thy orders, and make thyself always obeyed. Thy kingdom has no bounds; let it therefore extend to every thing I am possessed of; to my whole being, and to all the powers and faculties both of my soul and body. Thy kingdom is everlasting; suffer not the tyranny of passion, nor the usurped empire of sin to destroy it in me. Thy kingdom is infinitely perfect; may therefore its glory, its riches, and its magnificence shine forth in me by means of the eminent virtues thou shalt enable me to practice.

Oh! the happiness of having my Jesus for my sovereign Lord, and of seeing myself subjected to his power, and governed by his amiable laws. I prefer obedience to him to the empire of the universe. By his reigning over me, he makes me a sharer in his kingdom, power and wealth; or rather, he himself becomes

An Exercise for Sunday.

comes my kingdom, my crown, my power, my wealth and my treasure. What an accumulation of glory and happiness is this for me! Preserve as the most precious of treasures, O my soul! the possession of this admirable kingdom which thy Jesus this day consigns over to thee. And thou, my Jesus! secure to thyself the possession of the little kingdom, which I this day resign into thy hands. The proofs thou hast given me of thy love, by feeding me with thy body and blood, encourage me to hope for this favour from thee.

Thou art possessed, O great king! of other kingdoms besides this of mine which I have this day made over to thee. The church is thy kingdom; all the nations of the earth (Pf. 2. 2.) are thy kingdom, though the greater part do not acknowledge thee for their king; every soul in particular is also thy kingdom, though but few of them render thee the submission they owe thee. I recommend unto thee all these kingdoms, the catholic church especially, beseeching thee to preserve and defend her, and to maintain in her a strict observance of thy laws. I recommend unto thee so many nations that are strangers to thy holy name; I beg of thee to enlighten them with the light of thy gospel, and bring them over to thee. I recommend unto thee, so many souls now upon the earth, which do not render thee the honour which they owe thee: convert them, I beseech thee, that they may serve and obey thee. As to thy part, my soul, let nothing make thee forget to serve and honour thy king.

king. On this day, in particular, let it be thy only study to honour, in the best manner thou art able, thy adorable sovereign, saying with the apostle: *To the king immortal, eternal* (1 Tim. 1. 17.) *be honour and power everlasting.* Amen.

Remote Thanksgiving.

BLESSED be thou for evermore, O sovereign King of heaven! for thy goodness in visiting me this day, and giving thyself to me to be my king. May all the creatures in heaven and earth join in thanksgiving to thee for so great a benefit.

Reign, I beseech thee O my king! in my heart, and in all my faculties and powers. Do not suffer sin to bear any sway there after thou hast taken possession of it.

Triumph, O my sovereign Lord! in this thy new kingdom; beat down all thy enemies under thy feet, that they may serve thee as a footstool for mounting thy throne: may every thing yield and submit to thee: *The Lord reigneth, let the people tremble,* he *who is seated on the cherubims* reigneth in my heart, *let the earth quake for fear*; let the universe respect his presence, and let no creature presume to oppose his laws.

Remember, O Jesus! thy little kingdom which thou hast conquered and acquired at the price of thy blood; defend it against thy enemies,

enemies, and cause justice and sanctity to flourish in it.

Seek, O my soul! the kingdom of thy Jesus. It is not the kingdom of this world, but of the other: it consists not in the sweets of the present life, in eating, drinking and diversions; but in peace, justice and sanctity. To seek his kingdom is to seek his glory; seek then his glory here, if thou desirest to be admitted into his eternal kingdom hereafter.

Thou hast this day promised fealty, O my soul! to thy king; and wilt thou evermore presume to turn traitor and surrender his kingdom to his mortal enemies? Oh! beware of such base treachery; be faithful to thy promise, fight manfully in his cause and call him to thy assistance that he may protect thee.

MONDAY.

Consider Jesus Christ as thy Father, and propose at waking to return to him, though thou hast so basely deserted him: say with the prodigal son and in the like penitential disposition: I will arise and go to my Father.

Remote Preparation.

OH! to what a wretched condition do I find myself reduced? I am poor, naked, famished and destitute of help. Why should I tarry

tarry longer in so miserable a condition, whilst even the hired servants in my father's house live in plenty? I will go then to my father, I will cast myself at his feet and will implore him to treat me like one of them.

Awake, O fatherly heart! and listen to what thy tender compassion shall speak to thee in favour of this thy unhappy child, who hath so basely abandoned thee: let the sight of his misery move thee to compassion, and to receive him again into thy house.

Be of good courage, O my soul! for how base soever thou hast been, such is thy Father's goodness and mercy that thou hast reason to hope that this day will put an end to all thy miseries; and that forgetting thy past disorders, he will restore thee to favour, and fill thee with the good things with which his house is known to bound.

O the most tender and the most loving of all fathers! thou art then willing to receive this prodigal child who hath so highly displeased thee; to change his affliction into joy, his poverty into wealth, his misery into happiness: who can sufficiently admire such an excess of bounty?

O how I desire to return to my heavenly Father! All my thoughts, affections, desires and actions shall serve this day as so many steps towards my return to him by means of the zeal and love wherewith I purpose to discharge them.

Not satisfied with receiving me, O merciful Father! thou dost also slay the fatted calf
for

for feasting me. A signal mark this of thy goodness! But clothe me first, I beseech thee, as the prodigal child, with the *robe* of charity; give me the *ring* of faith and the *shoes* of hope, that I may partake worthily of this heavenly food, no other than thy precious body here exhibited in the state of mystical death.

But since thou art, O my soul! to partake of this delicious aliment, cast from thee the husks of swine, renounce all sensual pleasures, and maintain the glorious dignity of a child of God by a life led in conformity to thy high rank.

This divine aliment is the bread of children; to be qualified for a participation of it, it is necessary to be a child of the heavenly Father and to lead a pure and holy life. This holy bread is not designed for dogs, nor for slaves, that is, for unclean souls, such as live under the law of sin. Clothe thyself therefore with the spirit and the virtues of the children of God, before thou dost presume to partake of it.

Immediate Preparation.

BEHOLD, loving Father! behold here that prodigal child who hath treated thee so unworthily, who left thee against thy will, who squandered away thy substance in rioting and debauchery, dishonoured thy holy name by a course of life unworthy of his birth, and who hath given thee so much vexation and uneasiness.

ness. He returns to thee covered with confusion and loaded with misery. He ingenuously confesses that he deserves no more to be called thy child, since he has not obeyed thee as his Father, and since by his sins he has defaced the features whereby he resembled thee. He cast himself notwithstanding at thy feet, in hopes that thy paternal bowels will yearn upon him at the sight of his misery, and that thou wilt at least receive him amongst thy hired servants. His sorrow for having displeased thee, O loving Father, is exceeding great; the affliction his conduct has given thee, grieves him beyond measure; and he has a much quicker sense of the trouble he has given thee, than of the misfortune he has brought upon himself by his follies and disorders.

Reflect, O my soul! on thy infinite obligations to this Father. Consider well his goodness towards thee in given thee a being and preserving it when given; bearing with thee, when thou didst depart from thy duty, and receiving thee when thou didst return to him. He is on a three-fold consideration thy Father, having given thee life three different ways. First, by bestowing on thee natural life on thy coming into the world: Secondly, by giving thee the life of grace in the sacrament of baptism: Thirdly, by having restored thee to this same life of grace in the sacrament of penance, after thou hadst forfeited it by thy sins. And indeed, he is thy Father an infinite number of times over, having given thee an infinite number of times, nay every moment,

both

both the life of nature and grace which flow continually from him as the rivulet from its source. By the life of nature which he has given thee, he hath raised thee above all sensitive creatures, and rendered thee like unto the angels; and by the life of grace he has made thee his child, and heir of his kingdom and of all his possessions. Behold the excess of his love and goodness towards thee, by raising thee to so exalted a dignity!

But what deserveth thy particular notice is, that this loving Father did not give thee this life of grace but by suffering death himself, even the death of the cross. Thou art the child of his sorrows, whereas the angels are the children of his joys: because he begot thee amidst the griefs of his passion, whereas he gave being to the angels amidst the joys of his felicity. He still suffers continually a kind of death on our altars, to preserve unto thee that life which he gave thee on the cross. Could his love extend farther? Ponder well with thyself, how great thy glory and happiness is to have for Father, the creator of the universe, the sovereign Lord of all things, the God of majesty whose glory, power and riches have no bounds: and what an excess of goodness it was in him to have made thee his child by adoption, and to have suffered so many torments to merit for thee that quality!

Reflect at the same time on the ungrateful returns thou hast made for such extraordinary favours; thy whole life having been nothing better than a complication of disobedience and rebellion,

rebellion, of wrongs and injuries which thou haft been guilty of againft him: for indeed, thou haft fcarce ufed the leaft endeavour to pleafe him, or to give him any tokens of thy refpect on the flighteft occafions.

Is it poffible for thee not to admire the greatnefs of his love which makes him this day overlook all this bafe ufage, to come to feed thee, not with fuch food as other parents fupport their children with, but his own flefh and blood? It was his love that made thee come forth out of the bofom of his power, when he gave thee a being; and it is the fame love which induces him this day to come into thy heart to be united with thee. He does not throw himfelf about thy neck in embraces to exprefs his tender regard for thee, as the father did to his prodigal fon; he goes farther, penetrating even to the bottom of thy heart to unite himfelf therewith, and there to repofe himfelf amidft the delights of thy heart. Muft not fuch an excefs of goodnefs make thee afhamed of thy paft conduct, and by exciting thee to a deteftation of it, engage thee to anfwer the ardours of his love by a due return of the fame on thy fide?

I deteft therefore with the greateft abhorrence, O merciful Father! all my paft diforders; I beg a thoufand pardons for them with a heart pierced with forrow, and a face covered with confufion; and I am determined rather to die a thoufand times than evermore to give thee the leaft difpleafure. I will for the time to come entertain that refpect, love, fubmiffion miſſion and gratitude towards thee as ſhall be a means of as much ſatisfaction to thee, as my paſt ingratitude and rebellion have been a ſubject of affliction.

Thou hadſt loſt this child whom thou didſt love ſo tenderly, O Father of mercy, but I hope that thou wilt this day regain him. Come then to him to take him with thee, come and honour him with thy divine preſence: come and repoſe thyſelf in his boſom, and make him repoſe himſelf in thine. He preſents himſelf before thee quite tranſported with love, gratitude and tender affection that thou mayeſt poſſeſs him for ever. He feels for thee ardours and tranſports which he cannot find words to expreſs; but being ſenſible that theſe diſpoſitions are not yet ſufficiently perfect to qualify him to appear before thee in a manner ſuitable to the exceſs of thy loving kindneſs, he offers thee to ſupply for this deficiency, all the love, obedience, reſpect and other eminent virtues of the ſaints and angels in heaven, and of all thy true children. Do not delay then, O loving Father! to viſit this thy child, that thou mayeſt put an end to his miſery, to reform in him thy image, to make him reſemble thee and remain for ever united with thee. Ah! I am thine, and I beg thy grace that I may be ſo for ever. Come therefore unto me, take poſſeſſion, I beſeech thee, of this thy child; his heart melts with love and tenderneſs when he ſees thee coming; to be united to thee, and to live with thee, is the ſum of all his deſires.

Immediate

Immediate Thanksgiving.

I POSSESS thee then, O amiable Father! in the midst of my heart, in the centre of my being. What an excess of goodness, in having so easily forgotten my past ingratitude and disobedience! What a prodigy of love and forbearance, in taking no other revenge on me for the horrid outrages I have been guilty of against thee, than by granting me the most signal of all favours, that of giving me thyself for food and nourishment! It is now that I am much more sensible than ever of my guilt in offending so kind a Father. I ask again thy pardon for it with a heart pierced with grief, and eyes melting into tears.

But what shall be my return of thanks, O my heavenly Father! for the favour thou hast just now granted me. *May my heart and all that is within me* (Pf. 102. 1.) *bless thee; may all my bones* (Pf. 34. 10.) proclaim thy praises; may all thy creatures of heaven and earth thank thee with, and for me. Since it is my happiness to possess thee within me, O heavenly Father! it is thy will that I should acquit myself of my obligations to thee. I therefore cast myself at thy feet, to testify my profound respect for thee, and to pay thee the honour that I owe thee. I adore thee with the deepest sentiments of veneration and submission, and I offer myself unto thee to execute henceforward, with an unreserved and constant obedience,

An Exercise for Monday.

dience, whatever thou shalt require of me; I acknowledge no other Father but thee. If there be a man upon earth whom I call by this name, I consider him in no other light than as the instrument thou hast made use of to give me being. But how great is the difference between Thee and this father? He begat me without knowing me; but thou didst know me before thou wast pleased to create me, and thou didst not create me but because thou hadst known and loved me before I had a being. This father begat me but once, amd perhaps afterwards left me forlorn; whereas thou producest me incessantly by an uninterrupted conservation, and hast never abandoned me. This father, in fine, gave me only a human being, but thou, by the means of grace, hast given me a divine (2 Pet. 1. 4.) being, It is thou alone therefore that art truly my Father; and thee alone do I own as properly such and whom I will henceforward obey.

His follies and disorders had robbed thee of this thy child, O bountiful Father! and thy love gave thee an extreme regret for his loss; but behold him now returned to thee, quite shamed of his ill-conduct, and fully resolved to repair it by the most sincere respect for thee, and the strictest obedience to all thy commands. Possess him, keep him always with thee, and hinder his going from thee any more, or his falling into the hands of thy enemies.

Alas! what did this foolish creature promise or warrant to himself by quitting thee? What has

has he found, out of thy houſe, but affliction, trouble and poverty? O how true it is, O amiable Father! that there is no happineſs, no ſatisfaction but with thee, Nothing but immediate miſery muſt be his lot who deſerts thee; the moment a man leaves thee he is loſt,

Behold, O tender Father! the wretched and forlorn condition to which thy enemies have reduced thy ſon! how they have disfigured him and effaced every feature of reſemblance he bore to thee! how they have tarniſhed his beauty, enfeebled his ſtrength, covered him with wounds, loaded him with ignominy, and ſtript him of all his valuable poſſeſſions and ornaments! May thy paternal heart be touched with compaſſion at the ſight of his miſery. Reinſtate him, I pray, in his former condition, retouch his features, reſtore to him his primitive beauty; heal his wounds, repair his decayed ſtrength, wipe away thoſe marks of ignominy which diſhonour him, and clothe him ſuitably to his birth and condition.

This child, O Father of mercy! is now in thy hands, Inſtruct him, I beſeech thee, correct him, conduct him, provide for him and defend him; keep an eye always upon him to prevent his departing from his duty, and to preſerve him from whatever may be hurtful to him: give him a true filial diſpoſition towards thee, and make him worthy of ſo great and ſo holy a Father, by animating him with thy ſpirit. And do thou, O my ſoul! give all due and proper attention to thy Father's advice

vice and inſtructions, and make them henceforward the rule of thy conduct.

Thou doſt very juſtly infiſt, O Father! upon this child's giving thee his heart, and placing his intire confidence in thee: he does ſo; for indeed, how ſhould he refuſe to comply? Yes, he gives thee all his love, all his eſteem, all his reſpect; he places in thee his whole confidence; he reſigns himſelf intirely into thy hands; he humbly ſubmits to all thy diſpenſations, and will for the future take every thing as from thy paternal hand: Yes, heavenly Father, as often as any thing proſperous befalls me, I will ſay, This is an effect of my Father's favour; and as often as any difaſter happens to me, I will ſay, This is his chaſtiſement. When diſturbed with temptations, I will call them trials of my fidelity. In ſhort, I will conſider every thing that ſhall happen to me as coming from my Father, and as teſtimonies of his love for me; and in all my actions I will ſeek nothing but his glory, and the fulfilling of his adorable will.

I will endeavour above all things to copy after thy infinite holineſs and thy other divine excellencies; I will ſtrive to be holy and *perfect* (Matt. 5. 48.) *as my heavenly Father is perfect*, and to be a ſubject of glory to thee by a life led in conformity to thine, particularly by the practice of ſuch and ſuch a virtue, and by the amendment of ſuch and ſuch a fault. But it is from the almighty power of thy grace, and not from my own ſtrength which is no better than weakneſs, that I hope,

O divine Father! for all this; grant me then I beseech thee, all the succours I stand in need of for accomplishing these good purposes.

I recommend unto thee also, O holy Father! thy other children which are dispersed throughout the world. Preserve the good in a punctual discharge of their duties, and make them grow in grace and advance daily in virtue and sanctity. Bring back from their errors and wanderings those that have deserted thee, give them grace to join the former in paying thee all due honour and obedience. As to myself, I promise thee that I will henceforward endeavour to acquit myself of all my duties in the best manner I am able, and will from this moment lay nothing so much to heart as the accomplishment of thy adorable will, this shall be my main business and employment; in every action I perform I will say: *My food, and my sweetest delight is to do the will of my Father.*

Remote Thanksgiving.

MAY immortal thanks be given to my divine Father for his goodness towards his fugitive and rebellious child, by receiving him this day into favour, by treating him with such magnificence and feasting him on the most delicious dainties he could set before the angels and blessed spirits in heaven.

My

An Exercise for Monday.

My heart breathes for thee alone, O amiable Father! it feels no pleasure but in thinking on thee, in cleaving to thee, in labouring for thy glory: all its desires and inclinations are to please thee. I renounce from this day, O worldlings! all conformity with your corrupt and unwarrantable ways; I loathe the enjoyment of the pleasures you present me with, I no longer live but for the sake and service of my Father, I have no other pleasure but in pleasing him.

O the sweet name of heavenly Father! my heart tastes a sweetness not to be expressed when my tongue pronounces it; it finds nothing so agreeable upon earth as to repeat it frequently, saying, *Abba, Pater!* Father! Father!

O holy Father! forget not the child of thy adoption; defend him against his enemies who are ever seeking after his destruction and provide for all his wants.

Leave me not alone, O loving Father! but abide always with me as thou hast promised, lest I should lose myself again.

Keep thine eyes constantly fixed upon me to watch over my ways, and lead me by the hand like a little child, lest I fall or lose myself.

Forget not, my soul, thy Father's greatness; live in a manner worthy of thy birth; thou hast God for Father, lead then a life altogether divine, do the works of thy heavenly Father.

Is it possible, O my soul, that after so many protestations of love, reverence and obedience to thy divine Father, thou shouldst ever again break through them, and be guilty of injuring him afresh? Ah! let it never be said that thy ingratitude and perfidiousness have risen to such a pitch. Observe therefore with an unshaken fidelity whatever thou hast promised him.

TUESDAY.

Consider Jesus Christ as Teacher, and purpose with thyself to learn his divine Doctrine.

Teach me, O Lord, thy divine ordinances.

Remote Preparation.

IT has been thy misfortune, O my soul! to have hitherto lived in darkness and ignorance, to have suffered thyself to be seduced by errors and lies. But behold here the teacher (Matt. 22. 16.) of the way of God in truth, who this day comes to undeceive thee, and to instruct thee in his divine doctrine. Let it be thy most earnest desire that he would vouchsafe himself to be thy instructer.

Come,

An Exercise for Tuesday.

Come, O heavenly master! come O teacher of nations! come and teach me the way of truth and the science of salvation, the only science I desire.

I have made choice of the way of truth I am resolved to walk no longer in that of falsehood. But come, O eternal truth! and instruct me in thy ways; thou alone canst teach me them.

Blessed, O Lord! *is that man whom thou instructest and teachest out of thy law.* Oh! do me the favour to instruct me out of it, and to teach me what it prescribes.

Let us go, O my soul! *let us go up to the mountain of the Lord, and to the house of the God of Jacob*, (Isai. 2. 3.) *and he will teach us his ways*; let us go and give ear to the oracles of this master who is come down from heaven, whom his Father commands us to hearken to, saying: *Hear ye him.*

But do thou, O Jesus, give me a docil heart, that I may receive thy doctrine with all due respect; give me understanding that I may comprehend it; give me wisdom that I may relish it, love it and be guided by it; send forth thy holy spirit to prepare my soul for receiving it.

Thy former errors, O my soul, must be renounced, if thou art desirous of understanding the doctrine of this divine master, without this thou wilt never be able to penetrate or relish it. Yes, Lord, I renounce and detest those errors from my heart, I am resolved never to follow any doctrine but thine.

The euchariſtical bread is a *bread* (Ecclus. 15. 3.) *of underſtanding*, which fills with the light of the ſublimeſt wiſdom thoſe who partake worthily of it. It is the genuine fruit of the tree of knowledge, which makes us perfectly intelligent in the ſcience of the ſaints. Go, my ſoul, and receive it with an ardent deſire of being filled with the heavenly light it will infuſe into thee.

Immediate Preparation.

IS it then poſſible, O Eternal wiſdom, O divine Word, light of the Father, the only begotten Son of God! is it true that thou condeſcendeſt to come and viſit this day from heaven, and to inſtruct in perſon this vile creature? Heretofore thou didſt inſtruct thy people by the mouth of thy patriarchs and prophets, but thou art pleaſed this day to do me the favour of taking upon thyſelf to be my inſtructer. And who or what am I, Lord, to deſerve that thou ſhouldſt addreſs thyſelf to me! I am no better than a vile wretch, who have offended thee a thouſand times, who have a thouſand times ſlighted thy doctrine, and have therefore ſo often rendered myſelf unworthy of being inſtructed by thee. But how much do I lament my having treated thee in this manner! how am I aſhamed and confounded at ſuch my behaviour! My heart is ready to burſt with ſorrow on this account,

and

and cannot sufficiently express its abhorrence of its wickedness. It humbly craves thy pardon for it, and intreats thee to blot it out of thy remembrance; promising to repair for the future the injury thereby done thee, by the profound respect and veneration it shall ever entertain for thy divine oracles.

I cannot sufficiently admire, O Lord, thy exceeding great charity towards me by condescending to be thyself my instructer; notwithstanding all my ingratitude and my base behaviour towards thee. I see, indeed, that those men, who are raised a little above me, look down upon me with contempt, though I never gave them the least offence, and even think it beneath them to speak to me. Yet thou, O Lord! who by the excellency of thy being and greatness of thy majesty, art so immensely raised above me, and whom I have so often offended, thou, I say, disdainest not to come down from thy throne to teach me the truths of salvation. O what a charity is this!

Reflect now, O my soul! with all due attention, on the excellence of the master who comes to thee this day to teach thee his doctrine; he is the sovereign of the universe, in whom are contained all the treasures (Col. 2. 3.) of the divine wisdom and knowledge. He is the source of all knowledge both in heaven and earth, and from whom angels, men and all creatures derive whatever gifts they possess of this kind. He that seeks not for knowledge in this living fountain, must remain in ignorance and error; and he that does, is sure of

being

being bleſſed with truth. This divine maſter is not like other maſters whoſe ſucceſs in teaching depends much on the diſpoſitions and capacities of their diſciples; he teaches his *as one having authority,* (Mat. 7. 29.) with influence over the powers, and whenever it pleaſes him he himſelf makes them learned. Oh! how ſoon is learning acquired, when he vouchſafes to teach!

Conſider alſo the perfection of his doctrine, which infinitely ſurpaſſes all other doctrines whatſoever; as by its *nobleneſs,* becauſe it is celeſtial and divine; by its *certainty,* becauſe infallibly; by its *extenſiveneſs,* becauſe it compriſes all things; by its *utility,* becauſe it beſtows happineſs on all thoſe that hearken to it; and by its *neceſſity,* becauſe to be ignorant of it, or to deſpiſe it would be to expoſe ones ſelf to eternal perdition.

Reflect how much thou ſtandeſt in need of receiving inſtructions from this maſter who is come down from heaven, ſince thou art as a child that cannot diſtinguiſh between the right hand and the left, between good and evil; nay, as an irrational creature, and void of underſtanding: and does not thy behaviour oftentimes ſpeak thee ſtill more unwiſe than the very brute itſelf? For *the ox knoweth his owner* (Iſai. 1. 3.) and the aſs his maſter's crib; *the ſwallow and the ſtork* (Iſai. 9. 7.) *know their appointed ſeaſons,* and obſerve the time of their coming and retiring; but thou hadſt not the ſenſe to decline the danger that threatens thee. A beaſt coming to the brink of a precipice

ſtops

stops short, but thou willingly castest thyself headlong down it.

Admire how great the kindness must be of this adorable sovereign, to induce him to come and instruct thee. What other master besides himself would stoop so low as to become thy teacher? He comes to thee, nay he incorporates himself with thee with the view of writing his instructions on thy heart with the characters of his own. Who besides himself would take a pleasure in familiarizing himself with thee and teaching thee the sacrets of his wisdom? What other master, in fine, would reward thy attention to his instructions by heaping on thee riches on this account? Other masters expect to be paid for their care in teaching their scholars; but this master, to induce his disciples to learn his doctrine, promises and gives them all his wealth, as a reward of their docility. O Lord, how great is thy goodness! how amiable thy charity! how happy am I in such a master!

Blest as thou art, O my soul! with so great a master, is it not thy duty to pay him all due respect? Being so good, oughtest thou not to love him? His doctrine being so pure, and perfect and divine, does it not challenge thy highest esteem? and withal so necessary, is it not thy interest to learn it? I adore thee therefore, O sovereign master, with the most profound respect imaginable; I love thee with all the ardour of my soul. I set the highest value on thy doctrine, and desire nothing so much as to learn it, and I hope that this day

day thou wilt make me a thorough proficient in it.

Prepare thyself, O my soul, to receive with all suitable respect and love, the doctrine of thy divine master. Thou art this day to become, in some repect, the school in which he is to teach, the pulpit in which he is to preach, and the book in which he is to write. Prepare thyself on all these accounts to embrace and adhere to his doctrine.

But how vain and fruitless will all my endeavours be, O Jesus! for these purposes, without thy assistance? Prepare then, I beseech thee, this heart for receiving thy divine instructions: make its inward ear attentive that it may listen to thee; soften its hardness, that thy documents may make a deep impression on it; give it a relish for thy maxims that it may love them; and send forth thy holy Spirit, that he may give it docility and every other disposition with which thou desirest they may be received and entertained: and to supply for what is wanting on my side, I offer unto thee the docility and every other suitable disposition of thy saints and angels. Come therefore, O divine master! for my heart pants after thee with extreme earnestness: come, I promise that it shall hearken to thee, that thy doctrine shall be received in it with respect, and that it shall be there faithfully followed. Come, love, wisdom, light, divine truth! come, I pray thee, I have no other desire but to be instructed by thee.

Immediate

An Exercise for Tuesday.

Immediate Thanksgiving.

THOU haſt then granted my requeſt O Teacher of the apoſtles! and art come into my ſoul. How great is my happineſs and what a favour have I received! But what ſhall I do to teſtify my gratitude? May infinite and eternal thanks be returned to thee by all the creatures of heaven and earth; may every being adore, glorify and praiſe thy moſt holy and moſt adorable name for the ineſtimable benefit which thou haſt granted me. I adore thee, I praiſe and thank thee together with them, with all the ſentiments of reſpect, love and gratitude my heart is capable of.

But ſince I enjoy the happineſs of having thee within me, O my beloved maſter! ſpeak to me, inſtruct me, I beſeech thee, for I will never more have any other maſter but thee; I will never more liſten to any other doctrine but thine, teach me then, I moſt humbly intreat thee.

Suffer me, O divine maſter! to place thyſelf with all due reſpect at thy feet as another Mary (Luke 10. 39.) that I may attend to thy divine oracles. Graciouſly be pleaſed to accept from me my heart, my underſtanding, my memory, my affections, my ſenſes both internal and external, that they may be formed and modelled by thee.

Here is then my heart which I give thee to be thy diſciple; teach it to ſerve thee, to do every thing in its power to please thee, never to seek itself, to walk at all times in thy ways and never to follow its own; and to fulfil always thy adorable will preferably to the suggestions of its own. Teach it to love the cross, mortification and penance; to regulate all its desires and actions by the maxims of thy gospel; to abhor and despise the honours, pleasures and riches of the present world, and to place its whole esteem and love in the goods of the world to come; in short, to desire nothing but virtue, to rejoice in nothing but doing good, and to put its whole confidence in thee.

Here is likewise my mind which I desire may be thy disciple. Teach it to know thee and to know itself; to judge of all things by the light in which thou beholdest them, and not according to that in which they appear to the eyes of men. Take from it that veil which hinders its clear perception of the vanity of the things of this world, of the excellence of those of heaven, of the deformity of sin, of the beauty of virtue, of the folly of those who run after visible and temporal things of the wisdom of such as shew no eagerness but for those that are invisible and eternal. In fine, discover to it the truth and beauty of thy ways, and the error and misery of the ways of the world.

Here too are my memory, my imagination, my desires, my senses and all the faculties of my soul and body, which I give thee in like manner to be disciplined and instructed by thee. Teach my memory to bear thee continually in remembrance, my imagination to form

An Exercise for Tuesday.

form images which may lead me to thee, and to reject all such as may withdraw me from contemplating thy perfections. Teach my defires to govern all their motions by thy laws, and to repress all such as are not conformable to them. Teach my eyes to behold thee in every thing; my ears to listen only to thee; my smell to delight only in the odour of thy perfumes; my feeling to be sensible only of thy divine impression; my tongue to speak only of thee; my hands to be employed only in thy service, and my feet to walk only in thy ways.

O divine master! on thee alone it depends to make me perfect in thy doctrine; for it is thou alone that givest knowledge and understanding. Leave me not therefore in my ignorance and my errors. Though I have been long in thy school, and received repeated instructions from thee, I am but too sensible of the little improvement I have made under such a master, being scarce acquainted with the first rudiments of thy divine doctrine; teach it me, Lord, I beseech thee, and suffer me not to continue longer in my ignorance. If I am still a stranger to thy ways and maxims, it is because my heart and mind are prepossessed and tinctured with the doctrines of the false writers and wise ones of this world. But do thou, O Jesus! efface every impression those false writers have made on my mind, that it may be thereby prepared for learning thy divine truths. They have bewitched my eyes, and enchanted my heart, to prevent my seeing and loving thy doctrine. Do thou, O Lord, remove this delusion, hufion, enamour me with thy divine precepts that I may love and value nothing but thy divine maxims. I utterly deteſt all ſuch as are repugnant to them.

Like a true Iſraelite, I will henceforward have thy law written on my heart, on my eyes, on my tongue, on my hands, on my feet, on every part of me; but write it thyſelf. O Jeſus! and write it in ſuch a manner that the characters may never be obliterated, and that every thing in me may concur to obſerve it with an inviolable fidelity.

Write it alſo on the hearts of all thy faithful, that they may religiouſly obey it; make it known to ſo many infidel nations that are ignorant of it. Inſtruct them, I beſeech thee in thy truth; diſſipate the darkneſs of their errors; enlighten them with the light of thy goſpel, that they may forſake the ways of death, and walk in the paths of life. And, thou, my ſoul, adhere always firmly, but particularly this day, to the doctrine of thy divine maſter, never abandon it upon any account; make it the inviolable rule of thy conduct becauſe *it is thy life.*

Remote Thankſgiving.

MAY endleſs praiſes, bleſſings and thankſgivings be rendered unto the great teacher of men and angels, for having vouchſafed this day to be my inſtructer and guide. Thou ſeeſt,

An Exercise for Tuesday.

feeſt, divine maſter, the neceſſity I am under of being taught by thee; abandon me not, I beſeech thee, but when by the alteration of the ſacramental ſpecies thou ceaſeſt to be corporally preſent with me, deprive me not at leaſt of thy ſpiritual preſence to teach me to walk in thy ways.

Speak, O divine maſter! ſpeak to the inward ears of my heart; make it hear thy voice; repeat to it thoſe divine leſſons which thou haſt this day taught it; convince it of their truth and importance, and never ſuffer it to forget thee.

O divine light! diſpel my darkneſs, I pray thee, that *I may not ſleep* (Pſ. 12. 3.) *the ſleep of death*; ſhew me the ways of life, and teach me to love and ſerve my God.

Treaſure up in thy memory, O my ſoul! the valuable inſtructions thy amiable Jeſus has this day communicated to thee. He has taught thee to contemn all that the world admires; he has recommended to thee the love of the croſs, humiliation, poverty, mortification, obedience and penance. This is the doctrine that thou art to follow.

Depart from me, ye prophets of Baal, falſe doctors and pretended wiſe men of the world! I acknowledge no other but Jeſus for maſter; I will be for ever his diſciple, and will faithfully adhere to his doctrine.

I have made thee a ſolemn promiſe, O my Saviour! never to embrace any doctrine but thine, and never to forget thy divine precepts;

and I am determined to obferve it faithfully with the affiftance of thy grace.

WEDNESDAY.

Confider Jefus Chrift as Phyfician, and defire earneftly to be cured of the many dangerous difeafes thou art afflicted with, cry out continually to him; Heal me, O Lord, (Jer. 17. 4. and I fhall be healed.

WRETCH that I am, with how many diftempers am I afflicted? I am, all at once, blind, deaf, dumb, paralytick, leprous, covered with fores from head to foot; my bowels are putrefied, gangrenous, and my whole body is confuming by a burning fever. O what friendly hand will deliver me from fuch a complication of diforders! None but thine, O heavenly phyfician! who art this day to vifit me.

Suffer not thyfelf, O my foul! to be caft down by fadnefs, or the defpair of a cure. How grievous and defperate foever thy diftempers appear, they do not furpafs the abilities of the phyfician who is this day to come to thee; one word from him, a look a flight touch (Mark 5. 27.) of his garment is fufficient to reftore thee to perfect health.

Come then, O divine phyfician! come, and heal me. Have pity on my mifery; let my manifold infirmities excite thy compaffion, and suffer me not to continue longer in so deplorable a condition.

Let us betake ourselves then, my soul, without delay to this sovereign physician, for the recovery of our health; let us hope for a cure from his goodness. He will infallibly effect it if thou place an entire confidence in him.

Yes, I confide entirely in thee, O my Saviour! I trust in thy goodness that thou wilt this day heal me. And have not I good reason to expect health from thee, when I consider the efficaciousness of the remedy thou appliest, no other than thy sacred flesh and precious blood?

Dispose me, O sovereign physician! dispose me thyself to receive benefit from the sovereign and precious remedy thou dost this day intend to administer to me. And thou, my soul, endeavour on thy side to receive it to thy benefit; avoid every thing that may hinder its due operation on thee; have a lively sense of thy disorders, conceive an utter abhorrence of them, and ardently wish to be cured.

Immediate Preparation.

O CHARITABLE physician! who from thy throne of glory in the highest heavens beholdest the extremity of my miseries and the dreadful consequences they must be attended with: there is no other but thyself to help me out of them: they

they infinitely furpafs the fkill of all other phyficians, and the power of all their remedies, but they are not out of the reach of thy healing power: nothing being eafier to thee than to heal me; a word of thine will fuffice to reftore me to perfect health.

But wouldft thou fpeak this word, Lord, for the recovery of one who has made himfelf fo unworthy of fuch a favour, having employed all the ftrength he could exert in the fervice of thy enemies? Nay the diftempers I have contracted are all of them the confequences of my having joined with thefe enemies in waging war againft thee: and when urged by their pain and aching fmart I had recourfe to thee or remedy, I neglected to follow thy prefcriptions, and defeated the power and efficacy of them by my irregular living. Wouldft thou then cure fuch a perfidious, ungrateful and profligate wretch? I deferve it not I own; but I hope notwithftanding to obtain it from thy boundlefs charity; thy compaffionate difpofition gives me room to hope for this favour.

For why fhouldft thou come to me, divine phyfician, if thou hadft no defign to cure me? to what purpofe fhouldft thou work fuch wonders in order to vifit me, unlefs thou didft intend to reftore me to health? Ah! thy mercy towards finners fufficiently convinces me that thou doft defign to put an end to my wretched condition.

Thou didft formerly, O Jefus, go about every where in queft of the diftempered, and didft cure them of all their ailments. There
went

went virtue out of thee (Luke 6. 19.) *and healed all* those that approached thee: I comfort myself with the hopes of a share in the effects of this all-healing power, since it is thy infinite charity that induces thee to come to me.

I have been hitherto so void of sense and understanding as to be fond of my infirmities, however severe and dangerous they have been, and to obstruct the endeavours of such charitable persons as were solicitous for my cure. But now that I am recovered of this frenzy, I have a quick sense of the distresses I labour under. My soul shudders with horror at them: I detest my wicked conduct which occasioned them; I beg pardon for it of that divine physician whose remedies I made slight of. I earnestly long for health, and promise to observe with great punctuality whatever he shall hereafter direct for my recovery.

What other physician but thee, O my Saviour! would not be afraid to come near a patient so infected as myself? What other physician besides thee would bestow his own body and blood on his patient, in order to cure him? what other physician would sacrifice his own life to preserve that of his patient, as thou dost upon the altar to preserve mine? O incomparable charity! O unparalleled goodness!

But what return canst thou expect, O Lord! for administering to me so precious a remedy, and for procuring me health at the expence of thy own life? Knowest thou not that I am a wretched creature from whom thou canst hope for nothing? But it is not interest, O most

charitable

charitable physician! that influences thee. So far from requiring any thing of thy patients, thou dost thyself confer upon them infinite rewards for suffering themselves to be cured by thee. Who can sufficiently admire such an excess of goodness?

Enter, my soul, enter by a lively faith into the heart of thy divine physician, there to contemplate the sentiments he entertains for thee. See how he pities thy disorders, how earnestly he desires thy cure, how affectionately he comes himself with the remedy which is to restore thee to health, a remedy, composed of his body and blood. The one he afflicted by infinite labours, the other he shed to the last drop to cure thee. He took upon himself all thy pains and infirmities (Pf. 2. 14.) to procure then health. Answer the greatness of his love by a proper return, honour the skill of this admirable physician whom thou standest so much in need of; place thy whole confidence in the power of his art; go to him with the same earnestness he comes to thee, and with a desire of recovering health equal to that which he hath to bestow it on thee; let thy abhorrence of the distempers be the same with his? assure him that thou wilt employ in his service the health he shall give thee, and solicit him affectionately to bestow speedily on thee so precious a gift.

Come then, O charitable physician! come to this poor patient's relief; come and deliver him out of the wretched condition to which he finds himself reduced; come and bestow on him

him the remedy of thy sacred flesh and of thy precious blood, before he die, *Lay but thy hand upon him and he shall live.* Ah! come in, come to me; for health, strength, life, and every good thing I can wish for will come in with thee; thy presence will put an end to all my miseries, and will enrich me with all sorts of blessings.

Immediate Thanksgiving.

THOU hast then visited me, O adorable physician! what thanks shall I give thee, for not disdaining to come to this poor patient? It is not one of thy servants, one of thy prophets, one of thy apostles, or one of thy angels thou hast sent to cure me; thou art come thyself: may infinite thanks be given to thee for ever by all creatures for so great a condescension; may heaven and earth proclaim for ever thy goodness.

Behold, O charitable physician! the number and dept of the wounds I have received from my enemies. Behold how I live in a restless conflict at once with pride, ambition, avarice, impurity, anger, envy, gluttony, and many other spiritual distempers. See what a load of corruption there is in my heart; how much my mind is fraught with error and delusion; how disorderly is my imagination, how headstrong and irregular my passions, how licentious my senses! I labour under a complication

cation of all diseases, and to such a degree, that all human remedies are ineffectual to a cure. And indeed, O Lord! the cure of a sick person in so deplorable a condition as mine cannot fail of redounding exceedingly to thy glory, thou being the only physician that can effect it. Heal me therefore, I beseech thee, in order to display thy power, and to shew forth the glory of thy holy name.

All powerful efficacy of the flesh and blood of my Jesus, which I have just now received in the nature of food! work an effectual cure on me. Ah! my Saviour, the least touch of thy sacred hand or of thy garment, the least word of thine formerly cured all sorts of diseases; why then should not the receiving of thy body and precious blood produce a like effect upon me, which thou dost administer to me as food, that I may more effectually be sensible of their power and all healing virtue?

Thy glory, O divine physician! is concerned in my cure; for what will thy enemies say, if after having undertaken it by means of that most powerful of all thy remedies, thy patient is no better for its application? And why, Lord, shouldst thou not cure me, it being so easy to thee to restore me to health? an act of thy will is all-sufficient for the purpose; thou needest say but the word (Mat. 8. 8.) *and my soul shall be healed.* The most grievous and most obstinate distempers are not less obedient to thy voice, than soldiers are to their commanding officer: the moment thou givest the word of command they vanish. Command them,

An Exercise for Wednesday.

then, Lord, this band of diseases that annoy me to depart, and they will quit me in a moment; if thou but will to cure (Ibid. 8. 2.). me, I shall be cured that instant.

But thou, my soul, who hast recourse to thy divine physician for health, art thou sincerely desirous of being cured? He now puts this question to thee as he formerly did to the paralytick at the pool of Bethsaida. Thou canst not answer with the paralytick, (Ibid. 7.) that thou dost indeed desire it, but art in want of a person to give thee the assistance required; thy divine physician being at hand and ready to do thee this charitable office. My answer therefore shall be: O Lord I desire it, and most ardently too; and as a proof of my sincerity, I submit with pleasure to every painful operation thou shalt judge expedient in order to my cure. I resign myself entirely into thy hands, I submit to all thy divine prescriptions; order me the regimen thou wouldst have me observe, and thy direction shall be punctually complied with: command me, O Lord, to refrain from this or that gratification, to avoid certain occasions, to perform such an exercise, and thy orders shall be faithfully obeyed.

O Jesus! who in this adorable sacrament art both my physician and my remedy, be thou also my health, my strength, and my life. Abide with me, and unite thyself to all my powers to give me life and strength, and to cure me entirely. Dwell then in my heart, and it shall be healed of its corruption; dwell in my mind and it shall be cured of its blindness; dwell in my imagination and it shall be cured of its folly: dwell in my sensitive appetite and its irregularities and excesses shall be corrected and restrained; dwell in all my senses, powers and faculties, and being then cured of all the disorders they labour under, they will be restored to health, strength and vigour.

What return can I possibly make to thee, my true physician, that may be worthy of thee for this thy charitable visit to thy patient, and for the divine remedy thou hast this day brought to him? But what can I give thee that is worthy of thee, but thyself? I therefore make an offering of thyself to thee. I offer to thee all thy divine excellencies and perfections, and more especially that infinite charity which induced thee to come and cure me. I make an offering to thee at the same time of myself and of all that I can call my own; and the health thou hast bestowed upon me. I consecrate to thee, to be employed entirely in thy service.

Being now, my soul, restored to health, by this heavenly physician, relapse no more into thy former infirmities; thou wouldst injure his glory if thou didst. Keep thyself therefore for the future in a vigorous state of health. Thy health is thy charity, thy strength is thy fervour and zeal: cherish then within thee an ardent charity, and exert all possible zeal and fervour in whatever the honour of God may be concerned.

O what numbers of sick there are in the world, O divine physician! that are in the greatest

greatest want of thy help? I recommend them all to thy infinite charity, particularly *N.* and *N.* and all such as I am bound to by ties or obligations, or in whose behalf thou desirest I should offer up my prayers.

I promise thee, O holy physician! that I will henceforward, and on this day in particular, refrain from every thing that may occasion a relapse into my former sickly state, and avoid not only sin but likewise whatever bears the appearance of it.

Remote Thanksgiving.

I CANNOT forget, O divine physician! the inestimable favour I have this day received by thy making a remedy for me of thy sacred body and most precious blood: I thank thee for it with my whole heart, and do pray all the saints and angels to thank thee for it on my account. It must have been a goodness such as thine, O charitable physician! that could induce thee to come down from heaven to heal me; may the heavens, earth, the sea and all the creatures in them praise and thank thee for it. Dwell with me, O heavenly physician! leave me not a moment lest I relapse into all those disorders of which thou hast cured me; rule me and guide me to prevent my contracting others which may throw me into a worse (Jo. 5. 14.) situation than that out of which thou hast delivered me.

Fruit of the tree of life ! whose property it is to restore our decayed strength, to heal our infirmities, and to preserve us from the death of sin, exert thy power within me; furnish my soul with fresh supplies of life and vigour, and preserve it from death.

Where is then the virtue of the admirable remedy, which thou hast this day administered to me, O Jesus ? Alas ! I scarce feel any effect from it ; I am not less weak and infirm than before; but suffer me not, I beseech thee, to receive it unprofitably : grant that it may operate in me a perfect cure.

Why complainest thou, my soul, of receiving so little benefit from this sovereign medicine ? is it not thyself that hinderest its operation, by obstructing its virtue ? Break off thy attachments to creatures, mortify thy senses, avoid the occasions of sin, apply thyself to thy duties, and thou wilt see that it will give thee perfect health. Remember, O my soul! that thou hast promised thy divine physician to abide by the regimen he prescribed thee : it consists of self-denials, austerities, mortifications, retirement from the world, humiliation, prayer and recollection. Be faithful in these duties, and thou wilt be assuredly cured.

But if thy perfect recovery be attended with difficulties and delays, be not astonished nor dismayed; disorders so grievous and inveterate as thine are not immediately cured. Time must be allowed for remedies to operate ; and in waiting for the effect with patience, let it be thy business to place thy confidence in the
skill

skill and power of him whom thou hast this day received. Let thy desire of recovery be sincere, and thy health will be infallibly restored to thee.

THURSDAY.

Consider Jesus Christ as Shepherd, and resolve to return to him after having strayed from his flock. Return to the shepherd of thy soul.

Remote Preparation.

I AM a strayed sheep, wandering about in a frightful wilderness, and constantly in danger of being devoured by every beast of prey. Take pity of me, O divine shepherd! I will not cease crying out to thee to come to my relief, and to lead me back to the fold. *I have gone astray like a lost sheep, seek thy servant.*

O thou shepherd of my soul! who hast fatigued thyself so much in seeking after this lost sheep, listen favourably to its cries; come and put an end to its wanderings, and leave it not a prey to the savage beasts that seek to devour it.

What an unfortnate sheep am I, for having quitted my loving shepherd! I am now convinced by my own fatal experience that there is no happiness like that of being with him. I have suffered myself to be deluded and decoyed from him by strangers, but I am determined to return to him and never more be guilty of such a folly.

Arise, my soul, and let us go to this loving shepherd, who forgetting, by a goodness not to be equalled, thy past disobedience, is willing to receive thee this day into the number of his sheep, to heal thy wounds, and to feed thee with an infinitely delicious food.

O heavenly pasture! O divine aliment! how vehement is my desire to feast on thee? My soul is as sheep that totters and falls to the ground through hunger and weakness; there is none but thyself that can restore it to its strength, and satisfy its hunger.

Purify, O divine shepherd! my heart and all within me, that I may have a true relish for the heavenly pasture thou art pleased to admit me into this day; and that I may also receive the happy effects it produces in well disposed souls.

And thou, my soul, remove far from thee every thing that may be an hindrance to thy profiting by this divine nourishment: renounce all earthly and sordid affections.

Immediate Preparation.

THOU comest then this day, O divine shepherd, to this strayed sheep! Thy goodness, indeed, must be exceeding great, not to reject it for its malice and rebellion. For what else has

has this ungrateful and malicious sheep hitherto done, what else has it been employed in, but in giving thee grievous displeasure? It has a thousand times slighted both thy favours and thy threats; it has fallen foul upon the other sheep of thy flock; it has made several of them by its solicitation to go astray with itself; it has infected some by its ill example, it has poisoned others by its evil speeches. Yet thou forgettest all this, and art so gracious as to come again to it to prevent its final perishing. O ineffable goodness! O incomprehensible charity!

But what need hast thou, O rich and powerful shepherd! of this wretched and perverse sheep? Are not all the saints and holy angels, all the just upon earth thy sheep? Do not likewise all creatures belong, in some measure, to thy flock, since it is thou that upholdest them, and art their master? What wouldst thou lose by suffering me to perish? wouldst thou not be still equally rich and happy? Yet thou seekest after me as if I was thy whole stock, and thou leavest thy flock in heaven to come to me on the earth, as if thy whole happiness depended on possessing me. Oh! what an excess of love!

Wilt not thou suffer thyself to be at length gained over, O my soul! by so much goodness? wilt not thou at last enter into thyself? wilt not thou resolve to make amends for thy past ingratitude and malice, and from henceforth at least to be a subject of consolation to so good a shepherd?

It

It is with this intent, O Jesus! that I come to cast myself at thy feet, my face covered with shame and confusion, and my heart pierced with grief, to beg thy pardon for all the displeasure and uneasiness I have given thee by my wanderings and rebellions against thee. How sensibly is my heart afflicted for such sinful behaviour! Never, never more will I be guilty of the like, with the help of thy grace; being determined to be henceforward an obedient and faithful sheep, which shall never again go astray from thee,

But should not I also greatly wrong myself by not abiding with so good and charitable a shepherd? Who is able to comprehend the tender love thou bearest thy sheep and the great care thou takest for their welfare? Thou hast thy eye always upon them to protect them; thou leadest them into fat and delicious pastures, and to the fountains of living water; thou providest them with comfortable shelter, where they may refresh themselves and are secured from the scorching heats of the summer, and the pinching colds of the winter: thou healest them when they are sick; thou carriest them upon thy shoulders when they are not able to walk; thou waitest for them when they are not in a condition to keep pace with thee; thou bringest them back when they go astray, and thou protectest them when in danger of being worried by the infernal wolfe.

Other shepherds sometimes make themselves a garment of the skins of their sheep, in order to procure their love and to be an inducement

to

to their following them; but thou haft taken upon thee the very nature of thy fheep by becoming man, that they might be animated with a more tender love for thee, and become more zealous to tread in thy fteps.

Other fhepherds feed on the milk of their fheep, but thou feedeft thine with thy own flefh and blood; other fhepherds clothe themfelves out of their fleeces, but thou clotheft thy fheep with thyfelf; they fell or flay them for their own ufe and profit, but thou fufferedft thyfelf to be fold to redeem thine, and deliveredft thyfelf up to a cruel death to fave their lives.

Who can refrain from loving fo good a fhepherd? a fhepherd poffeffed of a love fo tender, fo ardent, and fo generous for his fheep. Behold, my foul, what frefh marks he gives thee this day of his love? He once more comes down from the holy mountain, that is, from heaven, to recall thee from thy wanderings; he facrifices his life anew on our altars for thy falvation; he re applies to thee the fruit of his fufferings for healing thy wounds and curing thy diftempers; he gives thee anew his own blood for recuiting thy ftrength, and wilt thou refufe him thy love who teftifies fo much love for thee? No, loving fhepherd! this would be carrying ingratitude to the higheft pitch. Accept, then I pray thee, of my love entire and undivided, thou fhalt be henceforward the fole object of it; and all my care and attention fhall henceforward be employed in zealous endeavours

deavours to please thee and to obey thy commands.

O charitable shepherd! thou hast for a long time been in quest of this perverse sheep, which maliciously avoided to come in thy way, but it shuns thee not this day; on the contrary, it finds an unspeakable pleasure in returning to thee. Thou hadst long deplored the loss of it, but it is now desirous to be a comfort to thee by its return to its duty; lo! here it is. Come then good shepherd, come and take possession of it; come and make thyself master of its heart, that it may make thee some amends for the immense labours and fatigues which thou hast undergone in seeking after it with no other view than to make it happy. Come and feed it on that delicious pasture thou hast prepared for it; and be thou its strength, its joy and its delight. Thou art at the same time its shepherd, its pasture, and its life, O shepherd! O pasture! O life! come unto me and take possession of me, to feed me and to give me life.

Immediate Thanksgiving.

ADORABLE shepherd, who feedest both angels and men, and who providest every living creature with suitable food! it is thyself then whom I now possess within me, and who now dost give thyself for spiritual food to this wretched sheep. How is it possible that thou should have descended from heaven, and stooped so low

low as to come to this ungrateful and rebellious creature? Can so great a condescension be ever sufficiently admired and extolled? But what requital shall this poor sheep make for so great a mercy? Why, from this moment, it offers and consecrates to thee all the sentiments of love and reverence which it is capable of conceiving, and all the inward acts of praise and adoration it is able to bring forth; most earnestly intreating all thy creatures to join in love, praise and thanksgiving with it, and for it.

But since thou hast had the charity, O divine shepherd, to come and visit this helpless sheep, cast an eye of pity, I beseech thee, on the distressed and melancholy condition to which it is reduced. It is sick, graciously be pleased to cure it; it is blind give it sight; it is dying with hungar, feed it; it totters with weakness, strengthen it; it is stubborn and disobedient, correct and chastise it; it is apt to stray, prevent its doing so; it is wholly bent on escaping from thee, unite it to thee with the soft cords of thy love; the wolves are ever prowling about it to devour it, protect it by the almighty power, lest it fall a prey to them. Thou hast declared that none shall ever wrest the sheep thy Father has given thee out of thy hand; suffer them not therefore to rob thee of this sheep. I am but too sensible, O divine shepherd, that I have no certain knowledge of the happiness of being one of thy sheep; perhaps I only flatter myself with the notion of this happiness without really possessing it; perhaps I bear some outward resemblance to thy sheep, though destitute

titute at the same time of what essentially constitutes them such. If so, I beseech thee by all thou hast suffered for me, and by the blood which thou hast shed for me, to make me one of thy real sheep, by bestowing on me their genuine qualities of innocence, simplicity, meekness, obedience and fruitfulness; set thy mark upon me to distinguish me effectually from those which do not belong to thee.

Remember, O divine shepherd! how dear my salvation has cost thee; call to mind what fatigues thou hast undergone in seeking after me, the blood thou hast shed to redeem me, the death thou hast suffered to save my life; suffer not all this to become useless to me.

Divine shepherd! thou art my only hope, it is from thee alone that I expect life and salvation, and therefore I resign myself intirely to thy divine guidance and disposal. Do with me whatever thou pleasest, I am ready to execute all thy commands; I shall henceforward look upon every thing that befals me as coming from thy hand, and I will perform, purely to please thee, whatever thou requirest of me; I will walk faithfully after thee whithersoever thou goest, and will copy as near as I possibly can thy divine example.

I am very sensible and heartily regret it, that I have therefore slighted and disobeyed thee, O divine shepherd! to run after other shepherds; but I promise never more to be guilty of the like folly. I will henceforward obey no call but thine, and feed on no other pasture but thine, which is thy heavenly doctrine. Be gone from

from me, ye strangers! I own no other shepherd but my Jesus; I will pay no regard to any call but his, I will obey no will but his.

Heavenly shepherd! since it is thy love that prevailed with thee to come and re-take possession of this thy sheep, let me be wholly thine according to thy desire; enjoy what thou hast loved, place it in thy bosom, unite thyself to it in the most intimate manner, and may this thy possession be everlasting, never suffering any one to rob thee of it; bind it to thee by ties of love so strong and lasting, that it may never more withdraw itself from thee.

I recommend to thee also, O divine shepherd thy flock which, is the church: preserve, govern and feed it: increase the number of its members by the conversion of infidels, hereticks, and scismaticks. I recommend to thee in particular N. N. of thy flock. My endeavour shall be to act the part of a good and faithful sheep, in obeying thy call and fulfilling thy divine will; *I will hear* (Pf. 84. 8.) *what the Lord shall speak within me.*

Remote Thanksgiving.

SHEPHERD of my soul! immortal thanks be given to thee for thy goodness in coming this day to visit this poor sheep: but may it please thee not to leave it in the forlorn condition thou didst find it in; grant it may long continue

continue to feel the good effects of thy precious visit.

Thou hast this day owned and treated me as one of thy sheep, O divine shepherd! I beseech thee, to protect me, guide me, and provide for all my wants. Leave me not to my own management, O charitable shepherd! because being so left I shall certainly perish: be thou always with me, to rule and guide me.

I have promised thee, O good shepherd! to give ear to no call but thine, to obey none but thee, I continue in the same disposition; lay thy commands upon me, whatsoever they are they shall be punctually executed and fulfilled.

Hearken not, my soul, to the world; hearken not to the suggestions of flesh and blood; hearken not to the insinuations of thy self-love, for thy heavenly shepherd forbids all this. He will have thee to be guided in all things by his Holy Spirit.

Wouldst thou again provoke thy good shepherd's displeasure by straying from him? Be exact therefore in the discharge of thy duty to him; separate not thyself from his flock, nor absent thyself from his person; forbear associating with the herd of his avowed enemy the devil, who would infect thee with their evil dispositions, and involve thee with themselves in endless torments.

FRIDAY.

Consider the divine Jesus as Redeemer. Conceive at waking an earnest desire of being rescued this day from the slavery of sin and Satan, to become a devoted servant of Jesus Christ. Cry out with the Prophet: Have Compassion on me O Lord, and redeem me.

Remote Preparation.

THOU hast hitherto groaned, O my soul, under the most oppressive and most cruel of all kinds of slavery, that of sin and Satan; but thy redeemer is come this day to rescue thee out of it: sigh after his coming, and desire with great ardour to be set at liberty.

Come, O divine redeemer! come and break my chains, and deliver me from the tyranny of this cruel master, to whom I have foolishly sold myself for a trifling satisfaction, a vain honour, a sordid interest.

Thou, O Jesus! art my creator, my king and my Father. Come, O my creator, and deliver thy poor creature; come, O gracious sovereign, and deliver thy unfortunate subject; come, O my Father! and deliver thy unhappy child.

Shameful slavery! cruel thraldom! shall there never be an end to thee? shall it never be in my power to shake off thy heavy yoke? Yes, I hope this day to be able to compass it, through the infinite liberality of my redeemer.

The price of thy ransom is now ready, O my soul! the divine Jesus is about to put it into thy hands at the holy altar, that thou mayest present it to the Eternal Father; prepare thyself for shaking off the yoke of thy servitude, and for being restored to the glorious liberty of the sons of God.

Give ear, my soul, to the voice of thy divine Jesus, who cries out to thee with his prophet: (Isai. 52. 2. 3.) *Shake thyself from the dust; arise,—loose the bands from off thy neck, O captive daughter of Sion!—you have been sold for nought, and you shall be redeemed without money.*

Immediate Preparation.

BEHOLD, O my soul! the loving kindness of thy redeemer. He this day comes down from heaven upon our altars, with the design to deliver thee out of the hands of thy enemies. He employs none of his servants in this concern; he undertakes it himself in person. What charity! what goodness! He had already prepared and paid the price of thy ransom by his labours and sufferings during his mortal life, by those ignominies and torments he underwent, by the blood he shed in the garden, at the pillar, on the cross, and by the death he underwent on it. He now comes to apply to thee the

the merit of all this in this myſtery, with the view of breaking thy chains and reſcuing thee from the ſlavery of Satan. And what is more, he comes to be again himſelf a ſlave to procure thee liberty, and to die myſtically for ſaving thy life. What generoſity! what love!

Other ranſomers pay down money to redeem ſlaves, but this ranſomer gives himſelf as the price of their ranſom. Other ranſomers of ſlaves, having paid down the price of their ranſom, let them go about with the diſagreeable marks of their paſt ſlavery, ſuch as wounds, nakedneſs, poverty, hunger and wretchedneſs; but this heavenly ranſomer, not content with procuring them their liberty, heals their wounds; clothes them with coſtly robes, feeds them with his fleſh and blood, and enriches them with his treaſures. Other ranſomers, in fine, after having procured liberty for their ſlaves, diſmiſs them to their reſpective countries; or if they allow them to continue with them, it is in a low and obſcure condition: but this redeemer admits thoſe he has ranſomed into his family, on the footing of brethren, nay he makes kings of them all, and co-heirs of his kingdom. Who can refuſe loving ſo good and ſo generous a redeemer? I will love him with the moſt ardent affection as long as I live, and my heart ſhall never cleave to any thing but him.

Come then, O moſt amiable redeemer! and releaſe me from the ſlavery of ſin and ſatan, and ſubject me to thyſelf: come and break my bands aſunder and bind me with thine; reſcue me out of the hands of the cruel tyrant who has hitherto poſſeſſed me, that I may belong to none but thee. Come and ſatisfy my hunger, heal my wounds, cover my nakedneſs, enrich my poverty, and turn my miſery into happineſs. Come unto me, I beſeech thee, O divine maſter! take poſſeſſion of me; I will never more have any other maſter but thee.

Immediate Thankſgiving.

I HAVE now received thee, O divine redeemer! into my breaſt, but doſt not thou loathe a ſituation ſo unworthy of thee, where thou art ſhut up, as it were, in a dark priſon? My ſoul muſt have been exceeding precious in thy ſight to take ſuch a ſtep in her favour. Who would not be aſtoniſhed that the God of majeſty and the ſovereign of the univerſe, ſhould vouchſafe to come to ſo wretched a creature and give himſelf for its ranſom? Ah! bleſſed for ever be that infinite charity which engaged thee to confer on me ſo ſignal a favour. May all the ſaints and angels, and all creatures join with me in everlaſting praiſe and thankſgiving for it. But what return, Lord, can I make for ſuch a mercy? Though I were to yield myſelf up to thee a thouſand times to be thy ſlave, how far ſhort would all this fall of what I owe thee?

I caſt myſelf in ſpirit at thy feet, O my divine redeemer! I kiſs and embrace them moſt

An Exercise for Friday.

tenderly to give thee some slight token of my gratitude; I thank thee with the most tender affections of my soul for thy infinite goodness in coming to redeem me. I offer and dedicate myself to thee, to be for ever thy servant; and I sincerely confess before thee, that though I were every moment to sacrifice to thee my body and soul, my life and all that depends on me, I could never make thee any return which could be in the least proportionate to so great a benefit.

What would have been my present condition, O divine redeemer! if I had been treated according to my deserts? Hell would have swallowed me up, I should have been sunk into the bottomless pit; the enemy would have seized and carried off my soul, he would have buried me in that dreadful gulph of unquenchable fire. How great then is my obligation to thee for not suffering me to perish like so many others, who have deserved it much less than myself, and for having added this day to thy former mercies that of giving thyself anew for the price of my ransom?

It being thy design, O divine Saviour! by coming to me to procure my liberty, carry this thy design, I beseech thee, into immediate execution: permit me not to continue any longer in this cruel slavery, under the weight of which I have groaned so long. Break all those chains the enemy has loaded me with, the chains of vice and passions, of my ill habits, of my hankering after the occasions of sin, of the obstacles and difficulties I find in the

dif-

discharge of my duty; break them all, I beseech thee, O Jesus! by the almighty power of thy arm.

Eternal Father! I have now within me the body and blood of thy only Son which he gave to redeem me out of my deplorable bondage; I offer them to thee for my ransom, grant me therefore I beseech thee, my liberty: I confide that through thy mediation, O Saviour! he will grant it to me, for it is with this view that he has sent thee to me.

To make me perfectly free, bring under thy subjection all my powers and faculties. By subjecting to thee my mind, thou wilt deliver it from its errors; by subjecting to thee my will, thou wilt free it from its inordinate affections; by subjecting to thee my appetites, thou wilt rid them of their violent cravings, by subjecting to thee my senses, thou wilt curb their bent towards sensible objects.

But let it not suffice, O Jesus! to deliver me from the chains of my enemies, may I be so happy as to put on thine. Chain my heart by the chains of thy love, my mind by those of thy truth, my passions by those of thy Justice, and my senses by those of thy mortification.

Having now applied to me, O adorable Saviour! the price of my redemption, keep me, I pray thee, in thy service, and suffer me not to exchange it for that of any other master. I have cost thee very dear, let not therefore that be taken from thee which thou hast purchased at so high a price.

Tho'

An Exercise for Friday.

Though rescued heretofore out of the hands of thy enemies by the power of grace, O divine redeemer! I have but too often forsaken thee to return to my former slavery, by incurring the guilt of fresh crimes; may this, I pray thee, never more befall me, but bind me with such powerful bands that I my never more unloose them by falling back into sin: may the stamp of thy divine seal be impressed so deep upon me, that no strange master may ever dare attempt to force or decoy me from thy service. Yes, Lord, do thou stand by me, and secure me so affectually against such as seek to bring me back into my former slavery, that none may dare to attack me.

I glory in being at this time the devoted servant and property of my Jesus. Yes, I am his, I belong to him, he is my master, him alone will I serve, it is for him that I will labour; it is his graceful and amiable yoke that I will bear, his divine commandments I will observe. I will never serve any other master but him; neither pride, nor covetousness, nor impurity, nor gluttony, nor any other vice shall ever bear sway in my soul: Jesus Christ alone shall rule and govern there, he alone shall reign supreme Lord and master over it.

Happy is that freedom, O Jesus! which thou bringest to a soul when thou takest possession of it as thy own. Ah! how precious, how desirable is it, how worthy of our ambition! It is a thousand times more valuable than the empire of the whole world. Grant

it

it me, O my divine redeemer! and preserve it to me when granted.

I beseech thee, to bestow it also upon all the children of the church, thy spouse, and graciously extend it to so many nations which are out of her pale, by rescuing them from the slavery of the devil, and subjecting them to the sweet and easy yoke of thy gospel. Such and such persons in particular I recommend to thee. It shall be my special care henceforward to watch over myself, to *stand fast in the liberty with which Christ has made me free, and not to be entangled again in the yoke of bondage*.

Remote Thanksgiving.

THOU hast this day ransomed me, O Jesus! by the application of the merits of thy precious blood, and by the repeated oblation of thy sacred body. Immortal thanks be given to thee by all creatures in heaven and earth on this account. Remember, Eternal Father, that thy Son has this day redeemed me and has paid down the price of his blood and life for my ransom; suffer not therefore my enemies ever more to usurp any power over me.

And thou, O my Saviour! remember what thou hast given this day for my ransom; permit not therefore, after this that my enemies should detain me any longer in a state of bondage.

Wouldst

An Exercise for Friday.

Wouldſt thou, my ſoul, ever more be inſtrumental to thy ſaviour's forfeiting the price of his blood, by robbing him again of his property in thee to transfer it to thoſe cruel tyrants whom thou haſt formerly had for maſters? Oh! grieve him not at this rate, be not guilty of ſuch a flagrant injuſtice againſt him, be not ſuch an enemy to thyſelf.

Be gone, then, be gone, from me, all ye worldly grandeurs, pleaſures, riches, diverſions which hitherto have been the fatal chains that deprived me of my liberty! depart from me, I renounce you for ever. My Jeſus ſhall henceforward be my only maſter; I will wear no other chains from this day but thoſe of his love.

Thou falſe liberty of the world, that conſiſts only in following the unhappy bent of corrupt nature, and gratifying the deſires of the fleſh! I renounce thee for ever. The ſweet obligation, my Jeſus impoſes on me of reſiſting my corrupt inclinations, and of denying my own will, ſhall be henceforward my chief delight, for it is herein that I find true liberty.

SATURDAY.

Consider the divine Jesus as Spouse, and let it be thy first thought in the morning, that this adorable Saviour is this day to espouse to him thy soul: I will betrothe thee to me for ever. *Sigh after this union, and endeavour by thy purity and fervent love to qualify thyself for such a spouse.*

Remote Preparation.

BEHOLD, my soul, the divine *bridegroom cometh* to thee; arise, and *go out to meet him*; but first be solicitous to wash away thy stains. Clothe thyself with thy most costly apparel, and adorn thyself with thy richest attire.

But how shall I cleanse myself, O divine spouse! who am so filthy, and have withal so forbidding and deformed an aspect? Where shall I find wherewith to adorn myself in a manner worthy of thee, who am not even provided with rags to cover my nakedness? It is thou alone canst cleanse, adorn and array me in such a manner as may make me agreeable in thy sight.

Oh! when will that happy hour come which is to unite me to my spouse? When shall I have the happiness of possessing him? O how long every moment seems till I see him!

Shew

Shew me thy face, O adorable spouse! let me hear thy sweet voice, and grant me the inestimable favour of possessing thee.

My heart burns with the desire of being with thee; it can relish no pleasure but in the delightful thought of being this day admitted to that happiness. O may this adorable spouse give me the kiss of peace and friendship, may he embrace and possess me, may his divine heart be intimately united to mine! This is the sum of my desires, and the height of my ambition.

Immediate Preparation.

THE greatest of kings, courts thee this day, O my soul! to make thee his bride. He desires to engage with thee in the most perfect alliance that ever was, but altogether spiritual and divine. He is the greatest of kings, as being the sovereign monarch of the world, and the God of all nature. He is the Almighty, who seeks you and loves you, who is worthy of all love, as being infinitely wise, infinitely holy, infinitely just, infinitely good, infinitely powerful, infinitely tender, infinitely meek, infinitely faithful, in short, infinite in all perfections. But how is it possible, O Lord, that thou shouldst cast thy eye upon so vile and so wretched a creature as myself for thy bride?—Was there ever so unequal an alliance, ever so great disproportion between the contracting parties? Thou art all, and I a mere nothing. Thou art greatness, and I meanness; thou art opulence, and I poverty; thou art goodness, and I malice; thou art justice, and I iniquity; thou art wisdom, and I am folly; thou art happiness, and I am misery: in a word, thou art perfection by essence, and the assemblage of all perfections; and I am imperfection itself, and an assemblage of all blemishes and defects. How then is it possible, thou most celestial spouse! that thou shouldst entertain the least thought of a person for thy bride, so disproportionate to thee in all respects?

But the immense inequality and disproportion between us in point of condition, is not the only impediment to the proposed alliance. Alas! I have made myself most unworthy of it by my ingratitude and perfidiousness: for thou didst heretofore wash me from original sin in baptism, and with this view didst redeem me at the price of thy blood, deliver me from eternal death by laying down thy life for me; cure me of my infirmities, embellish, adorn, enrich, ennoble me, and treat me, in fine, with all tenderness and love. But I, on my side, instead of suitably corresponding with such uncommon favours, have betrayed thee, base, ungrateful and perfidious wretch that I am!

I cast myself at thy feet, O my adorable spouse! and embracing them affectionately, I crave pardon with my eyes bathed in tears for my past ingratitude and repeated acts of perfidy; my heart is oppressed with a more vehement

ment sorrow than I am able to express. I here make before thee a solemn protestation that I will undergo the greatest torments, rather than ever return to my former disorders.

Such being thy goodness towards me, O adorable spouse! notwithstanding my having so often deserved to feel the most rigorous effects of thy just indignation and resentment, it shall be my serious endevour to make the best return of love in my power for the excess of thine towards me. May my heart then love thee with all the tenderness, ardour, and might it is capable of. O that it glowed with an ardour of love equal to that of the seraphims, and with all the perfection of that of thy blessed mother and of all the saints in heaven! I offer to thee all their love together with the love of thy own divine heart, to make amends for the imperfection and coldness of mine.

I chose not thee, O adorable Saviour! for my spouse, but it was thou that chose me for thy bride. But since thou hast vouchsafed me that honour, I pray thee to make me worthy of being united to thee. Thou art not like other bridegrooms who suppose merit in their brides to which they have not contributed, for thou art the very source of all the merit that is found in thine. Grant me therefore, I beseech thee, all that grace, beauty, purity, wisdom, fidelity, submission: in fine, all those perfections thou desirest to find in me: clothe me suitably to thy dignity, in a word, make me such as I ought to be, worthy of thee and agreeable in thy fight. Regard is not to be had in this matter to my perſon but to thine; becauſe it is for the intereſt of thy glory that thy bride ſhould be poſſeſſed of the moſt excellent qualities, and of a merit anſwerable, in ſome meaſure, to thy own.

It is therefore my firm reſolution, O divine ſpouſe! to be faithful in the diſcharge of my duty to thee. A bride is to leave parents, friends and acquaintance, and to cleave to her ſpouſe; all theſe I now quit and abandon to enjoy the happineſs of being with thee. A bride is alſo to diveſt herſelf of every thing ſhe before held as her property, to make it over to her bridegroom, I do the ſame from this moment in the deſire of my heart, and make a tender of it to thee: ſhe is to ſurrender her heart and her mind to him; in like manner do I conſecrate both to thee: ſhe is to live with him; I will rather die than ſeparate from thee: She ought to be ſolely his; and I would ſooner undergo the ſharpeſt torments than fail in fidelity to thee.

Come then, my adorable bridegroom! come and take poſſeſſion of thy ſpouſe; come and poſſeſs her, whoſe entire love and affection centre in thee. Come, my joy, my crown, my riches, my happineſs, my all! my heart can live no longer without thee; it pines, it languiſhes, it dies away with the deſire of poſſeſſing thee: Come and let me be for ever united to thee by the ſtricteſt ties of everlaſting love.

Immediate

Immediate Thanksgiving.

I HAVE *at length found him whom my soul loveth*: I have at last found the dear object of my affections and of all my delight. Long have I desired and sought after thee, O adorable spouse! and at last have found thee, and do now possess thee in the very centre of my being. Happy moment this! which has put me in possession of so amiable an object. Felicitate me, O ye daughters of Jerusalem! you holy souls, for having found my beloved, and that I am at length possessed of the dear object of my wishes.

Suffer me, O adorable spouse! who art also my Lord and my God, to cast myself at thy feet to pay thee my homage and adoration, to thank thee for the inestimable benefit thou hast this day conferred upon me, and to beg once more thy pardon for my past infidelities. Wherefore, prostrate at thy feet, I adore thee with the most awful reverence and perfect homage, at least in desire, that a creature is capable of paying to its Creator. I annihilate myself before thee by the most sincere acknowledgment of my nothingness. I return thee for this favour all the thanksgiving that gratitude can inspire, and I once more beg pardon for all my past transgressions.

But since thou hast done me the favour to espouse me, thou justly requirest that I should give thee my heart, nay my whole self, as being indebted to thee for all I am and all I poffefs. I accordingly furrender to thee my heart and all the love and tendernefs it contains. I give it to thee intire, and do proteft and folemnly declare before thee, that no other object but thyfelf fhall evermore have any fhare in my affections. I fhould look upon myfelf as a thoufand times unworthy to live, if after the favour thou haft done me this day, I were ever to accept of any other but thee for my fpoufe.

Take full and entire poffeffion of me, I befeech thee, O my adorable fpoufe. Poffefs my heart, my mind, my memory, my powers and faculties with every thing belonging to me; and fuffer none but thyfelf to poffefs me. A bridegroom ought to be jealous of the affections of his fpoufe, fo as to make no allowance for any other to attempt to ufurp any fhare in them.

Vouchfafe me thy love, O adorable fpoufe! Keep me conftantly near thee by a union with thee, and by uninterrupted prayer; fupport me by the food of thy holy doctrine, clothe me with the robes of thy juftice, lodge me in the bofom of thy mercy, guide me by thy divine laws, protect me under the fhadow of thy wings, heal me by the fovereign balm of thy blood, bear with my weaknefs, comfort me by the prefence of thy Holy Spirit, and grant me all the fuccours I have occafion for.

But if I afk of thee the tendernefs and protection of a bridegroom, I promife thee on my fide the moft dutiful behaviour of a bride;
that

that is to say, the moſt profound reſpect, the moſt ſincere love for thee, and entire confidence in thee; a perfect obedience to thy commands, and a never failing obſequiouſneſs to thy will and pleaſure.

What elſe, O adorable ſpouſe! was thy portion while here upon earth, but toils, affliction, ſcorn, poverty, contempt, croſſes, torments and death,? The like I deſire may be mine. I would gladly partake with thee here in the bitter cup of thy ſufferings, that I may have a ſhare with thee hereafter in the cup of thy joys and delights; *I will follow thee whitherſoever thou goeſt.* Grant me, I beſeech thee, both the will and the ſtrength to do ſo.

I recommend to thee alſo thy ſpouſe, the Catholic Church, and all holy ſouls, which are alſo thy ſpouſes. Grant them the grace of a perfect love, and exact fidelity in the diſcharge of their obligations. Make likewiſe worthy of thee the ſouls of ſinners, whom thou ſeekeſt for ſpouſes; reſcue them from the power of the devil who has taken them from thee; re-unite them to thee, I pray, by thy grace. My care and concern this day ſhall be to pleaſe my adorable ſpouſe, and to love him with an undivided affection; for on him alone, without the leaſt reſerve, I place all my affections.

Remote Thanksgiving.

WHAT ruturn shall I make to thee, O my Saviour! for the inestimable benefit with which thou hast this day favoured me in taking me for thy spouse? The love, adoration and praise due for such a favour far exceed my utmost efforts.

Praise and proclaim, ye blessed spirits in heaven and you just upon earth! the goodness, love, generosity, magnificence and every other perfection of my adorable spouse; and join me in thanking him for the divine union he has been pleased to cement with me this day.

Thou requirest of me, O divine spouse! that I should give thee my heart: I give it thee with pleasure, I consecrate it to thee a thousand times: it has no warmth, no affection, nor inclination but for thee: thou hast captivated it by thy divine gifts, O adorable spouse! I now feel no more of it abiding with me; it has quitted with me to take its flight towards thee and to dwell with thee.

Abide always with, and near me, O holy spouse! to be my joy, my treasure, my comfort, my happiness and my all.

A short Method for hearing Mass.

THE preparation, the oblation, the participation of the victim and the thanksgiving and praise offered to God after partaking of it, constituted the four principal parts of the ancient sacrifices which were offered to God. These are, in like manner, the principal duties required of us to assist devoutly at the holy sacrifice of the Mass, which is the most august act of the christian religion, and the most excellent prayer that can be offered to God. A form of these acts is hereafter set down. The rest of the time may be employed either in meditating on the mysteries of our Saviour's passion, or attending to what the priest says at the altar, or in devout prayer, mental or vocal, or, in fine, entering into the spirit of the church at each ceremony or part of the Mass.

For instance, when the priest goes down to the foot of the altar to say the Psalm *Judica*, a person may lament the fall of the first man, and give thanks to the Eternal Word for coming down from heaven to raise him up again, as also human nature which had fallen with him——At the *Confiteor*, make an humble confession of his sins to God.—When the priest goes up to the altar, he may form an act of hope for being reconciled to God—At the *Introit* sigh with the Patriarchs after the coming of Jesus Christ.—At the *Kyrie*, invoke the mercy of God.—At the *Gloria in Excelsis*, rejoice

joice for the birth of Christ.—At the *Collect*, join with the church in beseeching God to accept of this sacrifice.—At the *Epistle*, beg of him to imprint in our minds the truths he has revealed in the Old Testament.—At the *Gradual*, pray him to dispose us for receiving the doctrine of the gospel.—At the *Gospel* he may beg of him to replenish our souls with the divine light of his truths contained in it, and that he would extend his mercy to all infidel nations.—At the *Creed*, he is to adhere with a firm and lively faith to the articles it contains. —At the *Offertory*, he may offer up himself together with the rest of the faithful, as a mystical victim for being transformed into Jesus Christ.—At the *Lavabo*, pray to be cleansed from his sins.—At the *Preface*, raise his heart to God, to adore and glorify him with the holy angels.—At the *Canon*, form the act of oblation hereafter inserted.—At the *Elevation*, he is to adore Jesus Christ upon the altar and upon the cross, beseeching him to communicate to him the benefits of his sacrifice.—At the *Pater noster*, or Lord's prayer, he is to recite devoutly the several petitions it contains—At the *Agnus Dei*, to beg of Jesus Christ to forgive us our sins, and dispose us for receiving him in our hearts. Afterwards may be said the prayer hereafter inserted for a Spiritual Communion, unless a person is to communicate sacramentally. While the prayer, called the *Post Communion* is saying, we may return thanks according to the form hereafter also inserted.— At the priest's Benediction, beg of Jesus Christ

to

for hearing Mass.

to bestow on us his blessing.—At the *last Gospel*, beseech him to make us worthy to contemplate after this life the glory which he is possessed of in the bosom of his Father. This method however, is not so strictly prescribed, as to give it the preference to any other to which a person may have more devotion, and from which he may reap greater advantage.

Act of Preparation for hearing Mass.

GRANT me, O Lord! I beseech thee, the necessary dispositions for assisting with all due reverence and devotion at the holy sacrifice of the Mass, that I may reap from thence the benefits thou hast designed I should. Purify me from my sins; keep my senses under proper restraint; banish from my mind all vain and earthly thoughts; raise up my heart unto thee and shed upon it the beams of thy light, that it may be wholly employed during this most august act of religion, in contemplating the greatness of the mystery; inflame it with thy love, and finally enable me to enter into the spirit of Jesus Christ and of his church, with which spirit I now desire to join in the performance of this duty.

Act

Act of Oblation after the Sanctus.

MOST adorable Trinity, I offer to thee, with Jesus Christ and his church by the hands of the priest, this divine sacrifice, as an act of homage to thy infinite greatness, of thanksgiving for thy benefits, of atonements for my sins, and for obtaining from thee all those helps I stand in need of in order to my salvation. I offer it in honour of Jesus Christ, his passion and his other mysteries; in honour of the blessed Virgin Mary, the holy angels, saint John Baptist, the apostles, martyrs, confessors, virgins, and all the other saints in heaven; those in particular whose memory is this day celebrated by thy church, or who on this day have been called to the possession of eternal bliss. I offer it to thee for the whole church, for its pastors and my own in particular; for my kindred, my friends, my benefactors and my enemies; for such as I am particularly connected with, or for whom I ought to pray or who have desired my prayers, or for whom thou desirest I should pray. I offer it also to thee, for the perseverance of the just, for the conversion of sinners, the comfort of the afflicted and for the support of all those who are in any danger, for all the necessities of the public, and for my own in particular; that thou wouldst be pleased to make me victorious over all my vices and passions, and endow me with all virtues, more especially with charity,

rity, humility, patience, and bestow on me the gift of final perseverance. I offer it up likewise for the conversion of hereticks, schismaticks, infidels and Jews; and to beg of thee to send zealous labourers into the vineyard of thy church, and to animate with thy spirit those whom thou hast already sent.

I likewise offer it to thee for the repose of the souls in purgatory, and in a more particular manner for those of my kindred, friends, benefactors, and such as I have occasioned to fall into sin, and for all those who may be destitute of help.

I recommend unto thee, O adorable victim! all our wants, whether spiritual or temporal; begging of thee to obtain a gracious relief of them from my Father: to whom I also make an offering of myself, to thy Father, together with thee and the whole church, as making but one and the same victim with thee; and in the same spirit and with the same intentions with which thou offerest thyself.

To make a spiritual Communion in the time of Mass.

DIVINE Saviour, who hast vouchsafed us thy presence on this altar, that thou mayest be the nourishment of our souls! I could ardently wish to receive thee; but my unworthiness hinders me from enjoying the effects of this desire. Being defiled to the degree I am, I dare

I dare not approach a body fo holy as thine: but if I am unworthy to partake of thy body, grant at leaft I may partake of thy fpirit; if I cannot have the happinefs of being incorporated with thee by receiving this Euchariſt, make me at leaſt become one fpirit with thee by the grace of the fame facrament. If, in fine, I cannot feed on the fleſh of the victim which I have juſt now offered by the hands of the prieſt, allow me at leaſt to be a ſharer in the benefit of the facrifice. Come, therefore, O Saviour! come into my heart by thy Holy Spirit; come and make me a partaker both of the fruits of the facrifice and of the grace of this facrament; come and reconcile me to thy Father, and bring to me the fuccours I ſtand in need of; come and feed me, cure me, enlighten me, inflame me, fanctify me, enrich me, and transform me into thyfelf. Let it not be faid henceforward that I live by my own life, will and fpirit, but that Jefus lives in me. May he then be the foul of my foul, and the only principle and moving fpring of all my thoughts and actions, that I may never move nor act in any thing hereafter but by the impulfe of his will and love.

Thankfgiving during the Poſt-Communion.

I THANK thee, Lord, for the honour thou haſt done me in fuffering me to aſſiſt at the facrifice juſt now offered to thee, and for the ſhare thou haſt granted me therein.

I thank

I thank thee alſo, O Jeſus! for vouchſafing to be ſacrificed anew for me on this altar; grant, I beſeech thee, that the efficacy of this divine ſacrifice may always operate in me, may ever produce in me effects worthy of its excellence, and make me reſemble thee by a life of virtue and ſanctity. *Amen.*

ELEVATIONS
TO
JESUS CHRIST,

When the bleſſed Sacrament is expoſed.

First Elevation.

Come unto me all you that labour and are heavy laden, and I will give you reſt. Matt. 11. 28.

WHOSE is that ſweet and comfortable voice, which with ſo much charity invites all that are in miſery to come for relief? Is it not thine, O divine Jeſus! whom I ſee expoſed on this altar? Is it not thou who from our tabernacles cryeſt out to all mankind to have recourſe to thee for a remedy of their diſorders, and doſt ſolicit me in particular to ſeek from thee comfort and redreſs in mine.

Thou ſayeſt, Come: But is it poſſible that thou ſhouldſt think of ſo vile and wretched a creature as myſelf, and that thy benevolence ſhould

should be so extensive and condescending as to invite me to thee to ease me of my miseries!

Thou commandest me to come: But O God of glory! how shall I presume to appear in thy sight? Heaven and earth tremble with fear in thy presence; the most exalted among the heavenly intelligences veil their faces, and do not even lift up their eyes before thy tremendous majesty, being overpowered by the dazling lustre of thy glory; how then shall I be able to support the splendour of it?

Come: But how dare I approach thee who am conscious to myself of so much guilt, by having so many ways transgressed thy divine law? My whole life has been one continued series of sins and disorders; with what face then shall I dare present myself before my judge under such a complication of guilt?

Come: But my Saviour, it is out of my power to take one step towards thee, being oppressed and enfeebled by diseases, and paralitick in all my limbs. I am, besides, laden with the insurmountable weight of my concupiscence, and with-held by the chains of my criminal habits; how then shall I be able to answer thy kind invitation of drawing near to thee?

Thou sayest, Come: The command I lay upon thee, so far from being oppressive, will afford thee strength and vigour sufficient to enable thee to obey it; and thou shalt find in me, not a God whose majesty fills with fear and trembling those that approach his throne, but a God whose goodness affords infinite comfort to all such as have recourse to his clemency: not a judge ready to inflict punishment on thee for thy crimes, but a father who stretches out his arms, and opens to thee his bosom to receive thee into his tender embraces after all thy wanderings.

Come: It is thy God, thy king, and thy redeemer that calls thee: it is thy Father, thy spouse and thy master that orders thee to approach; do not all these rights, titles and relations vest him with sufficient authority over thee to require thy attendance?

Come: because it is my desire that thou shouldst come: for though I have no need of thee, being infinitely happy in myself; such notwithstanding is my love for thee, that I am infinitely delighted to see thee come to me, and this on no other motive and with no other view, than the desire I have to make thee a partaker of my happiness.

Come: because I reside on this altar, that I may converse with thee, and because I have divested myself of all my glory to make myself accessible; having thus veiled and shrouded myself in condescension to thy weakness. Having done all this to draw near to thee, canst thou on thy side refuse coming to me?

Come: I wait for thee on this altar; be not afraid that I will withdraw when I see thee appear, or what will deprive thee of the liberty of speaking when thou shalt present thyself before me to lay open to me thy wants. I am not like the kings of the earth, difficult of access, and from whom it is so hard to obtain a favourable

favourable hearing. I have so ordered myself as to be immoveable on this altar, to convince thee that thou art sure of there finding me; and I there keep a profound silence, that thou mayest not doubt of my being always ready to give thee a hearing.

Come, whilst thou hast such free access to me; thou wilt not always have the same advantage. The time may come when thou wilt wish to be heard by me, but wilt not have that favour granted thee; make use therefore of the opportunity while thou hast it.

Come: since it is an honour I do thee, which I have refused to thousands. How many millions are there alive at this time who refuse to know me, and whom therefore I leave in the darkness of error and ignorance, not allowing them the least access to me, much less the grace I make thee the offer of; wouldst thou not be very culpable in not availing thyself of it?

Come: what is it that keeps thee at a distance? Is it a frivolous pleasure, a vain honour, some transitory possession, some unhappy connection? But how canst thou for such trifles resist a God that invites thee, and deprive thyself of the inestimable riches he desires to heap upon thee?

Come: because I am thy only resource; thou wilt find nothing elsewhere but treachery, perfidiousness, a want of power or inclination to serve thee; harshness, affliction and misery: I am the only one thou canst confide
in,

in, and from whom alone thou canst receive help and comfort.

Come to me, for I intirely consult thy interest, I have nothing else in view but thy own happiness: thou hast hitherto gone after those who sought nothing but thy destruction; who have laid violent hands on thee, stript, dishonoured, wounded, and loaded thee with chains, and who are now preparing for thee everlasting punishment. Be convinced of, and own thy mistake; forsake them from this moment, and come to me who desire nothing but thy salvation.

Come to me, because thou wilt find with me all that thou canst wish for or desire. If hunger afflict thee, I am the bread of heaven; if thirst torment thee, I am the fountain of living water; if darkness surround thee, I am the true light; if poverty oppress thee, I am sovereign wealth; if weakness deject thee, I am strength itself; if death threaten thee, I am life eternal.

Come, and I will ease thee of that complication of disorders thou dost labour under, and for which thou canst find no remedy. I will ease thee of the heavy burden of thy iniquities, which are ready to weigh thee down into the *lower hell:* I will ease thee of the weight of thy concupiscence which makes thee totter at every step, and those motions thou findest so much difficulty to withstand; I will ease thee of the chains of thy ill habits, which keep thee bound and shackled and hinder thee from advancing in the road to heaven; I will ease thee

thee of the yoke of this world, which, by its maxims, counfels and folicitations, the bufinefs, it loads thee with or throws in thy way, ftrives to draw thee into fin.

I will relieve thee from the hard and painful labours brought upon thee by the inceffant conflicts thou haft to maintain againft thy invifible enemies, ever implacably intent upon compaffing thy ruin both by ftrength and ftratagem. I will eafe thee of the troubles and difficulties thou findeft in the difcharge of thy duties, and in the practice of virtue. I will endow thee with a ftrength which fhall raife thee above whatever can thwart or difturb thee. In fine, I will fupport thee under the continual labours and vexations of this life, wherein poverty, contempt, perfecution, injuftice, ficknefs and many other calamities which form as it were an uninterrupted fucceffion of miferies, afford thee not the leaft refpite; but I will either mitigate their violence, or will enable thee to fupport them in fuch a manner, as fhall be conducive to thy future glory, and add to the luftre of thy crown.

Well, fince thou art pleafed, O divine Saviour, to invite me to thee with fo much goodnefs, lo! I accept of thy gracious invitation, and do now prefent myfelf before thee. It is with pleafure that I break off all my engagements with creatures to come to thee, becaufe thou art my only good, my only hope, and my only confolation.

I come to unload myfelf, at thy feet, of the heavy burden of my fins; there I lay them dow down, my Saviour, and do moſt humbly beg of thee that I may not be called to account for them at thy tribunal

I come to obtain of thee ſtrength for reſiſting that domeſtic enemy, my concupiſcence, and for repreſſing the violence of my paſſions and conquering my bad habits.

I come to aſk for ſuccour in the riches of thy mercy, that by it I may be preſerved from the corruption of the world, and withſtand the malignant impreſſions made on my heart and my mind by opinion, cuſtom, bad examples by the inſinuations and importunities of its abettors, and the ſeducing charms of riches, pleaſures and earthly grandeur.

I come to throw myſelf before the throne of thy mercy there to ſeek a ſure refuge againſt the rage of my inviſible enemies, ever watchful to deſtroy me by violence or artifice, which I cannot reſiſt by the mere force of nature.

O my divine Jeſus! who haſt invited me with ſo much tenderneſs, wilt thou reject me, now I am come to thee, attracted by the ſweetneſs of thy love and the infallible certainty of thy promiſes? Alas! what will become of me if thou caſt me off? whom ſhall I have recourſe to if thou forſake me? who will defend me againſt my enemies if I fail of thy protection? who will cure me of my diſeaſes, if thou doſt not apply a remedy to them? who will deliver me out of ſo many dangers I ſee myſelf inceſſantly expoſed to, unleſs guarded and protected by thee? I muſt be utterly loſt unleſs thou ſave me. I therefore throw myſelf

self into thy arms, and into the bosom of thy infinite charity. Receive me into this bosom, O Jesus! as one of thy sheep according to thy promise by thy prophet; (Ezech. 34.) hold me fast in thy arms, and suffer none to force my soul from thee: have compassion on my weakness, and bear me on thy shoulders, (Luke 15. 5.) as thou didst the strayed sheep, to thy heavenly fold. *Amen.*

Second ELEVATION.

The Lamb that was slain is worthy to receive power, and divinity, and wisdom, and strength, and honour, and glory, and blessing. Apoc. 5. 12.

LAMB of God, whom thy love for men has laid on our altars in a state of mystical death! I there adore thee, not only as living, but also as the source of my life; and join in one accord with that numberless host of blessed spirits whom the Beloved disciple saw in his Revelation, acknowledging with them that thou art worthy to receive power, divinity, wisdom, strength, honour, glory and blessing.

The world makes no account of thee in this mystery; it ranks thee amongst the dead of whom it has lost all remembrance, or rather amongst the things that never existed, as refusing to believe and acknowledge thy real presence fence in this facrament. But in fpite of their forgetfulnefs, I will always think of thee; in fpite of their incredulity, I will always believe with a firm faith that thou art there really prefent; in fpite of their contempt, I will ufe my beft endeavours to render thee in this facrament all the honour I poffibly can; and I will every where proclaim, that to thee belong power, divinity, wifdom, ftrength, glory, and bleffing.

Oh! that my voice was equal to that of thofe numberlefs angels and bleffed fpirits, to make thy praifes refound throughout the univerfe, and to declare unto all creatures that thou waft never more worthy than thou art in this ftate of annihilation, that they fhould all join in acknowledging and adoring thy power, thy divinity, thy wifdom, thy ftrength, thy glory, and thy other perfections.

Thou art worthy of this acknowledgment on account of the infinite excellence of thy perfon, becaufe thou art the fame God with thy Father who begat thee from all eternity out of the bofom of his effence, and has communicated unto thee, by thus begetting thee, his divinity, his power, his wifdom, his ftrength, his glory, and all his other perfections,

Thou art worthy; becaufe thou art the principle and fource from whence is derived all the power, all the wifdom, all the ftrength, all the glory, and all the other perfections creatures are endowed with; and for which they

are

are bound to do thee homage, and to acknowledge that they hold them from thee.

Thou art worthy; becaufe thou art the end of all things; for if thou haft made creatures to exift, it was for the glory and praife of thy holy name. The power, wifdom, and might thou haft endowed them with, are given to make known to us thy divinity, to caufe thy power to be dreaded, thy wifdom to be adored, thy ftrength to be admired, and to lay us under an indifpenfable obligation of having nothing in view but thy honour in all our actions.

Thou art worthy; becaufe thou didft fuffer death in obedience to the command of thy Father, to repair by it the injury he had received from the fins of mankind The zeal thou didft exert in his caufe, and thy painful labours for the re-eftablifhment of his glory, well deferved his giving thee an abfolute power over all creatures; (Matt. 28. 18.) his crowning (Pf. 8. 5.) thee with honour and glory, and his making thee to be adored throughout the world.

Thou art worthy; becaufe by dying on the crofs thou haft redeemed mankind from hell, delivered them from the dreadful captivity of fin and the power of Satan, repaired the lofs fuftained in heaven by the fall of the angels and re-eftablifhed all things. The many bleffings thou haft conferred on the world juftly challenge from all creatures a moft fincere confeffion of thy divinity, a voluntary fubjection to thy power, a due admiration of thy wifdom, and a most studious endeavour to honour thee to the full extent of their faculties.

Thou art worthy; because thou hast, to appearance, divested thyself on our altars of all thy perfections, and dost suffer there a kind of second death for the salvation of the world. The honour thou dost us in making thyself there present; the goodness thou there exhibitest such signal proofs of, by laying aside all the ensigns of thy greatness, and the blessings thou dost there procure for us by thy sacrifice, deserve that we should use our utmost efforts to restore to thee, in some measure, by our subjection and respect, the power, divinity, honour, and might, of which thou hast in a manner stript thyself for the love of us.

Thou art worthy; because thou hast opened for us the Book (Apoc. 5. 8.) of the mysteries relating to thy divinity and thy humanity. Thou hast broke open the seven seals (Ib. 5. 5.) that shut it up from us, by making known to us the truth of the seven principal mysteries contained in this admirable book, and which had been foretold by the prophets; which are the incarnation of thy divine person, thy passion, thy resurrection, thy ascension into heaven, the sending of the Holy Ghost, the calling of the gentiles, and thy last coming.

Thou art worthy: because thou hast opened the mysterious book of providence, by disclosing to us the adorable secrets of its conduct towards the elect. Thou hast taught us that the miseries and afflictions, which are by God's permission their portion in this life, are sent in order

order to purify them from their sins, to preserve them from the corruption of the world, to lead them to an eminent degree of virtue, to enable them to merit rich crowns in heaven, and to make the efficacy of thy grace triumph amidst all their weaknesses.

Thou art worthy: because thou hast opened the book of our own conscience. This book is written both *within and without* (Apoc. 5. 11.) and contains an account of the sins both internal and external which we commit with so little scruple and remorse; and it is sealed with seven seals by the darkness wherewith our passions and self-love overspread our mind, and hide from it the knowledge of our sins: but thou hast broke open these seven seals by the light thou hast shed upon it, which discovers to us both their number and their enormity, inspires us with an utter abhorrence of them, and induces us to expiate them by penance.

Thou art worthy; because thou hast opened for us the book of the divinity by opening to us the gates of heaven, and by meriting for us the possession of eternal happiness. This book was sealed with seven seals, the seven capital sins we are guilty of having shut the gates of heaven against us: but thou hast also broke open these seals, by meriting for us the forgiveness of our sins and the eternal fruition of God himself.

Thou art worthy, O divine Jesus! upon all these accounts, and by reason of such a profusion of graces and favours thou hast procured us through thy merits, to receive power, divinity, wisdom, strength, honour, glory and blessing, not as if thou didst not already possess all these in thyself, but because thou dost not possess them in the minds of ungrateful and rebellious men, who refuse to own thee for what thou art. Thou art worthy to have all these qualities ascribed to thee by them, and that thy Father should make them sensible thereof, that they may adore and obey thee.

Thou art worthy to receive *Power*; because thou deservest that all the nations of the earth should own thee for their sovereign monarch, and obey thy laws; and that the throne of Satan, who had usurped the goverment of the world, should be overthrown to make way for the establishment of thine.

Thou art worthy to receive *Divinity*; because thou deservest to be every where acknowledged as the only true and living God together with the Father and the Holy Ghost, and to have temples built to thee, and divine honours paid thee; that the worship of devils in all parts of the world being abolished, thine alone may take place and be established for ever.

Thou art worthy to receive *Wisdom*; because thou deservest that all men should acknowledge thee to be supremely wise, and even wisdom itself; that they should embrace thy doctrine as the only true one, and be guided intirely by its dictates, as the only one that is incapable of leading them into error.

Thou art worthy to receive *Strength*; because thou deservest that the whole world should

acknow-

acknowledge that thou art the strength of thy Father; that thou dost whatever thou wilt in heaven and earth without controul; and that thou makest use of the feeblest things to destroy the mightiest, of the lowest and most contemptible to confound the highest, and (1 Cor. 1. 28.) of that *which is not to bring to nought that which is*.

Thou art worthy to receive *Honour*; because thou deservest that all creatures should be employed in honouring thee with all the testimonies of sovereign respect, and make it their whole business and study to find ways and means of giving thee constantly fresh marks of their profound veneration.

Thou art worthy to receive *Glory*; because thou deservest that the glory of thy holy name should be every where displayed; that men and angels should join in admiration of thy divine actions and boundless perfections; and that they should confess that there are none like thee in heaven or on earth, and none who are not indebted to thee for whatever excellence and virtue they are possessed of.

Thou art worthy to receive *Blessing*; because thou deservest that all mankind should bless thee, praise thee and thank thee for all the graces they have received from God, it being only through thy merits that they have been bestowed on them; and that they should also omit no endeavours to make reparation, by their praises and blessings, for the blasphemies and curses which the impious vent against thee in this divine mystery.

May therefore men and angels join in one accord, O divine lamb! to come and make thee all these acknowledgments and to celebrate these thy praises. May they come and acknowledge thy power, by submitting to thy authority and doing thee homage for their own. May they come and acknowledge thy divinity by adoring thee as their God, and by confessing that it is through thy merits they have been graciously made partakers (2 Pet. 1. 4.) of the divine nature. May they come and acknowledge thy Wisdom, by embracing thy doctrine as the only one worthy of belief, and by doing homage to thee for all the knowledge they are possessed of. May they come and own thy Strength, by confessing that nothing is impossible to thee, and by expecting all from thy gracious assistance. May they come and render thee Honour, by all the testimonies in their power of sovereign respect, and by making a sacrifice to thee of their own honour. May they come and Glorify thee, by every where proclaiming thy wonderful perfections and by sacrificing to thee their own glory. May they come, in fine, to Bless thy holy name by acknowledging that it is through thee that they have been favoured with the blessings of heaven, and by paying thee a just tribute of thanks for the same.

O how earnestly do I wish, O adorable Saviour! that all the nations of the earth would come and make thee all these acknowledgments before thy euchariftical throne; it sorely grieves me to see that so few acquit themselves wor-

thily

thily of this duty. I have but too much reason to lament my own backwardness and defieiencies heretofore in these particulars; but I now come to make some reparation for my failure. I do therefore declare in the presence of heaven and earth that I do here acknowledge thee under the sacramental veils for my God, my king, my master, my protector, my redeemer, and my all. I make a solemn declaration before men and angels, that I adore thy Divinity, that I subject myself to thy Power, that I account it my duty to follow the dictates of thy Wisdom, that I place my intire confidence in thy Strength, that I consecrate my whole being and all I possess to thy Honour, that I desire nothing but thy Glory, and in fine, that I own myself indebted to thy merits for all the blessings I have received from heaven.

But since, O divine Saviour! I acknowledge thee for my God, make me sensible of the power of thy divinity by transforming me into thyself, by making of my heart a temple worthy of thy greatness. Since I acknowledge thee for my king, assert thy power over me by establishing thy kingdom in my heart and suffering none of those strange masters who have hitherto ruled in it, evermore to exercise any power there, since I acknowledge thee for my instructer, teach me thy heavenly doctrine, infuse into me the lights of thy divine wisdom, discover to me the falshood of the errors of the pretended sages of this world. Since I place my intire confidence in thy strength, re-

cover

cover me out of my feeble state, and support me against the powerful efforts of my enemies. Since I consecrate my whole being, and every thing thereto belonging to thy honour, protect me against those that seek my destruction. Since I every where proclaim thy glory, suffer me not to fall into the infamy of sin. In fine, since I acknowledge the excellence of thy merits, make me experience their efficacy by new and more powerful graces which may bring me to a thorough reformation of my life, the practice of christian virtues, and a faithful discharge of the duties of my state of life, and enable me to merit the crown of glory which thou hast prepared for me in the kingdom of heaven. *Amen.*

Third ELEVATION.

He hath set his Tabernacle in the Sun. Pſ. 18. 5.

O THOU glorious Sun! whom I behold exposed on this altar, permit me to approach thee that I may contemplate thy beauties, admire thy splendours, enjoy thy light, be enriched with thy virtue, and receive the happy influence of thy salutary beams.

How gloriously dost thou shine forth, O divine Sun! in the midst of this tabernacle? The cloud of the accidents which should seem to cast

cast a veil on thy light, do not in the least obstruct or weaken its effulgence. Faith finds thee under them as bright and glorious as thou art in heaven on thy throne! O with what a bright day dost thou delight the whole world by virtue of this mystery! The earth is blessed thereby with a fore-taste of the felicity of heaven, it enjoys a day which dispells all its darkness, and is never succeeded by any night; because thy continual presence on our altars eases all our troubles, and forms a continued day throughout the world. Thy first appearance in the flesh brought light into the world; for the proceeding ages were a time of obscurity, like that which preceded the creation of light. But from the time of thy appearance upon earth by the mystery of thy incarnation, and of fixing thy abode amongst us by that of the holy eucharist, thy light has been in regard to the world as the light which succeeded that primitive darkness; which darkness and light form the day of the present life.

Thee, O divine Sun! God himself has placed in the firmament of the church, that by means of thy light and thy influence thou mightest preside over the performance of all her works. For with a little attention we may observe that whatever the sun operates in the material world, thou performest the like by this mystery in the spiritual.

The sun is the source of all the light of the former: it enlightens at the same time both the sky and the earth, by communicating light to the planets and sublunary bodies. And thou,

thou, O Jesus! in this mystery, art the source of all the light the spiritual world enjoys; thou at once dost enlighten in it both angels and men. All that we know is derived to us from the light thou sheddest on us;. without this light we should remain in perpetual darkness.

The sun communicates heat to our world by the warmth of its rays; it is as the heart of all nature to which it gives heat and motion, and which could no more subsist without its influence, than an animal can live without its heart. And thou, O Jesus! residing as thou dost on our altars, kindlest the warmth of devotion in the hearts of men by the ardour of thy charity; thou art there as the heart of the church, imparting warmth, life and motion to all her members. Without this mystery, the religion thou hast established could not subsist, it being its foundation and the pillar that supports it.

Those who have more curiously considered the nature of the sun, have remarked that it resembles an ocean of fire, in which there is a kind of perpetual ebullition, and as it were a continual ebbing and flowing of flames. It constantly imparts its heat and light to other heavenly bodies that move round it, and they reflect it back to it, as it were to do it homage. Those in like manner who have made the secrets of this mystery their particular study, have observed therein as it were an ocean of divine fire which is in a kind of perpetual ebullition, ever ebbing and flowing, and communicating its flames to the heavenly luminaries of the church,.

church, which are the faints and the juft, in order to enlighten them, to inflame them and to impart to them its virtue and its efficacy: and thofe myftical luminaries reverberate alfo their light and their fire by a reciprocal love and by an unreferved confecration of their whole being.

The fun renders fruitful both the earth and the waters. In the former it contributes to the production of numberlefs fpecies of plants and animals, and in the latter to as great a variety of fifhes. It may be faid to contain within itfelf the lifegiving power or virtue of whatever poffeffes any fpecies of life: this power or virtue it communicates by its rays to matter in order to the formation of living creatures. And thou, O Jefus! doft in this myftery beftow fruitfulnefs on our fouls and bodies, that they may produce a variety of different forts of holy actions and living works. The lifegiving power, which imparts life to all we do, is contained in thy body and in thy precious blood, and this thou infufeft into our fouls by Communion, that all our works may be works of life.

The fun attracts vapours from the earth, and raifes them to the higheft region of the air, where piercing them with its rays, it fometimes fhapes them into a crown for itfelf, or forms of them other agreeable meteors and fometimes the appearances of other funs. The life of man (Jam. 4. 14.) is compared to a vapour; but thou, O Jefus! by virtue of this myftery raifeft this vapour above every thing of a fimi-
lar

lar nature to it, thou filleft it with the fplendour of thy rays, and makeft of it a crown or fome other bright ornament in the firmament of thy church: nay thou doft fometimes tranfform it into a fun in making it, in fome meafure, an image of thyfelf, by a perfect imitation of thy virtues.

The fun by its heat is productive of winds and rains, the winds for purifying and refrefhing the air, and the rains for watering and mellowing the earth and making it fruitful. And doft not thou, O divine redeemer! refiding in this myftery! produce in our hearts the facred breath of the Holy Ghoft, which purifies and fanctifies us? doft not thou there fupply us with a choice rain of graces and bleffings, enabling us to bring forth fruits of juftice and fanctity?

The fun by virtue of its rays is faid to produce in the bowels of the earth gold, filver, and other metals; alfo diamonds, rubies and other precious ftones: and thou, O Jefus! produceft in our fouls, by virtue of this myftery, the gold of charity, the filver of purity, the rubies of fervour, the diamonds of fortitude, and the metals and precious ftones of all other virtues.

The fun, in fine, is the joy, the glory, the riches, the life and the happinefs of all nature. Every thing is cheered, every thing flourifhes, teems, and is happy on its appearance; whereas every thing mourns, fades, fails, dies, perifhes, when it withdraws. And thou, in this myftery, art, O Jefus! the joy, the glory, the riches,

riches, the life and the felicity of our souls. It is by their union with thee that they live, are filled with comfort, are raised to a high pitch of glory, are enriched with every kind of blessing, and become happy; whereas by withdrawing from thee, they droop, mourn, and are involved in darkness, ignominy, poverty, wretchedness and death.

I now enjoy the favour of beholding thee by being suffered to approach thee, and in having the favour granted me of contemplating thy beauties, of admiring thy perfections, and of receiving the effects of thy benevolent, and kindly influence: Ah! how happy do I esteem myself on this account? but that my happiness may be compleat, make me experience, I beseech thee, the wonderful effects thou art wont to produce in our souls. Cure me of my languors, enlighten my darkness, inflame me with thy ardours, endue me with thy strength, render me fruitful in good works, and make my life conformable to the glorious pattern thou hast set me in thine.

I here consider myself, O Jesus! in the nature of a frozen and barren soil! or as a tree void of sap and consequently incapable of bearing fruit. I am come to place myself within the reach of thy salutary beams, that the soil of my heart being warmed and cherished by thee, may become fruitful and enabled to produce the flowers of all virtues. I come to enjoy thy favourable aspect, that it may make my soul fruitful and enable it to bring forth the fruits of justice. Bloom then in my heart, and diffuse

diffuse your fragrant odours in the presence of this divine Sun, O ye delightful flowers of all virtues! And you, O fruits of justice! bud forth happily in all the powers of my soul, that I may thereby become a sharer in those great rewards God has promised to bestow on his faithful servants. *Amen.*

Fourth ELEVATION.

The love of Christ constraineth us.

THE love, thou givest me such signal proofs of, in the adorable mystery of the eucharist, constraineth me, O my Jesus! yes, it too forcibly constraineth me to be able to refrain from coming to give thee some tokens of mine, and to consecrate to thee all the affections of my heart. I am no longer myself, O divine Saviour! when I consider the sacred excess of thy love for us by exhibiting thyself on our altars; and I never think of it but with new astonishment and fresh transports.

This love constraineth me, as often as I reflect on the infinite dignity of him who does me the favour of being desirous that I should be the object of it. For it far exceeds my comprehension, O Jesus! how a God of infinite majesty can love with so much ardour so vile and wretched a creature as myself?

This

This love conftraineth me, as often as I reflect on the great unworthinefs of the perfon thou loveft. For alas! I have a thoufand bad qualities which render me utterly hateful and abominable in thy fight. I am an ungrateful and perfidious wretch, who have defiled myfelf by numberlefs crimes, and fo often infulted thee in the moft outragious manner. How canft thou, who art effential fanctity, and haft an infinite abhorrence of fin, love one fo deeply infected with it? how canft thou, who art juftice itfelf, and canft not therefore bear iniquity, love one that is ready to fink under the weight of it? Thou muft undoubtedly find the motive of this thy love in thyfelf, there being nothing in me but what muft difguft any other but thee.

This love conftraineth me, on account of the wonders it induceth thee to operate in order to make thyfelf prefent in this facred myftery. The leaft difficulty I meet with in coming to thee keeps me back; but thou workeft wonders without number or precedent, wonders repugnant to the laws of nature, that thou mayft come to confole me in this mournful exile, to protect me againft the dreadful enemies I am engaged with and who have confpired my ruin; to help me in my preffing wants, to conduct me fafe amidft fo many dangers to the haven of falvation: and fince thou haft vouchfafed me thy prefence on this altar, I am very fenfible that it is with the view of ftretching out thy hand to me to draw me out of the deep abyfs of mifery in which thou seest me involved, and to afford me the opportunity of laying before thee my petitions in order either to their being granted to me, or to have something much more advantageous afforded me in their stead.

This love constraineth me, by reason of thy constant continuance with me which it is the cause of. Thou dost not pay me cursory visits, neither dost thou tarry only for a time on the earth, though a place so unworthy of thee; but thou continuest there at all times that thou mayst abide always with me. Thou forsakest me not a moment, and by an unprecedented miracle thou multipliest thy presence in all parts that thou mayest be present wherever I am, to be there my support, my consolation, my riches, my glory and my happiness. What an excess of goodness is this! that a God to whom I am so unprofitable, and who is infinitely happy in himself, should be unwilling to leave me for a moment! and that whereas I shun his presence, and even find a kind of uneasiness in being with him, he should make it his delight, and repute it as it were his happiness in being always with me?

This love constraineth me, by the extreme humiliations to which it reduceth thee; as it occasions thee to come down from thy throne to engage thyself in a state of so great condescension. Thou dost there seem to divest thyself of thy glory, of thy power, of thy riches, to stoop to our weakness; in a word, to annihilate thyself as it were, in order to raise us, by thy humiliations, to the highest pitch of greatness,

greatness. Thou doſt to us in a very different manner from what we do to thee: If we make a ſacrifice to thee of our ſubſtance, of our glory, of our pleaſure, this ſacrifice is never entire, we always reſerve to ourſelves the better part of the victim; nay we often take back what we have offered: but thy ſacrifice is here moſt perfect and entire. Thou leaveſt all without reſerve, and for ſo many ages paſt that thou reſideſt on our altars, thou haſt never yet diſplayed in this ſacrament, the glory, or the greatneſs thou didſt here diveſt thyſelf of for the love of us. What an exceſs of love muſt this be, in the perſon of a God of infinite majeſty in behalf of ſuch vile and miſerable creatures!

This love conſtraineth me, by the extraordinary munificence it expreſſes; for it induceth thee, O my Jeſus! to make us a free and unlimited donation of all that thou poſſeſſeſt. Thou giveſt us thy body, thy blood, thy ſoul, thy perſon, thy divinity, thy labours, thy merits, thy kingdom, in a word, all that thou art poſſeſſed of. So great is thy love, that it would not be ſatisfied if thou with-heldeſt any thing from us. Oh! how wide is the difference between that and ours? When we make thee an offering, or beſtow any thing on our neceſſitous brethren, it is always ſome trifling matter, for the moſt part of no ſervice to us and what we are in want of; and yet, after parting with it, we often regret our having beſtowed it. But this is not thy method of proceeding, O Jeſus! in this myſtery, in which thy munificence

ficence and liberality exceed all bounds. Thou there withholdeft nothing from us, not even what is moſt dear and precious to thee, thy glory and thy very perſon : thou takeſt a delight in extending this thy munificence to all forts of people, and without fetting any bounds to thy liberality. There is no perſon howſoever involved in diſgrace and wretchedneſs, to whom thou art not infinitely bountiful. What a prodigy is this of love and goodneſs!

This love conſtraineth me, by the fortitude and generoſity wherewith it maketh thee to ſuffer, during ſo many ages, all the affronts, injuries, and indignities which the impiety, malice, perfidiouſneſs and madneſs of men are capable of. This love is not like that which we bear thee, which has ſo much in it of forecaſt, and takes ſo many precautions that nothing may befall us which is like to give us any trouble or uneaſineſs in what we undertake for thy ſervice.

O my Jeſus! to what a height doſt thou carry thy love, for ſuch a miſerable creature as myſelf? Could thy humiliations, thy privations, thy magnificence and thy zeal be carried further than thou haſt carried it in favour of me in this myſtery? Couldſt thou expoſe thy ſacred perſon to greater injuries and indignities than thou here doſt for the love of me?

Ah! my Saviour! didſt thou not do enough for me by creating the heavens, the earth, the ſea and all they contain for my ſervice? Did not thy liberality ſufficiently exert itſelf in my favour, by beſtowing on me all things here below?

low? by establishing me lord and sovereign over all the beasts of the earth, the fowls of the air, and the fishes of the sea, and by even giving charge to thy angels to guard and attend on me every where? Didst thou not sufficiently humble thyself for me, by coming down from heaven, and clothing thyself with human nature in the mystery of the incarnation? Didst thou not, in fine, suffer enough for my salvation during the course of thy mortal life and by thy death, to dispense thee from these further demonstrations of thy love for us upon our altars?

How is it possible, O Jesus! to withstand such powerful efforts, as those of thy love? I must either have no heart, or one colder than marble, or harder than adamant to be guilty of such an excess of ingratitude. If the meanest of men had done for me the thousandth part of what thou dost in this mystery, I could not help loving him: what then ought to be the sentiments of my heart towards thee, who art the sovereign monarch of the world and the God of all nature? Thou didst love me with so much ardour without the least desert on my side, though I had never done any thing for thee, though thou hadst no need of me nor couldst expect any thing from me. What return ought I not make to thee, O my Jesus! when I find moreover united in thy adorable person all merit and perfections imaginable, I who have partook so largely of thy liberality, who cannot subsist a single moment without thy succour, who find in thee my so-

vereign

vereign happiness, and expect from thy pure goodness an immense and eternal kingdom, abounding with unspeakable glory and felicity. May I love thee then. O Jesus! may I love thee, with all the ardour and all the perfection I am capable of! May all the members of my body be converted into hearts, and all these hearts into flames to be able to love thee still more and more. O that I had a million of hearts to be employed all in loving thee, to bear evidence of the sincerity and perfection of my love in return for thine! Ye angels and saints in heaven, and ye just on earth! aid me, I pray you, to love my Jesus. Lend me your hearts that I may consecrate to him all their affections, or do ye consecrate them to him yourselves, and love him in my behalf. Redouble your ardours, and augment them, if possible to an infinite degree, in return for the infinite love of my Jesus to me in this mystery. With this view I offer to thee, O my Saviour! all their love, particularly that of the angels, who here assist before thee; that of thy own divine heart, that which thy Father and the Holy Ghost bear thee, and that which thyself hast for them in the adorable Trinity. I love thee by, and with all this love.

Infuse, I beseech thee, O Jesus! a small portion of the love of thy divine heart into mine, that I may love thee myself in a manner worthy of thee. Send forth some sparks of that sacred fire which glows within thee, that I may be inflamed thereby One of them would be sufficient to cast the whole world into

a blaze;

a blaze; what wonder if the like favour beſtowed on me ſhould wholly inflame my heart? Behold then I ſtand before thee, O Jeſus! preſenting to thee my heart that thou mayeſt infuſe into it that degree and meaſure of love thou requireſt of me, as a grateful return for thine and for all thy benefits. But why does the liberality of my Saviour towards me exceed my power of making him a ſuitable return? or why, if it be his will to be ſo liberal to me, does he not give me a heart endowed with ſuch a degree of ſenſibility, and ardour, as may qualify me for the purpoſe? Ah! how vehemently do I deſire, O Lord, to teſtify to thee my gratitude, and to make thee a full retribution for all thy bounties? To this end I could wiſh, if it were poſſible, to poſſeſs an immenſe and infinite love thereby to make an adequate return for thy benefits which are without end or meaſure. I feel, O my Jeſus! within me a deſire to love thee which I cannot ſatisfy notwithſtanding all the ardour of my love; and ſo vehement are my wiſhes that all ſhould love thee, that I can neither ſufficiently enlarge nor ſatisfy them.

Thy deſign, O Jeſus! in becoming incarnate was thereby to bring down upon the earth the ſacred fire of thy love: this thou didſt begin to kindle in the hearts of men during thy mortal life, by thy words, by thy example, by thy benefits, and by thy ſufferings; but in this myſtery I may ſay that thou doſt kindle it by thy love itſelf, entering by communion into our hearts as a devouring fire to conſume fume them by the sacred ardours of thy charity. And we on our side ought never to receive thee at the holy table, without returning from it inflamed with thy love, as possessing within us that consuming fire which in heaven inflames all the blessed spirits with the ardours of a consummate charity; we ought never to appear in thy presence at the foot of thy altars, without being at the same time inflamed with thy divine charity. Thy altar is as the holy mountain on which God appeared to Moses (Exod. 19. 16. 18.) in a cloud of fire and lightning. Thou dost there form as it were a glowing furnace, whence issue continually streams of fire and flaming clouds, which happily burn and consume all within their reach. Lo! I am now with thee, O my Jesus! desirous of nothing more than to burn and be consumed by thy sacred fires. Send forth then, I beseech thee, a stream of this holy fire that it may consume and devour me. It shall be my constant endeavour to keep so near to thee that I may at length have the happiness of being consumed by thy divine fires. O love! O love! that dost burn for ever, and art never extinguished in the centre of this mystery, when shall I have the happiness of burning with thy divine fires? This is my only desire, I have no other in this world. But why dost thou suffer me to languish and wither away in expectation of what I so earnestly long for? I die with the desire of loving thee. Send forth then I beseech thee, O my Jesus! send forth into my heart thy Holy Spirit, which is that fire issuing

ing out of thine, that it may replenish me with the fulness of love. May I love thee by thy Holy Spirit, but order it so, I beseech thee, O Jesus! that my love for thee may have all the qualities of that which thou bearest me; and that it may be a love which may humble me, a love which may inspire me with self-denial, induce me to make a sacrifice of myself; a love, in short, which may act so effectually upon me, that I may give all, do all and suffer all for thy glory.

Thou exhortest me, O Saviour! (Apoc. 3. 18.) to purchase for myself that love which thou callest *fire-tried gold*; but what price, O Jesus, dost thou set upon it, and what dost thou require of me to grant me the possession of it? Am I to obtain it by making thee a sacrifice of my worldly substance, of my pleasures, my conveniencies, my repose, my happiness and my life? All these I am ready to forego for obtaining this love. Can I obtain it by being patient and resigned under detraction, calumny, contempt, injuries, affronts, sickness and persecution? I acquiesce in every thing of that nature that I may be possessed of it. Shall I, in fine, to obtain it undertake great things for thy service, as the leading an austere, penitential and mortified life; afflicting my body with toils and fatigues, and my mind with humiliations and denials? all this I will do with pleasure that thou mayst grant me thy love.

Others, O my Jesus, come hither to ask of thee prosperity, health, riches, honours, pleafures

sures and success in their affairs; but all that I petition for is thy love, all I desire is to be consumed by thy heavenly flames, and that my whole life may be spent in burning and dying for the love of thee; and this as a grateful return for the love with which thou dost burn and die continually for my sake in this mystery, and in union with this same love. My desire would be to end effectually my life at the foot of thy altars, and to die there of love in thy presence; but in whatever place soever it is thy will that I shall end my life, grant me at least, O Lord! to end it in the purest and liveliest ardours of thy love. *Amen.*

Fifth ELEVATION.

To beg of Jesus Christ in the Blessed Sacrament the cancelling of our Sins.

O THOU sovereign judge of angels and of men! who has graciously established the throne of thy mercy upon our altars, to afford us the means of being sheltered from the dreadful effects of thy justice; I come to cast myself at thy feet to beg I may be judged by thee at this tribunal of mercy, that thy justice may have nothing to lay to my charge at her own. It is my desire, with one of thy saints, " that I may have been already judged when I shall be presented at the bar of the divine justice,"
that

that nothing may then remain to be laid to my charge.

I am about drawing up a charge, and acting the part of an accuser against myself, to make room for thy mercy to pronounce in my favour the sentence of obliteration of my sins. I therefore acknowledge in thy presence, O Lord, that I am guilty of numberless crimes which deserve hell. I confess that my life is so full of them, that to what side soever I turn myself, I behold nothing but heaps of iniquity: such numbers of criminal thoughts, irregular desires, bad words and wicked actions present themselves before me, that in my whole life I scarce can find any one action, thought or word that has been wholly free from sin. Thou didst give me human body and a rational soul, and I employed them with all their faculties and powers in offending thee. Thou gavest me dominion over other creatures, and I made them instruments and incentives to sin. Thou didst redeem me from hell, and I made void the price of my ransom by engaging anew in my former servitude. I have been favoured by thee with more graces than thou hast vouchsafed to whole nations of pagans and infidels, but I abused them all by obstinately persisting in my disorders. I made no better use of thy lights and inspirations, thy benefits and thy chastisements, thy promises and thy threats, thy sacraments and thy most signal succours; all which I made the matter of new crimes: and what was an high aggravation of my wickedness, I was thoroughly sensible at the same time

time of the evil I committed, having been often reproached by thee for it, and as often promised thee amendment, and had it in my power to make good my promise. In a word, I here declare before thee, that no ingratitude, malice, and perfidiousness can be blacker than mine, and that I muſt confider it an infinite prodigy of goodnefs that thou haſt borne with me till now, and that thou haſt not long before this plunged me into the deepeſt pit of hell. But behold, O Lord, I do now deteſt all my paſt malice and diforders. I come with a heart pierced with grief, a face full of confuſion, and eyes bathed in tears to caſt myſelf at thy feet with the view of humbling myſelf before thee, to beg thy pardon of them. I know thou placeſt thy glory, not ſo much in puniſhing crimes as in pardoning them: I know thy clemency and mercy towards finners; that no finner ever yet had recourfe to thee with true forrow for his crimes but found mercy; that thou art upon our altars the lamb that takes away the fins of the world; that thou there performeſt the function of mediator and high prieſt to reconcile us to thy Father: that, in fine, we cannot pleaſe thee more than by throwing ourfelves on our knees before the throne of thy mercy. Thefe confiderations have emboldened me to come to thee, O my Saviour! to beg pardon for my crimes, and to intreat thee to pronounce a favourable fentence in my behalf from thy euchariſtical throne. Speak unto me therefore thoſe comfortable words thou formerly didſt to the man fick of

the

the palſey: *Thy ſins are forgiven thee.* (Luc. 5. 23:) May I hear that merciful ſentence from thy mouth which thou didſt order one of thy prophets to paſs upon Jeruſalem, that is, the penitent ſoul: *Her ſin is pardoned*; (Iſa. 30. 2.) or that which thou didſt commiſſion another prophet to pronounce over the repenting ſinner: *None of the tranſgreſſions that he hath committed ſhall be reckoned unto him.* (Ezech. 18. 22.)

O ſovereign judge of the univerſe! my bones dry up with fear when I think of the rigour of thy juſtice, which I have deſerved by tranſgreſſing ſo often thy laws. Enter not, I beſeech thee, into judgment with me as I cannot otherwiſe avoid being cruſhed by thy thunderbolts; reprove me not in thy wrath, becauſe I ſhould certainly periſh; let me not feel the weight of thy arm, leſt I ſhould be cruſhed to deſtruction by the blow. I confeſs that I am a wretch, who by having often abuſed the pardon thou hadſt generouſly granted me, am altogether undeſerving of ſuch a favour: I acknowledge that the multitude and enormity of my crimes cry aloud for a refuſal of it. But, Lord! what wouldſt thou gain by my deſtruction, what advantage would accrue to thee, from my blood (Pſ. 29. 30.) and death, ſince thoſe that go down into hell (Pſ. 113. 35.) will not praiſe thy holy name? Pardon me therefore, I beſeech thee, pardon me: Jeſus, the ſon of David, take pity on me; make me experience the effects of thy goodneſs and lenity, ſhewing in me an inſtance of thy great mercy.

mercy. I know that whoever returns to thee with true repentance is never rejected: I am therefore resolved to cry and weep, that my cries and lamentations, may prevail with thee, to grant my request. Weep, weep then, my eyes, melt into tears to soften your judge. And thou, my heart be rent with sorrow, and send forth thy sighs and groans before his throne to appease his wrath; wail and lament with the bitterest grief and sorrow to excite his tender compassion. O my Saviour and my judge! wilt thou not relent at the sight of my grief and affliction? But perhaps thou dost not find that I have as yet all the repentance and compunction I ought to have for my sins. If that be the case, behold I here present thee with my heart, that thou mayst fill it with the full measure of the grief and affliction thou requirest of it; break it into as many pieces as it hath committed sins; may the excess of its grief dry up the very marrow of my bones, and make me shed in tears even the last drop of my blood. If thou art not yet appeased, inflict on me all the miseries, afflictions and reproaches thou shalt think proper; only grant me the pardon of my sins, and do not reserve my punishment for the next life. Remember that thou art no less my Father than my judge; chastise me therefore as a loving Father and not as a provoked judge.

You holy angels who are here present, solicit I beseech you, my judge for pardon. Holy Virgin, be thou my advocate with thy Son to obtain for me mercy. You saints of heaven, and you juft upon earth, interpofe, I befeech you all, in my behalf, and ufe your endeavours to procure my pardon. And more particularly, you holy penitents who have heretofore obtained it for yourfelves, intercede with God that I may obtain it alfo; and for this purpofe offer up to him your forrows, tears and mortifications to fupply the deficiency of mine. All thefe I offer up to thee together with them, O my Saviour! as alfo the infinite abhorrence thou beareft to fin, and that of all thy angels to fupply the infufficiency of mine, together with all thy merits and fufferings to compenfate for the imperfections of my repentance. But grant, if it be thy pleafure, that I may depart from the foot of thy throne thoroughly cleanfed and purified by virtue of thy blood, and may never more be fo unhappy as to be defiled with fin: rather let me die here at thy feet, than ever fuffer me to fall again, it being my defire to die rather than offend thee any more. Reftore to me therefore the robe of innocence, as the father of the prodigal child reftored it to his fon, and preferve it to me when reftored, that it may entitle me to admittance into thy celeftial tabernacle. *Amen.*

Sixth ELEVATION.

To beg our conversion of Jesus Christ in the most holy Sacrament of the Altar.

How long, O Lord, wilt thou suffer me to lie buried in the deep gulph of my miseries? How long wilt thou abandon me to the irregular desires of my heart, and suffer me to wallow in the mire of my sins? Thou seest the wretched condition I have so long continued in. Corruption has reached even the marrow of my bones. My life is but one continued series of sins and disorders: every vice and passion hath established its dominion in my soul, and detains me captive under its cruel tyranny, pride and envy, avarice and impurity, anger, gluttony and sloth, by turns make me feel the effects of their rage: self-love and self-will, like a fatal leaven, spread their malignity over all my actions. In all my thoughts, desires and actions, concupiscence ever seeks to gratify nature and inclines me to vice and sin. Will not this my extreme misery move thee to compassion?

Thou hast already been pleased to separate me by baptism from this corrupt world, to rank me in the number of thy children and to call me to holiness of life. Thou hast also favoured me with several extraordinary graces, that I might acquit myself as I ought of the duties

duties annexed to that state of life in which thy providence has placed me. But what return have I made for all these favours? In what manner do I even now discharge the obligations of it? The greater part of them I culpably omit through neglect; and if I perform some, it is merely from motives of humour, interest or self-love. After what manner have I behaved in my prayers and spiritual exercises? has it not been with sloth, irksomness and voluntary distractions? After what manner have I laboured in the practice of solid virtue, and to attain the perfection my state of Christian requires of me? I scare give myself the least concern about these matters, though so important. Where is that pure love of my God with which I ought to be animated, and which seeks him alone without the least view to self interest or satisfaction? Where is that ardent zeal for whatever regards his interest and service? Where is that lively faith which fills the mind and heart with the truths of salvation, and keeps them always fresh in our minds for the due regulation of our actions? That firm hope which never desponds of receiving help from heaven, even when every thing seems desperate? That profound humility which prompts us to seek always the lowest place? The exact obedience which never fails in the least point of what is prescribed? That invincible patience which always remains unshaken? That insatiable love of crosses which sighs after suffering and ignominy? That continual prayer which never loses sight of God? That
perfect

perfect contempt of the world which regards all worldly goods as drofs? In a word, where are all thofe chriftian virtues which I ought to practife in a moft perfect manner? Tho' I may have fome idea of thefe virtues, I find myfelf notwithftanding obliged to confefs before thee, O my Saviour! that I am as remote from poffeffing them as heaven is from earth; and that when I examine and found myfelf, I find nothing in my foul but an ever-flowing fource of corruption, ordure and fin. But, O my Jefus! wilt not thou, to whom the depth of my mifery is much better known than to myfelf, take pity of me? will not thy compaffion be moved towards me at the fight of my extreme mifery?

I here place myfelf at thy feet, O adorable redeemer! to conjure thee to relieve me, and to requeft of thee the grace of a fincere and hearty converfion. Convert me therefore, O my Jefus! convert me, Stretch forth thy almighty arm to draw me out of that abyfs of fin and corruption into which I have caft myfelf; renew in my favour the miracles of former times, to cure me of thofe numberlefs diforders that I am afflicted with, and to change me into quite a new man. But when I beg of thee, O loving Jefus! to convert me, I do not afk of thee an imperfect converfion; that which I folicit is an entire and perfect converfion; fuch as may not only make me avoid great crimes, but even the flighteft faults committed with deliberation; a converfion whereby I may not only fhun evil, but practife good

in

in its purity, and exercise myself in the most solid and perfect virtues.

It is perhaps to punish me for the sins I have commited against thee, that thou permittest me to fall into other sins; and it may be also to punish me for being unfaithful to thy former graces that thou sufferest me to fall into the like offences. But hast thou, O my God! no other chastisements but that to inflict upon me, the consequences of which are not only fatal to me, but also highly prejudicial to thy interests? Ah! rather cut, hack, burn, tear; make me suffer whatever chastisement thou pleasest, provided thou dost not take vengeance on me by abandoning me to the irregular desires of my heart.

It may also be with the view of humbling my pride that thou sufferest me to remain in my sins, as I might presume too much of myself if I found myself delivered from them. But, Lord, hast thou not other ways to pull down my pride? Ah! thou needst only shed a beam of thy light on my mind, and it will at once discover to me the abyss of my misery and the depth of my nothingness: I shall then no longer entertain the least sentiment of vanity, because having no other foundation but falshood, thy truth will bring it to utter destruction.

Perhaps, in fine, thou dost defer converting me and granting me solid virtues to make me conceive the greater esteem for them, and to oblige me to cultivate them, when received, with the greater care and attention. But canst thou

thou not, O Lord, infpire me with this efteem and care without all thofe delays, fo derogatory unto thy glory and fo prejudicial to the affair of my falvation. Delay not, therefore, O Lord, delay not any longer to work in me this thorough converfion; haften, I befeech thee, to grant me this grace: I am here at thy feet to intreat it of thee, and fhall not depart thence without obtaining it. No, Lord, let the difcouragements I meet with be what they will, I fhall not go hence till thou haft granted it me, it fhall at leaft be the fubject of my requeft to my laft moments. May the blood of my Jefus, the merits of his life and death, the unbloody facrifice which he offers continually on altars, plead my caufe before him and obtain for me the grant of my petition.

Thou alfo, O Bleffed Virgin! ye holy angels, who attend here, all ye bleffed fpirits and faints in heaven, and juft on earth! make moft earneft fupplications to my God in my behalf for the grace of an entire converfion, and that I may become entirely a new man, altogether according to his own heart.

Seventh

Seventh ELEVATION,

To Jesus Christ in the blessed Sacrament to beg of him his Protection amidst the dangers of perishing which we are continually exposed to.

I COME, O Jesus! to prostrate myself at thy feet and before the throne of thy mercy, to beg that if I have found favour in thy sight, my life, the life of my soul, may be given me at my request: I come to beg of thee to protect it amidst the dangers that surround it, and to entreat thee not to suffer it to perish everlastingly.

Ah! Lord, all my bones quake, and my blood runs cold through fear, when I reflect on the greatness of the peril I find myself exposed to. I see under my feet a lake of fire and brimstone of a frightful depth, and glowing more intensely than molten brass or copper, wherein the damned lie buried and burning. I see the devils, who in order to redouble their punishment, throw themselves upon them with a violence and impetuosity, surpassing as much the force wherewith lightning falls on the earth, as the spiritual nature transcends the corporeal. I see, in fine, that place of torments, where thy infinite power has assembled all manner of evils, which those unhappy victims of thy wrath are to suffer, not by succession, but all at once and for ever, together with

with pains, which neither the eye has seen, nor the ear has heard, nor has it entered into the heart of man to conceive; and I see myself every moment ready to fall into this dreadful abyss of misery.

I am walking continually on the brink of the precipice that leads to it, and in roads so slippery and dangerous that it is scarce possible to escape falling in: tempests also and whirlwinds sweep passengers into it; the devils use their utmost efforts both by force and stratagem to push them in; a world of senseless people second the endeavours of these wicked spirits, and even throw themselves headlong out of mere frolick, and drag others after them; in short, the thick darkness one is encompassed with, is an occasion of a person's falling in without the least surmise or apprehension of danger.

Ah! Lord, where am I at this present time? am I on the right road, or having already gone astray, am I not on the brink of the precipice? Unhappy wretch that I am! I can have no certainty of my condition, because the thick darkness I am involved in, keeps me in a total ignorance of the matter. I flatter myself that I am going right and in the safe road to happiness, but perhaps I am so far advanced on the road that leads to hell, that there is nothing but the thin thread of life between my soul and that dreadful gulf; so that the moment this thread shall be broken by death, I may find myself irrecoverably swallowed up in it.

I may

I may fancy that I enjoy the happiness of being an object of thy love, O my God! but perhaps I am so unhappy as to be the object of thy just indignation; being certain of having heretofore committed a great number of enormous sins, but under great uncertainty of having obtained thy pardon? What security have I of having sufficiently wept, mourned, done penance for them, and repaired the injury done to thee or my neighbour to be entitled to forgiveness? But without mentioning what is past, do I not at this present time harbour in my heart some hatred, some secret vanity, some attachment to the things of this world, to pleasure, glory, health, life, or some other created object, which though I am insensible of, it may notwithstanding render me guilty in thy sight? The little love I bear thee, the little sense of gratitude I have for thy benefits, my slender attention to what regards thy service, my coldness in approaching the holy mysteries, do not all these particulars but too plainly speak me a child of wrath? In fine, among the several duties of a Christian, common to all states or peculiar to my own, is there no article of which I am wilfully and culpably ignorant, the neglect of which may deprive me of the happiness of thy friendship? This, O Lord, is what I cannot pretend to the knowledge of; all this is an impenetrable secret to me.

But though I were at this time so happy, as to be in thy favour, what assurance have I of persevering in it to the end, and of dying the death of the just? How small a matter is capable of making me fall from the state of grace into the state of sin? A thought that may spring up in my mind, a phantom that may cross my imagination, a desire that may start up in my heart, a passion that may rise in my appetite, a word which may slip unguardedly from my tongue, a carelessness which may occasion the omission of some duty, is capable of bringing me to a dreadful fall? How small a matter suffices to cast me down, weak reed as I am! A temptation somewhat violent, an opportunity somewhat encouraging to sin, an accident somewhat cross, an injury, an injustice, an ill turn from the hand of an enemy; a kindness, a favour, a service a friend may desire of me contrary to the law of God, is sufficient to overthrow me and make me forget my most essential duties.

My life being crossed by such a chain of misfortunes, my frailty so great, my enemies so powerful, and the snares they constantly lay for me so artful, can I promise myself to escape all those dangers, and to persevere in a virtuous course to the end of my life? Nothing less than thy almighty hand, O Lord! is capable of preventing my falling down the precipice; my own most attentive application and care, with all the helps creatures can afford me, will avail me nothing without thine: to deliver me from all these dangers, and to conduct me safe to the haven of salvation, thou must work, not one but many miracles. Thy power must with one hand support me
under

under my own weakness, and ward off with the other the powerful attacks of my enemies; it must on one side remove the impediments which obstruct my passage, and on the other supply me with strength and vigour to hold on in my course.

In a word, thou must afford me that series of succours both internal and external, without which no one perseveres, and with the help of which no one ever fails. This perseverance, O Lord! is a gift which thy mercy confers on whomsoever thou pleasest, but which none can lay any claim to, such notwithstanding is thy goodness that thou never refusest it to those that ask it of thee as they ought. This it is that compells me to cast myself at thy feet to beg it of thee with all possible humility, confidence and fervour. Ah! Lord, have pity on my misery, and suffer me not to perish, permit not the enemies of my salvation to carry off my soul, and to boast of having devoured it. Remember that I am the work of thy hands, the price of thy blood, the inheritance thy Father has given thee; (Ps. 2. 8.) that this same Father has made me his son by adoption; that his Holy Spirit has made choice of my soul for his spouse; and that thou thyself hast often fed me with thy sacred flesh and blood, and hast granted me other numberless and extraordinary graces, all tending to promote the great work of my salvation.

Finish therefore, O my Jesus! thy work, and conduct me safe to the heaven of salvation; suffer not all thou hast already done in my behalf

half to prove ineffectual through the malice of thy enemies, left they triumph over me by making my foul their prey.

Thou art here present on our altars to afford me thy protection against them; grant it me, I beseech thee, for the glory of thy holy name, by all the toils and labours of thy mortal life, by all the torments of thy death, by all the love of thy divine heart, and by all that is most dear to thee in heaven and earth.

What doft thou require of me, Lord, to incline thee to grant me this favour? Is it thy pleasure that I should ask it of thee continually? I will do it. That I should always humble myself in thy presence? I consent to it. That I should place an entire confidence in thee? I will not fail to do it. That I should avoid committing the slightest faults with full deliberation? I will avoid them? That I should shun the world and all occasions of sin? they shall be shunned. That I should lead a mortified, penitential and retired life? such a life shall be my choice. That I should undergo the sharpest afflictions, sickness, poverty, contempt, wrongs, persecution and death itself? I will undergo them in submission to thy will. Yes, Lord, I am ready to do and suffer whatever may be agreeable to thee, that I may avoid hell and possess thee for ever in heaven: I only beg of thee to enable me to accomplish what thou requirest of me, that I may at length become worthy of the favour that I sue for. *Amen.*

Eighth

Eighth ELEVATION.

For consecrating ourselves to Jesus Christ in the Holy Sacrament.

AFTER the several consecrations which I have already made thee, O Jesus! of my whole being, I am come to make a new one at the foot of thy altar, excited thereto by the ardent desire my heart feels to be intirely thine. I offer thee therefore, O my Jesus! my soul, my life, my senses, my powers and all that I am, as a whole-burnt-offering of love. Look down, I beseech thee, with a favourable eye upon the victim I here present to thee, and consume it in the flames of thy ardent charity; may that immense fire which burns in thy divine heart, come down upon it to consume it intirely. For I am not come to offer thee a common victim, such as was offered thee under the law, when the offerer shared the victim with thee and eat one part of it, while the other lay burning on thy altar; my intention being to sacrifice unto thee a perfect holocaust, where the whole victim is intirely consumed to the glory of thy holy name, without the least reservation of any part for myself.

I henceforward claim no share in my mind, my will, my senses, my body, my thoughts, my desires, my actions; in a word, in no one thing I have hitherto been possessed of. I in general

general divest myself of all manner of property, to make a sacrifice of all to thee. It is my desire to be for the future, at once both a dead and a living victim; dead to all creatures, and living to God: I will live no longer for the world, but intirely for thee alone who art my God and my all, and I will be eternally consuming in the flames of thy love. It has been my misfortune, notwithstanding my promises of being wholly thine, to have been hitherto a victim devoted to Satan; alive to the world, but dead to God; a slave to my passions and lusts, and ever burning in the flames of concupiscence: but, by the assistance of thy grace, I will be henceforward a victim, dead to the world, living and devoted to God, and evermore burning with the sacred fire of charity.

I am therefore from this moment dead unto thee, O world! I no longer entertain any thought, desire, or fondness for whatever may be the objects of ambition in thy votaries. Speak no more to me of thy joys and pleasures, the dead are quite insensible and regardless of them; make me no more a tender of thy wealth and possessions, the dead are feelingly sensible of their emptiness: flatter me no more with the hopes of thy glory and felicity, the dead have no expectancies from thee. All my thoughts, desires and inclinations are now fixed upon thee, O my Saviour! because I live for thee alone, It is in thee that I place all my joy and consolation, all my wealth and treasure, all my glory and my happiness. I will

will entirely employ all the faculties of my soul and body in honouring and serving thee. My mind shall be so occupied in contemplating thy divine excellencies, that it shall harbour no thought but for thee; my heart shall so entirely consecrate to thee its affections, that thou shalt be the sole object of its desires; my sensitive appetite shall have no inclinations but for thee; my eyes shall behold nothing but thy wonders, my ears shall hearken to nothing but thy oracles; my tongue shall proclaim only thy praises, my hands shall be employed only for thy glory, and my feet shall walk only for executing thy commands.

I will not only exert all my powers in honouring thee, but I will employ them to the utmost extent of their ability. My understanding shall entertain such an esteem for thee and give thee such a preference to every thing else, that it shall conceive nothing but contempt for all earthly grandeur; my will shall be so warmly affected towards thee, as to have all other things in abhorrence; my eyes shall be so intent upon considering thy interests, as to be blind to every other object; all my faculties shall be entirely laid out in thy service, as to have no abilities for being employed but for thee.

I will fly like lightening to perform every thing that may be instrumental to the advancment of thy glory. I will be so earnest in my endeavours for this purpose, that at all times and on all occasions, I will procure thee all the glory I possibly can, without suffering either

the

the love of pleasure, the dread of pain, the complaints of nature, the importunities of friends, or the persecutions of enemies, to retard or cool my zeal. I will ever do that which I shall judge most acceptable to thee, and esteem most perfect; sufferings and reproaches shall be my delight, in the view of their redounding to their glory: I will be so obedient to thy commands, that to gain the whole world I will not depart one tittle from the punctual observance of them. It shall be entirely thy will which I will consider in whatever befalls me, and which I will make the rule of my own. The love I bear my body, my life, my health and the worldly substance thou hast given me, shall not take its rise from the satisfaction, comfort and interest which nature finds in them, but from my being convinced that it is thy will that I should love them with moderation, and because thou hast charged me with the care of them. Life and death, sickness and health, plenty and scarcity shall be indifferent to me; my preference of the one to the other shall be under the direction of thy adorable will, and as it shall please thy divine wisdom thus to glorify thyself in me. If I apply myself to the duties enjoined me by my superiors, it shall not be because vanity and self-love may find therein the comforts, conveniencies and advantages they seek after, but because it is thy will that prescribeth them for me. All employments shall be alike to me when dictated by thy will, convinced that it is that alone which gives them their value, and which ought to be the sole

sole motive in performing them. Whether the discharge of them be attended with success, or whether disappointments and adversity, I will be resigned to thy will; considering nothing else in either but the accomplishment thereof, and the glory that may thence redound to thee. I will check the sentiments of vain joy in the former, that I may take no pleasure in any thing but in the manifestation of thy goodness and magnificence; and I will suppress the sentiments of grief and affliction in the latter, that I may rejoice in seeing thy justice satisfied and the bands broken asunder that attached me to creatures. I will make the best use of the small talents with which thou hast entrusted me, without envying others, or repining on account of the greater it has pleased thy wisdom to favour them with. Perfectly satisfied with the distribution of them which thy wisdom has thought fit to make, and the measure of thy glory which thou art pleased to acquire by me, I shall rejoice more in seeing great talents fructify in the hands of those on whom thou hast bestowed them, than remain barren in the hands of one so negligent and slothful as myself. In a word, my only comfort, joy and happiness shall be placed in accomplishing thy adorable will, and it shall be my only care and concern to make my own conformable to it.

But if I am bold enough to make thee all those promises, O my Saviour! it is entirely in expectation of thy succours, convinced that being nothing of myself but inability and weakness,

ness, I can lay no stress on my own performances. I hope therefore that as thou hast already inspired me with the desire of being wholly thine, thou wilt also vouchsafe me the strength requisite for accomplishing it. Grant me this grace, I beseech thee, O thou victim of love! Thou who art eternally consuming in the flames of charity, make me a partner in thy sacrifice; make me to die to this corrupt world, and to live to thee, burning as thou dost in a furnace of love.

And do thou, O my soul! endeavour to unite thyself as closely as possible with this divine victim; die, burn and be consumed therewith; sink down into, and be swallowed up for ever in the immense fire of his love; let my life henceforward be no other than a faithful copy of the life he leads upon our altars, that is, an eternal immolation and consecration of himself to the glory of his Father; an immortal flame ever ascending towards heaven, a devouring and consuming fire which nothing can extinguish. Yes, O my Jesus! to burn and to die of love for thee and with thee, to dissolve by the most immense ardours of thy divine charity, to place my greatest pleasure in being consumed, destroyed and annihilated in those sacred fires, shall henceforward be my life and my sole occupation. *Amen.*

An ELEVATION,

To the divine heart of Jesus in the Holy Sacrament of the Altar.

1. HAIL, O divine heart of Jesus, in the most Holy Sacrament of the Altar, which art the centre of all hearts, where they find their rest, their joy, their happiness, and out of which they are ever miserable! Hail, O admirable vessel! which art the most excellent work and master-piece of the most high, where his power, wisdom and goodness, infinite as they are, seem exhausted. Hail, O theatre of wonders! which alone does contain a greater number than the whole world besides. I love thee with all the affections of my heart, O heart infinitely amiable! which art the object of all the complacency of thy heavenly Father, and dost also deserve to be the object of the love of all creatures. I adore thee, O heart sovereignly perfect! which art the king of all hearts, as being bound to submit to thy sovereign authority and obey thy laws. I bless and thank thee, O heart infinitely charitable! for the love with which thou dost burn for me, for that goodness with which thou bearest me in the midst of thee, and for thy continual care of every thing that concerns me. I unite myself to thee and to all thy divine operations, O adorable heart! I join in all the love, respect,

praise and glory which thou art eternally giving to God, I centre in thee all the love, reverence, praises and adorations of angels and men: permit me to unite them in my homages to thee, that I may be able to love my God with all this love, revere him with all this respect, extol him with all these praises, and bow down before him with all these adorations. I dedicate myself entirely to thee, O sacred heart! to be employed in nothng but thy service and to labour with all my might for the advancement of thy glory. I place all my hopes in thee, O heart full of goodness! which art always ready to receive me into thy protection, to succour me in my distresses, and to heap on me thy benefits. To thee I have recourse, O infinite abyss of perfection! which art the principle, the centre and the model of all the virtues and of all the perfections of creatures; and am come to beg of thee to infuse them into my heart. Infuse into it charity, obedience, purity, patience, mortification, meekness and all other virtues. I will come daily to receive them from thee as from their source, nor will I depart without being enriched with a large share of them.

II. Thou source of mercy, which art ever flowing, I come, oppressed with misery, to seek refreshment from thee! Thou fountain of living water, ever open to the thirsty, (Joh. 7. 37.) and whose water springeth up (Ibid. 38.) even to life eternal! I come to thee to quench the thirst that parches me up. Sun of glory that enlightenest the whole world, and whose light

suffereth

suffereth no eclipse or diminution! I come to thee that thou mayst dispel my darkness, and let me enjoy the beams of thy amiable light. Furnace of love! that causest both heaven and earth to glow with thy fires, I come to beg of thee to melt down the ice of my heart, and to inflame me with thy divine ardours. Principle of life, that impartest life to all the members of Christ's mystical body! I come to beg of thee to make me a partaker of that same life, that I may become a living member, worth preserving, and not one dead or rotten, and fit only to be cast away. Holy school, in which one hath the happiness of being instructed by the heavenly Father! I come to thee to learn the truths of salvation. Divine mercy seat, at the foot of which all repenting sinners receive the forgiveness of their sins! I come to thee to obtain the pardon of mine. Ocean of all good, from whence flow incessantly streams and rivers of grace and mercy, which water the whole world! I come to thee to have my soul replenished to the full extent of its powers by thy divine effusions.

III. When I reflect on thy inconceivable beneficence towards us, and the engaging favours thou incessantly dispensest to mankind, O most perfect and most charitable heart: I find myself quite transported with love and gratitude towards thee. Thou art the ark of the covenant that procurest us a happy fellowship (1 Jo. i. 3.), with God, and obtainest for us at all times numberless favours from heaven. Thou art also, in a mystical sense, the ark of Noe,

in which alone salvation can be hoped for, and out of which a man must necessarily perish; an ark, into which thou receivest, as into thy bosom, not a small number of persons, but even as many as are desirous to enter, provided they forsake the corruptions of the world. Thou art the chariot of fire, that transportest into heaven, not Elias (4 Reg. 2. 11.) only, but all the faithful who unite themselves to thee by throwing aside the mantle of all terrestrial affections. Thou art the treasure of the world that enricheft both men and angels, and to which every one may have free recourse to take thereout whatsoever he has occasion for. Thou art the temple of the Lord, ever filled with his (3 Reg. 8. 11.) glory, where any one is free to enter to adore his infinite majesty. Thou art the holy altar on which alone God accepts of offerings, and whither he orders us to carry ours. Thou art the only holocaust perfectly agreeable in his eyes, that sanctifiest our holocauft by thy union therewith, and givest them their worth by consuming them with the same fire wherewith thou thyself dost burn. Thou art the universal Priest, that presentest to God not holocaufts only, but all the offerings of men of what kind soever; that paffing through thy hands they may be acceptable to him. Thou art our advocate and mediator with the heavenly Father, who art continually pleading our cause (Heb. 7. 25.) before his tribunal, and reconciling us to him. Thou art the book of life (Apoc. 21. 17.) in which the names of all the elect are written, and in which,
every

every one, in order to be saved, must have his name entered. Thou art a paradise of delights, where pure souls dwell, and where they enjoy unspeakable pleasures. Thou art a heaven, ever open to all that are willing to enter into it, and to forsake the creature for the sake of possessing and enjoying the Creator. Thou art, in fine, the holy city, the dwelling place of all the Angels, and Saints, and where I have made choice to dwell, saying with the royal prophet : *This is my rest for ever, here will I dwell, for I have chosen it.* Whoever is in search after me, let him repair to the adorable heart of Jesus to find me, for I am determined never to quit it.

IV. O heart of exceeding great goodness and clemency ! thou art on this account my sure place of refuge against the pitiless cruelty of the hearts of men : thou art my shelter, when they reject me ; thou relievest me, when they forsake me, thou comfortest, me, when they afflict me. O most holy heart ! thou art by thy holiness my support against the corruption of the children of this world ; thou inspirest me with contempt for it, when they endeavour to fix it in my esteem ; thou inclinest me to mortification, when they would engage me in pleasure ; thou raisest in me a heavenly flame, when they strive to destroy me by an infernal one. O most generous heart ! it is in thee I find abundantly wherewithal to repair all my losses. By thy humility, I repair what I have lost by my pride ; by thy obedience, what I have lost by my rebellion ; by thy fervour, what I have loſt by my ſloth; and by all thy virtues, what I have loſt by my vices. O moſt charitable heart! thou art by thy charity a very abundant ſupply in all my wants; thou loveſt and honoureſt my God for me; thou makeſt atonement to him in my behalf; thus making him ample amends for my failure in all theſe duties: thou watcheſt over me, when I ſleep; thou workeſt for me, when I enjoy relaxation from labour, and thou haſt care of my affairs, even whilſt I give little attention to them. O moſt benign heart; thou faithful friend of mankind! thou art all my comfort, for I find no other pleaſure upon earth than in uniting and conſecrating myſelf to thee. Thou art my only hope, it being from thee alone that I expect ſuccour and ſalvation; thou art my only refuge, becauſe I have no other ſupport nor reſource but thee. O thou ſecure harbour of thoſe who know not where to put in for ſafety! I come to take ſhelter with thee in my diſtreſs, where I may be ſecured from all the evils that threaten me: I come to thee, that thou mayeſt ſerve me as a buckler againſt the wrath of my heavenly Father which I have kindled againſt me by my crimes; as a bulwark againſt the rage of my inviſible enemies, always ſeeking to deſtroy me; and a ſupport under my own weakneſſes and frailties, which threaten me every moment with death.

V. O ſource of love, light, grace, and holineſs! infuſe I beſeech thee, into my heart this love, this light, this grace, this holineſs;
make

make it meek, and humble like thyself, upright, patient, obedient, diligent, disengaged from all sensible things, as thou art; soften its hardness, bend its obstinacy, check its sallies, regulate its affections, make it a partaker of thy purity, communicate to it thy integrity, kindle in it thy fervour, inspire it with fortitude, impress on it all thy motions, and suffer it at no time to follow any other. It belongs to thee, as the chief and sovereign of hearts to govern, regulate and conduct mine.

VI. Yet take one step farther, O divine heart! by coming thyself to occupy the place of my heart in order to communicate unto all my members life, heat and motion. This heart of mine is so tainted, that its corruption is almost past cure; and though a remedy were applied with success, I fear it would be to no purpose, on account of its proneness to relapse, through inconstancy, into its former disorders. Come then, O divine heart! and take thyself its place; come and warm, quicken and govern all my members; come and communicate to me thy love, grace, and holiness. Ah! what a happiness will it be to me to be possessed of a heart, so holy and so perfect? I shall then be in no dread of failing in love for God and my neighbour, as having within me the source of all charity: I shall then no longer be under any apprehensions of falling into sin, as possessing the source of all justice: I shall then no longer be anxiously disturbed by a servile fear of hell, as having within me the

the source of all the happiness of heaven, which will give me a foretaste of its sweets in this life, as a pledge of enjoying them in their fullness, and for ever in the life to come. *Amen.*

This, as well as any of the Eight foregoing Elevations, may also serve for an Exercise of Devotion before the blessed Sacrament, though it be not exposed.

Eight SUBJECTS

OF

MEDITATION

BEFORE THE

BLESSED SACRAMENT,

Whether exposed or not.

In order to receive the Benefit from the ensuing Considerations and Affections, a Person should apply himself thereto with Zeal and Spirit, and endeavour to dive to the Bottom of their Subject Matter, and to imprint deeply on the heart the Affections that may be drawn from them. For this Purpose they may be repeated several times, but this should always be with
an

an additional degree of fervour. Each point may furnish out matter for a Meditation of any length : but those who find a difficulty in this, may add thereto some other point. And in order to help the memory, a person may have before him the Book, to pass from one Affection or Consideration to another.

I. CONSIDER Jesus Christ as God : say to him with the royal prophet : *Thou art my God.* His own people, the Jews, refused to accept him in that quality ; but to repair this injury, acknowledge him as such in the blessed Eucharist. Confess with Peter and Martha, (Jo. 11. 27.) that he is the Son of God ; adore his divinity with most profound reverence ; join thy adorations to those of the holy angels there present ; continue in a state of annihilation at the foot of his throne ; conceive the highest esteem possible for his majesty, power, wisdom, goodness, justice, mercy, sanctity and his other perfections which are all infinite ; profess unto him that there is no other God but himself together with the Father and the Holy Ghost, acknowledge him as the Creator of all things ; thank him for the being he has bestowed on thee ; beg his pardon for having polluted the work of his hands by thy sins ; beseech him to reform it, to make thee a new creature, to build himself a temple, to erect for himself a throne, and to create for himself a dwelling in thee, there to take up his abode.

II. Consi-

II. Consider Jesus Christ as High Priest (Hebr. 9. 11.) that offers up unto God his victim, no other than himself: Consider the excellencies of this High Priest; he is *holy, innocent, undefiled, separated from sinners*, (Ibid. 7. 26.) *and made higher than the heavens*, perfectly agreeable to God, and abounding with charity for thee. Sink deep into his heart by a lively faith, there to contemplate the zeal with which he offers to his Father for thy salvation his person, his labours his death and his blood. He is present in the blessed Eucharist to receive all thy requests and to present them to his Father. Thank him therefore for his solicitude for thee, and beg of him a continuance of it; beseech him to appease his Father's wrath against thee; to grant thee the succours thou standest in need of; making an offering of him to his Father, and offer thyself likewise with him, or rather beg of him that he would offer himself in thy behalf, and thee at the same time and all that belongs to thee with himself. Assure him that thou wilt henceforward lead the life of a victim, by dying to every thing that is not God, and that thou art resolved to avail thyself of his precious blood.

III. Consider Jesus Christ as Friend. *He himself is my friend.* (Cant. 5. 16.) Reflect on the merit of this friend, his power, importance, wealth, generosity, and the love he bears thee. He is present in the Eucharist to afford thee ease and comfort in thy afflictions. Thank him for his bounty to thee; acknowledge that thou hast made thyself unworthy of it by thy past infide-

infidelities; afk his pardon, place all thy confidence in him, lay thy heart open before him and expofe to him all thy wants, and beg of him to relieve them; make a folemn proteftation to him that thou wilt henceforward be faithful to him, and wilt love none but him, or for his fake; confecrate to him all the affections of thy heart, and pour forth the moft fervent acts of love thou canft poffibly form.

IV. Confider Jefus Chrift as Guide: *Thy God, he it is that is thy Guide.* (Deut. 31. 6.) Reflect on the excellence, the charity, the ability and fkilfulnefs of this guide. He fhews thee the ways of life, he accompanies thee therein, he makes the road fmooth, he carries thee in his arms, he feeds thee with his flefh and blood, and he protects thee againft all thy enemies. Confider the importance of all his benefits; thank him for his charity, afk his pardon for having fo often turned afide from his ways to walk in thofe of Satan, and make him a folemn promife to walk in them faithfully for the future; beg a continuation of his charity; keep clofe to him that thou mayft not go aftray and be loft. He is not only thy Guide to fhew the way, but the light alfo that directs thy fteps, the way in which thou walkeft, and the path thou tendeft to, which is life eternal.

V. Confider Jefus Chrift as Comforter; *I myfelf will comfort you.* (Ifai. 51. 12.) Reflect on the goodnefs and power of this divine comforter. His goodnefs gives him a lively fenfe of all thy miferies, and induces him to come down from heaven upon this altar to adminifter comfort to thee;

thee; not like men after a cold and ineffectual manner, but with such power and efficacy as to afford thee all the relief and assistance thou art in want of. His power owns no superior to it, and he needs say but a word to put an end to all thy miseries; conceive a lively sense of them, of thy spiritual distempers, of the wounds thy enemies have inflicted on thee, of thy poverty and of thy inability, and represent them altogether to thy divine comforter; ask his assistance, place all thy hope in him, with an humble confidence wait for his divine consolations, and renounce those of creatures: confess that they are all vain and unworthy of thee, protest that thou desirest none but his, and beg of him to shed in thy heart his joy, his peace and his love.

VI. Consider Jesus Christ as Captain and Commander: *Behold I have given him for a leader and commander to the people.* (Isai. 55. 4.) He is thy captain and commander in that dreadful war thou hast to wage against hell. Consider the number, the power, the rage of thy enemies, who breathe nothing less than thy destruction: consider thy natural inability to make head against them; the importance of the victory, and the need thou hast of the conduct and help of this divine captain: observe his wisdom, which defeats all the stratagems of thy enemies; his power, which frustrates all their efforts, and his charity which induces him to come from heaven to thy assistance. It is he that supplies his soldiers with armour for fighting, gives them victory in battle and a crown

after

after conquest. Beg of him to clothe thee with the armour of justice, and grant thee victory over thy vices, thy passions and thy other enemies; ask his pardon for having so often deserted his service and enlisted under the banners of his enemy against him; promise to fight faithfully and courageously for the future under his standard and in his cause,

VII. Consider Jesus Christ as Pattern: *Whom he* (God) *predestinated to be made conformable to the image of his Son.* (Rom. 8. 29.) He is in effect the pattern of all the Elect. Behold the excellency of this divine pattern whose perfections are above all conception: observe the virtues he practices on our altars; his charity, his obedience, his humility, his patience, his disinterestedness. Return him thanks for the excellent examples he sets thee: ask his pardon for having so ill followed them, and for having laboured only in disfiguring more and more in thee his divine image; promise him to copy them faithfully for the future; beg of him to impress himself as a divine seal upon thy heart (Cant. 8. 6.) and upon thy arm to communicate unto thee all his virtues, and to make thee practise them both by inward and outward acts; petition for those virtues in particular which thou hast most occasion for.

VIII. Consider Jesus Christ as Judge: *He hath given all judgment to the Son.* (John, 5. 22.) He hath established upon our altars the tribunal of his mercy. Go and cast thyself at his feet; confess unto him sincerely, and with a lively sorrow all thy sins, and ask him pardon for them;

testify

testify to him thy gratitude for not having already condemned and punished thee like so many others less guilty than thyself; thank his Father for having given thee thy best friend for thy judge; acknowledge his authority and willingly submit to all his decrees; beg him to be favourable to thee in the sentence which is to decide thy eternal lot; resolve to make it thy endeavour to acquire his benevolence by thy respects and services; join with him from this moment in condemning the world, by a life led in opposition to its maxims.

DEVOTIONS
TO
JESUS CHRIST,
WHEN THE
BLESSED SACRAMENT
Is carried in Procession.

LORD *when thou goest forth in the sight of thy people, the earth is in motion*; its inhabitants are overjoyed to see, not indeed the ancient ark of the covenant, which was no more than a chest of cedar-wood overlaid with gold, and where God resided only in figure; but the new ark which is thy sacred humanity, wherein are contained all the treasures of grace and glory, and in which, by means of the hypostatical union, the *fulness of the godhead dwelleth bodily* and in truth. We are overjoyed to see our king and our God, our redeemer and our Father in the midst of us; his presence strikes terror in our enemies, banishes all our anxieties, and makes us forget all our miseries.

It

It is chiefly on this occasion, O Jesus! that thou literally fulfilleſt the promiſe thou didſt make by one of thy prophets, that thou wouldſt, in time to come, walk in the midſt of thy people. The accidents indeed, or outward appearances of bread and wine conceal thee from our bodily eyes in this ſacrament; but no cover can conceal thee from the eyes of our faith, which penetrates every thing, diſcovers every thing, and diſcerns thee howſoever ſhrouded under the ſacred ſymbols, with greater certainty, than if thou hadſt manifeſted thyſelf to our bodily eyes. I own thee therefore really preſent in this myſtery, O divine Jeſus! I adore thee in it as my king and my God, with the ſame ſentiments of reſpect and veneration with which the ſaints and angels adore thee in heaven.

Come, ye people and nations, great and ſmall, young and old, rich and poor! come and adore your king and your God, and give glory to his name. Come and ſing unto him new canticles in admiration of the greatneſs and riches of his love; celebrate his power, proclaim the inventions of his wiſdom, and ſet forth all his other excellencies and perfections. *Let Iſrael rejoice in him that made him, and the children of Sion be joyful in their king.* Let them praiſe his holy name with concerts of muſick, and with the ſound of inſtruments; let them all appear to teſtify how happy they deem themſelves in having for their ſovereign, a Lord ſo powerful, and withal ſo gracious, and ſo tenderly affected towards his people; let them come and testify their sentiments of gratitude for all his favours.

We carry thee about, my Saviour, as in triumph on this solemn occasion, to declare our great joy in having thee for our king, and with what pleasure it is that we submit to thy amiable yoke: we boast of the honour of possessing thee, because thou art the glory, the crown, the life, the salvation, the delight, the wealth, and the happiness of thy people.

Thou dischargest this day in our favour, O Jesus, the office of a gracious monarch, who has nothing so much at heart as the welfare of his people: thou honourest this place with thy presence which has the happiness of belonging to thee. And now, thou art come to comfort us in our afflictions, to heal our wounds, to relieve our miseries, and to provide for all our wants; and thou goest here before us to conduct us to the fountains of life. Thou, O Jesus, art our only hope and resource; it is thou alone that canst deliver us from the evils that oppress us on all sides, and protect us against the powerful attacks of our enemies. Grant us therefore thy protection, we conjure thee, and favour us with all the good offices of a king who tenderly loves his people. We also, in quality of true subjects, resolve to acquit ourselves faithfully of all our duties; we make thee a tender of our homages and adorations, and promise thee obedience and fidelity. We consecrate to thee our bodies, our souls, our lives, our goods, and every thing in our power to be disposed of according to thy good pleasure;

sure, and we solemnly protest unto thee that we will be faithful to thy commands, and that nothing shall ever be able to separate us from thy service.

O amiable sovereign! what a glory and satisfaction it is for us to accompany thee with holy pomp on this solemn occasion, and with a kind of triumph which thy church celebrates to the honour of thy holy name!

We are all desirous, O my Saviour! of following thee whithersoever thou goest; we are all resolved to copy the great virtues thou givest us the example of in this mystery. *Draw us, I pray thee, that we may run to the odour of thy perfumes*; and do not suffer that the allurements of creatures, or the artifices of the devil may ever hinder us from following thee.

O glorious sovereign! whose glory and magnificence is every where conspicuous, make thy people this day sensible of the effects of thy liberality. Enrich them with thy gifts, heap upon them thy graces, that each of us may return home loaded with the effects of thy royal munificence. It is not the frail and perishable goods of this life that we sue for, but spiritual graces, the only true goods and which alone are worthy of thee. Inspire us with thy fear, fill us with thy love, impart to us thy light, arm us with thy fortitude, and heap on us thy graces and mercies. We venture also to put up our petitions for the relief of our corporal necessities; that disengaged from all temporal solicitude, we may serve thee with the greater assiduity and fervour.

Thou waſt heretofore, O. Jeſus! ignominiouſly dragged about the ſtreets of Jeruſalem, and followed by multitudes blaſpheming and abuſing thee; and thou haſt many times ſuffered in this divine ſacrament, from unbelievers and impious catholicks, a no leſs ignominious treatment than what thou didſt endure at thy paſſion. It is to make publick reparation for all theſe outrages, that the church has ordained thou ſhouldſt be carried with a holy pomp through our ſtreets, and that her children ſhould appear with lighted tapers in their hands in teſtimony of this atonement. It is alſo her intention by her hymns and canticles, to make atonement for the imprecations and blaſphemies which have been vented againſt thee; by her praiſes and adorations, to make thee ſatisfaction for the affronts and reproaches with which thou haſt been loaded; and by the concourſe of people gathered together on theſe occaſions, and who own thee for their king and their God, to condemn the injuſtice of the Jews in refuſing to receive thee as ſuch, and to make thee triumph over thoſe enemies of thine who ſtill refuſe thee this title. Triumph therefore this day, O adorable Saviour! over all the enemies of thy glory: over all that refuſe to own thee for their king and oppoſe the eſtabliſhment of thy empire, and over thoſe that refuſe to adore thee as their God, conſidering thee as a mere creature. May heaven and earth, angels and men join in adoring thy holy name, and may all the creatures of the

univerſe

universe acknowledge with one voice thy power and thy divinity.

My heart is so full of reverence for thee, O august sovereign! and I have so earnest a desire of contributing all in my power towards promoting the glory of thy triumph, that if the rules of decency agreed with my inclinations, I would not only spread my garments on the ground as the apostle did, where thou passed, but I would even prostrate myself before thee, that thou mightst as vanquisher and conqueror walk over a wretch who has been often audacious enough to rise up against thee by his crimes.

This procession, O my Saviour! in which we carry thee about with solemn pomp, represents to me that by which thou comest forth eternally out of the bosom of thy Father in the way of the knowledge, and returnest into the same bosom in the way of love whereby thou dost unite thyself to him. It also represents to me that which happened at thy incarnation, when thou camest down from heaven into this our lower world to redeem mankind, and after having redeemed them didst return to heaven on the day of thy glorious ascension. Lastly it reminds me of that which is to be at the end of the world, when attended by thy angels and saints, thou wilt once more descend from heaven, in order to judge the world, and after having judged it will reascend into heaven attended by all thy elect. It is our intention to do homage to the two first of these processions by that we are this day performing;

and

and we heartily entreat thee, O Lord! to grant us the grace of attending on thee, after thy judgment, in the third in company with thy faints and angels; that, admitted into heaven with them, we may there love, praife and glorify thee for ever. *Amen.*

During the Benediction.

LORD, fave thy people, and blefs thy inheritance, fhower down thy graces and thy bleffings on thy people; grant that we may be of that happy number whom thou haft bleffed, and to whom thou wilt hereafter fay: *Come ye bleffed of my Father.* May thy bleffing alfo protect and defend us from the curfe which thou wilt hereafter denounce againft the reprobate. *Amen.*

Devotions to Jefus Chrift during the time of accompanying the Bleffed Sacrament, when it is carried to the Sick.

IT is the voice of my beloved who knocketh. Yes, it is the voice of my beloved, who invites me to attend on him on this folemn occafion. He fays to me as to the Spoufe of the Canticle: *Arife, my beloved, make hafte and come.* (Cant. 2. 10.) He cries out to me as he formerly did to the chief of his apoftles;
'Come

'*Come and follow me*; leave thy houfe and bu-
'finefs for a few moments, to attend upon me
'to this fick perfon, who is in want of my af-
'fiftance which I am defirous to afford him'.
I will anfwer thee, O my Saviour! with one
of thy difciples, that *I will willingly follow thee
whitherfoever thou goeft.*

It is the character, O my Jefus! of thy true
difciples to follow thee at all times and never
forfake thee. The multitdes followed thee
only at certain times, either out of curiofity to
fee thy miracles, to be fed by thee or to receive other favours. But thy difciples conftantly followed thee as well in thy toils and labours,
as in thy refpits and confolations; they followed thee both by fea and by land, in tempefts
and in calms. It is in fuch a difpofition of
mind that I will now attend on thee to the fick
perfon thou art going to vifit.

The children, that is to fay, the friends of
the bride-groom (Matt. 9. 15.) accompany
him in all places without ever leaving him.
Thou art that bride-groom, O my Jefus! and
I have the happinefs of being one of thy children. I accordingly defire to bear thee company at all times, and never to forfake thee:
neither my bufinefs, nor my pleafures, nor my
conveniencies, nor the advantages I might expect elfewhere fhall ever prevail with me to feparate from thee. *How wonderful, O Lord!
is thy name over the whole earth! for thy glory is
raifed above the heavens,*, by the manifeftation
of thy goodnefs to the fons of men in the auguft facrament of our altars. Thou difdaineft

not

not to descend from thy throne to visit the most abject and despicable sick person, in his own house; to administer to him, by way of remedy, thy precious body and blood, and to protect him against the efforts of his enemies by becoming thyself a shield of defence to him, to seek after him in order to conduct him to heaven, and put him in possession of thy kingdom.

Let us go then, my soul, let us go to admire the wonderful love of this divine Saviour. Let us go and be spectators of the charity with which he bestows on this poor sick person, his precious flesh, and takes his sheep upon his shoulders to carry it to his flock.

I praise and bless thee, my Saviour, for all thy favours bestowed on this soul: I admire the love thou bearest her, I join in all the sentiments of compassion with which her misery affects thee; I thank thee for the divine love which induces thee to give thyself for saving her. Grant her, I beseech thee, a true spirit of repentance, that by an hearty detestation of her sins she may be thoroughly converted to thee: restore to her the robe of innocence should she have lost it by sin; clothe her with strength, fill her with faith, hope and charity and bestow on her all the necessary dispositions for receiving thee worthily. And to supply for whatever may be wanting to her in the way of preparation, I offer to thee all those holy dispositions with which thy saints have approached this mystery, together with thy own excellencies and perfections.

When

When the ſick Perſon communicates, ſay:

ENTER, O Lord, enter into this ſoul to cleanſe her, to ſanctify her, to heal her, to ſtrengthen her, to poſſeſs her, and to protect her againſt her enemies: ſhe is thy inheritance, the price of thy blood and thy conqueſt; ſecure to thyſelf the poſſeſſion of her, and ſuffer not thy enemies to rob thee of her.

After the ſick Perſon has communicated; ſay:

I Thank thee, O Saviour! for thy goodneſs in giving thyſelf to this ſoul; I bleſs thy holy name for it, and intreat all the creatures of heaven and earth to join with me in bleſſings and thankſgivings. I love thee, O Lord, bleſs thee and glorify thee in behalf of this ſick perſon, and I offer to thee in thankſgiving all the glory thou haſt received and will receive for ever from thy creatures.

Produce in this ſoul, O Jeſus, the intended good effects of thy viſit; pardon her ſins, reconcile her to thy Father, eſtabliſh thy abode and kingdom in her, confirm her in thy fear and love; give her ſtrength for bearing her illneſs with patience; preſerve her from the ſnares of the enemy, that ſhe may never more come under his power; raiſe her mind and heart to thee, that ſhe may ſanctify her ſufferings, think only

only of thee, love and defire nothing but thee: and in cafe her departing hour is at hand, grant her a death that is precious in thy fight. But if it be thy will to leave her fome time longer upon earth, reftore her, I pray, to her bodily health, that fhe may blefs thy holy name, and employ it entirely in thy fervice. I pray, O Lord, in thy infinite charity to reftore her to fpiritual and corporal health, and recommend her to thy divine compaffion. I conjure thee by all the love thou beareft her, and which induced thee to lay down thy life for her on the crofs, and by the love which thou requireft we fhould bear each other, to guide her always in thy ways, without ever forfaking her, till thou haft brought her to thy heavenly kingdom. To thy ardent charity, O holy Virgin! I earneftly recommend this foul, and to the protection of St. Jofeph thy fpoufe, of St. Michael, of her angel guardian, and of all the blefled fpirits and faints in heaven.

When the blefjed Sacrament is carried back, fay:

COME, my foul, let us attend on this ark into its tabernacle, and accompany the blefled Jefus to his temple. But while I attend on thee, O my Saviour, to this terreftrial temple, do thou conduct me to thy heavenly fanctuary: teach me the way to it, take me by the hand, be thou thyfelf my guide, make me worthy to dwell in it with thee, and to be one of thofe living

living stones (Pet. 2. 5.) of which it is to be built.

O my Saviour! who didst heretofore instruct thy disciples (Luke 18. 31. 32.) whilst thou wast journeying with them, and didst unfold to them the mysteries of the kingdom of heaven: who didst kindle a holy flame in the hearts (Luke 24. 27.) of those two disciples who were going to Emmaus, and didst open their eyes that they might discern thee; permit me to ask of thee the same favour, now that I have the happiness to accompany thee. Speak, Lord, instruct thy poor servant, teach him the maxims of thy gospel; make his heart to glow with the holy ardours of thy love, and enlighten his mind with the beams of thy light; grant that he may know thee and love thee, and that he may know and love nothing but thee, or for thee.

I here walk with thee, O Jesus! do thou at all times accompany me; leave me not alone, lest I fall, or lest the enemy seeing me defenceless, should assail me in order to reduce me to my former state of bondage.

O how sweet it is to be with thee! thou assuagest all pains, removest all dangers, givest strength and courage to follow thee, and those that do so thou fillest with joy and comfort.

So long as I have the happiness of being in thy company, I fear nothing: I will not fear darkness, because thou art the light; nor poverty, because thou art wealth; nor affliction, because thou art joy; nor infamy, because thou art glory; neither will I fear death, because thou

thou art life: there is but one thing which I fear, and that is left my frailty should separate me from thee. But prevent, Lord, I beseech thee, this fatal separation, and unite me to thee by such strong bands, that nothing may be able to break them asunder.

When the Blessed Sacrament is replaced on the Altar, and while the Benediction is giving, say:

THOUGH I have been abundantly rewarded, O my Saviour! for my attendance on thee, by the honour of being admitted to accompany thee; allow me farther to crave thy blessing. Give me then that blessing, O Lord! and let it be unto me a source of graces, and a safeguard against the temptations of the enemy, against the corruption of my nature, and against all the dangers of this life.

Thou art going, O my Jesus, to take up thy residence in the tabernacle: I offer to thee my heart for that purpose, come and take up thy abode in it for ever. My whole desire is to possess, and to be inseparably united to thee. Come then, I once more intreat thee, and fix thy abode in me; thou alone shalt be loved, honoured and served there.

A Formulary of Atonement, or Act of making reparation for any injurious treatment of the most Holy Sacrament of the Altar.

For THURSDAYS.

DIVINE Saviour, who, by an incomprehensible excess of the love which thou bearest to mankind, hast been pleased to bestow thyself upon us in the adorable Sacrament of the Altar; thou deservest, no doubt, as well by the infinite dignity of thy person, as by the signal benefit thou thereby impartest to mankind and the astonishing abasement thou hast reduced thyself to in their favour, that they should, in return, be very assiduous in honouring thee to the best of their power. But alas! by the blackest ingratitude, by the most flagrant injustice thou art repaid with nothing but contempt and outrage. One would imagine from their behaviour that thou hadst concealed thyself in this mystery to no other purpose than to be exposed to all their contradictions. I have too lively a sense, O my adorable redeemer! of the injuries and insults thou sustainest incessantly from them, and in which I bear so great a part myself, not to come to thee to testify my grief and to make thee atonement for them to the best of my power. I am come then, Lord, to the foot of thy throne, which is this altar on which thou art seated, I come in the condition of a criminal to make atonement to thee, for all the indignities which thou haſt ſuffered in this ſacrament ſince its original inſtitution at thy laſt ſupper to the preſent time. And in the firſt place, for all thoſe that I myſelf have been guilty of: for my little gratitude for ſo ineſtimable a benefit, for my want of zeal and fervour in diſcharging my duty to thee in this myſtery; for ſo many frivolous and idle thoughts which I have entertained in thy preſence; for ſo many vain, unprofitable and irregular deſires which I have given way to at that time; alſo for ſo many idle, unſeemly and ſuperfluous words which I have uttered; for ſo many levities and irreverences which I have committed; for ſo many bad actions I have been guilty of, and for ſo many ſcandals I have then given; for all the ſloth and negligence I have ſuffered to prevail over me in preparing myſelf for receiving; for all the ſacrileges I have committed by communicating in the ſtate of mortal ſin; for having ſo many times abuſed the grace of this ſacrament; in fine, for the many ways by which I have obſtructed its virtue and efficacious power. Ah! Lord, how great is my ingratitude, how grievous my malice, in having thus treated thee in a myſtery wherein thou art inceſſantly offering up thyſelf to thy Father out of pure love for me! What puniſhment have I not deſerved on all theſe accounts, if dealt with according to my demerits! Oh! how heartily do I bewail them, how ſenſibly is my ſoul afflicted for them when I call them to mind!

mind! Prostrate at thy feet, O Lord! I crave pardon, with a heart pierced with grief, and my face covered with confusion; grant it me, I beseech thee: I confess my injustice, I own my sin, I detest it and abhor it. Reputing myself on this occasion as a criminal devoted to make public satisfaction for his offences, I openly declare the indignity of my past conduct, and profess that nothing is more just and reasonable than that all creatures in heaven and earth should pay thee sovereign honour, and reverence. I do solemnly declare that thou art the light of the world, that thou lyest there concealed under the sacramental veils, yet that through the clouds which environ this thy mysterious abode, thy light breaks forth and enlightens all mankind. But do thou, O my Saviour! for thy mercy's sake which knows no bounds, consume my iniquities in the fire of thy love; out of thy remembrance all my past behaviour, which I am resolved to atone for by my zeal and fervour in paying thee on our altars my most dutiful homage.

But I don't mean to confine this my atonement to my personal guilt with respect to this august mystery, I also include in it all the like offences of other men. For since it is for the love of mankind, and that I might have the happiness of possessing thee that thou hast exposed thyself to so many outrages and affronts, it is but reasonable that I should deem it incumbent on me to make all the atonement in my power for them. I therefore extend this act of atonement to the making thee some reparation for whatever the malice of Jews, the fury of infidels, or the rage of hereticks, have attempted against thee in this adorable sacrament, by their obstinacy in refusing to believe the truth of this mystery, by their bitter taunts and scoffs at it; by their horrid blasphemies against thy holy name; by their most shocking treatment of thy sacred body in trampling it under foot, or causing their horses to trample upon it; in casting it into the mire, giving it to their dogs to eat, stabbing it with swords and poignards, throwing it into fire and water, and exposing it to the mercy of the winds. Also, by overturning thy altars, murdering thy priests, mixing their blood with thine, and expressing their irreverence many other ways.

I make thee all the reparation in my power for whatever the irreligious insolence, passion, malice and impiety of bad catholicks have made thee suffer in this mystery. Also, for the little esteem they have held it in; for their neglect in visiting and attending on thee; for their little respect for thee while in thy presence; for their indecent behaviour and for the crimes they have perpetrated at that time; for their disregard to thy holy table, and for their coldness and insensibility in approaching it; for the sacrileges they have been guilty of, by receiving thee in the state of mortal sin; for the horrid impieties they have incurred the guilt of by stealing the holy vessels, and casting thy sacred body into the streets and common sewers; for their execrable profanations thereof, by making

use

use of it for the purposes of enchantments and witchcraft. Most amiable Saviour! when I consider attentively what happens in so many parts of the earth in regard to this mystery, I cannot avoid being witness of the great contempt and the many insults, and outrages thou sustainest in it. Every day produces new sources of these by the fresh ignominies and affronts that are put upon thee; while few or none concern themselves about the matter, or think to come and apply to thee for pardon. Is it possible, O Jesus! that for the love of us thou shouldst expose thyself to such horrible usage during so many ages past? O ineffable goodness! O unparalleled love! How hard and insensible soever my heart may be, it is not so hard and callous as not to be sincerely affected by such an excess of goodness; not to entertain a deep sense of gratitude for the favour. My heart has also a very lively feeling of all that thou sufferest for the love of us upon our altars; it sympathizes with thee herein as much as possible, and is affected beyond what it is able to express. Ah! that I could, at the expence of my blood, prevent all these indignities and affronts! I would shed it with pleasure in that case to the last drop. Oh! that I could but at least, render thee as much honour in this mystery, as thou sustainest contempt in it, procure thee as much glory, as thou are treated with ignominy, and give thee as much praise as the impious vent blasphemies against thee? I adore thee, however, O divine master, in this mystery; I adore thee in it

with

with the most profound sentiments of reverence I possibly can: I confess that thou art my king, my God, and the sovereign Lord of all things, and that to thee alone belong dominion, power, honour, glory and adoration for evermore. I offer and consecrate myself to thee with all that belongs to me, as a perpetual holocaust of love. I join with thy angels and saints in heaven, and with thy just on earth to adore and glorify thee wherever thou resideft by means of this adorable mystery. I thank thee for all thou hast ever suffered in it for the love of me, and I will henceforth make use of it as a powerful motive to encourage myself to receive with submission and humility all the injuries which shall ever be done me, be they ever so outragious and undeserved.

But since it was the design of thy heavenly Father, in the institution of this adorable sacrament, that mankind should therein make thee atonement for all the injuries and affronts thou didst receive during the course of thy mortal life, and in particular in thy sacred passion; I am also come, O my Saviour! to make the best atonement in my power for all the contradictions, calumnies and blasphemies thou didst then suffer from thy enemies; for all their buffetings and spittings on thy sacred face, for the reed they put into thy hands as a mock-scepter, for the crown of thorns which they pressed into thy head, for the scourges by which they tore thy sacred body, for the ignominious death of the cross they put thee to, and for all the other insults and outrages they

heaped

heaped upon thee. It is therefore, with the view of repairing, to the beſt of my power, O divine redeemer! all thou haſt ſuffered, and all thou art yet pleaſed to ſuffer in this adorable ſacrament, that I come to offer unto thee all the honour, glory, and praiſe which all the creatures in heaven and earth render thee in time and eternity; and I could wiſh that it were in my power to make an infinite addition thereto in order to make thee a ſtill more ample reparation. I do moreover offer unto thee all that glory which thou poſſeſſeſt in thyſelf and in the boſom of thy Father; and I rejoice with thee that it is not in the power of thy enemies to tarniſh it, or diminiſh the leaſt part of it. May my chief care henceforward be to honour thee in this auguſt ſacrament, and to contribute all I can to promote thy being ſo honoured by others. Inſpire me, O Lord! with ſentiments worthy of thee, and fix deep in my heart the diſpoſitions I ought to be poſſeſſed of, to be able to give thee in it the honour that is due to thee. Grant the like grace to all the faithful, that we may all with one accord honour thee to the full extent of our abilities, Grant alſo that all the nations of the earth may know and adore thy holy name, and that the Bleſſed Sacrament of the Altar may be every where praiſed, honoured and glorified with a ſovereign deference and adoration for evermore. *Amen.*

An **ABSTRACT** *of the foregoing Form or Act of Atonement for such as have less leisure.*

DIVINE Saviour! who, by an incomprehensible effect of thy divine love for us, hast made thyself present in the Blessed Sacrament of the Altar; and who instead of the respects and adorations we ought to render thee therein, art most injuriously and contemptuously treated; I come to cast myself at thy feet, to make atonement to thee for all thou hast suffered, and dost daily suffer in this adorable mystery. And first, for all the irreverences, internal and external, which I myself have committed in thy presence, and for all the scandals and disedification I have given thereby; for the little fervour I have had in approaching the holy table and assisting at the holy sacrifice of the Mass; for my want of preparation and devotion on these occasions; for the little benefit I have reaped from it; for the sacrileges I have committed in receiving thee unworthily; and for all the other injuries I have done thee, or had any share in.

In the next place, I make thee this act of atonement for all the affronts, contempt and indignities, thou hast suffered in this august sacrament from the time of its original institution to this present day in all parts of the world, from unbelievers and wicked christians, who are ever perpetrating the most horrid acts of sacrilege and impiety against thee. In the third

third place, for all the injuries, calumnies, persecutions and insults thou didst suffer during thy mortal life, particularly in thy sacred passion. Prostrate at thy feet, I most humbly crave thy pardon for all this, owning thee to be worthy of all honour, glory and praise. I confess thee to be the king of heaven and earth, the God of the universe, and in this firm belief I pay thee my most humble homage and most respectful adorations. I consecrate myself to thee as a perpetual holocaust of love : I transport myself in spirit and desire to all parts of the world where thou resideth sacramentally; and I there render thee all the glory which thy angels and thy faithful there give thee, to which I join all that thou hast received from thy creatures during time, and wilt receive from them for all eternity. Oh that it may henceforward be the chief of my endeavours to honour thee upon our altars, and to omit nothing in my power that may contribute to the universal and eternal praise, adoration and glory of the most holy and most adorable Sacrament of the Altar! *Amen.*

An other Act of Reparation,

Which may be daily made by an unworthy communicant, in order to obtain pardon for his past sacrileges.

WHO *will give waters to my head, and a fountain of tears to my eyes, that I may weep and bewail, day and night,* the horrid sacrileges I have committed against my Saviour in the most Holy Sacrament of the Altar, by receiving him in a criminal state! Oh! how my heart is rent with grief, and my bowels torn with sorrow! Oh! may my mouth send *forth a wailing as the dragons, and mourning as the ostriches.* (Jer. 9. 1.) Let every place resound with my sighs and groans for the execrable injuries I have been guilty of against my God and my Creator. O wretch that I am! is it possible I should ever have carried my ingratitude and malice to such a pitch as to attack the King of angels seated on the throne of glory, to crucify afresh the author of life, to bury him in the poisonous sink of a heart loaded with crimes, to precipitate into an abode where satan presides, Him, who constitutes the happiness of the blessed in heaven! Ah! Judas that I am, and worse than Judas, who as far as lay in me put the blessed Jesus to death even in his state of immortality, and in the midst of a people who adore him as their God? Ah! wretch that I am! why did I not die in my
mother's

mother's womb? why did I not perish in the cradle, before I had it in my power to perpetrate so black a deed? But what was it that induced me to commit it? Why, a little confusion I might have been in by declaring my sins to a priest; a little violence I should have done myself by checking a loose inclination, or breaking off a bad habit. But that I should crucify anew my Saviour for such trifles! O ye heavens, do ye not shudder? are ye not seized with horror at the sight of so much malice? You creatures of the universe are ye not moved with indignation at the proceeding? I am myself so full of confusion that I dare not look up to heaven; I still consider myself as guilty of the death of my God; the image of my crime is ever before my eyes, and all creatures seem to be continually upbraiding me with it. But what shall I do in my unhappy situation? shall I despair? No, Lord, this would be doing thee a new injury. I come therefore, O great God! I come to cast myself at the feet of thy throne to cry aloud for mercy and to make atonement for my horrible impieties. I come to beg pardon for my sacrileges, in the condition of a criminal and penitent confessing his guilt, my head I should have covered with ashes, my face upon the ground, my heart pierced with grief, and my eyes bathed in tears: Grant it me I beseech thee, O Jesus I own myself indeed infinitely unworthy of it, and am convinced that my perfidiousness should move thee rather to arm all thy creatures to wreak their vengeance on my guilty head to my utter destruction.

But

But since thou didst pardon on the cross thy own executioners, and became even their advocate with thy Father, I dare hope from thy bounty that thou wilt not reject my request. I will employ, O Lord, the remainder of my days in deploring my crimes, and will endeavour as much as possible to repair them by my homages and adorations. From this moment therefore do I render thee on this altar, in desire at least, all the honour and glory a creature is capable of rendering: and I implore all the angels and Saints in heaven and all the faithful upon earth to join me in giving thee honour and glory, that I may expiate the sacrilege I have committed by receiving thee unworthily. I offer to thee, O divine Redeemer! all the glory that will accrue to thee both in time and eternity, in satisfaction for my crimes; and it is my fervent wish that thou mayst be eternally praised, adored and glorified in a manner proportionate to thy infinite excellence in the Holy Sacrament of the Altar. *Amen.*

A MORNING OBLATION,

Of the Actions of the Day.

MY Lord and my God, most holy and adorable Trinity, Father and Son, and Holy Ghost, the beginning, end, and centre of all things and my sovereign happiness! I believe in thee, I hope in thee, I love thee with all the
affec-

affections of my heart. I adore thee, I praise thee, I thank thee for all the blessings I have ever received from thy liberal hand, particularly for having been pleased to preserve me in the night past. I offer and consecrate unto thee my whole being; my body, my soul, my life, my thoughts, my desires, my actions, my words, my sufferings of this day, all the good that may befall me in it; and I offer them all conjointly with the merits of my divine redeemer Jesus Christ, and those of thy saints and angels, as also whatever will be this day performed worthy of thy acceptance, whether in heaven or upon earth. I offer to thee moreover all the glory, excellence, power, and felicity which thou possessest within thy own being, for which I rejoice with thee. I purpose to render thee every moment of this day and of my whole life, to the utmost of my abilities, all the glory which thou derivest from thyself and from all thy works both in time and eternity. All this I offer unto thee with Jesus Christ my Saviour, and with the whole church both militant and triumphant, in honour of the blessed Trinity, and by way of homage to the infinite majesty of God, to acknowledge his supreme dominion; also, in thanksgiving for all his benefits, whether of nature or of grace; in satisfaction for all my sins, and for obtaining from his goodness all the succours I stand in need of towards fulfilling the obligations of my state of life, towards corresponding with the designs of providence over me, and attaining eternal salvation. I offer it unto thee for the glory

glory of my divine redeemer Jesus Christ, and to thank thee for all the prerogatives, excellencies, and graces with which thou hast endowed his sacred humanity; in honour of the blessed Virgin and her chaste spouse Saint Joseph; of all the choirs of angels, that angel in particular whom thou hast appointed for my guardian, and of the tutelar angels of this kingdom, place and church: in honour of all the saints in heaven, that saint in particular whom thou gavest me for patron at my baptism; of my holy Patriarch, of my yearly and monthly patron; of the saints who entered heaven on this day, or whose memory is this day honoured by the church: Of those whose relicks are reposited in this city or church; and of those lastly, for whom I have a particular devotion, and whom I am accustomed to invoke. I offer it unto thee particularly in honour of such a choir of angels or such an order *(a)* of saints.

I return thee endless thanks for all the favours, blessings, and gifts both of nature and grace, thou hast ever bestowed on them, and I beg of them to intercede with thee in my be-

(A) The Angels and Saints may be classed according to the different days of the week: Thus a commemoration of this kind in regard to all the choirs of Angels may if agreeable, take place on Sunday: On Monday that of the holy patriarchs: On Tuesday that of St. John Baptist, and of all the holy prophets: On Wednesday that of St. Joseph, and of all the holy confessors: On Thursday that of ... Peter and Paul, and all the holy apostles and disciples of Christ: On Friday that of all the holy virgins, widows, and other persons eminent for the purity and sanctity of their lives. At the end of the oblation a short litany may be made for invoking in particular the Saints for whom a person may have most devotion.

half.

half. I offer it for the preservation and increase of the Catholick church, particularly in this kingdom and in this place; that it may please thee to send labourers animated with thy spirit into thy vineyard, to bless their labours, and to dispose mankind to profit by their instructions. I offer it for the perseverance of the just, for their progress in the ways of justice and their faithful concurrence with thy grace; particularly for N. N. with whom I am joined in an association of good works. I offer it thee for the conversion of sinners, infidels and bad christians; for my parents, friends, benefactors, enemies and persecutors, and for all those it is thy will I should pray: for the publick necessities, for all in affliction, for such as are in want, for all that are near their end and in their last conflict; I offer it for the souls in purgatory, the souls especially of my parents, friends and benefactors, those to whom I have been an occasion of sin, those also who are forgotten by men and are destitute of relief.

Vouchsafe I beseech thee, O my God! to shelter me this day under the shadow of thy wings, that I may be protected from all evil both of soul and body, and above all from sin. Give me thy holy spirit to be my guide in all my ways; and to direct according to thy law all my thoughts, words and actions. I, on my side, do renounce and disclaim every thing disagreeable to thee which may slip from me by inadvertence, surprise, frailty or otherwise.

I renew

I renew my baptismal vows and promises (*a*): I renounce the devil and all his works, the world with all its pomps and vanities, the flesh and all its concupiscences; and I thank thee most humbly for having called me to thy faith. I purpose to perform all my actions this day wholly to thy glory, to avail myself of all opportunities of doing good, to adhere at all times to that which is most perfect, to be particularly assiduous in the practice of such a virtue which I am endeavouring to acquire, and to reform such a fault which I am striving to master; but all this must be with the assistance of thy grace which I humbly crave through our Lord Jesus Christ. *Amen.*

An Abstract of the foregoing Oblation.

MY Lord and my God! I adore, praise, and thank thee for all thy benefits, particularly for having preserved me the night past from all evil. I consecrate myself intirely to thee, and make an offering to thee of my actions, thoughts and words during this day in union, with the merits of Jesus Christ my Saviour, and those of all the saints and angels. I offer to thee all these merits and whatever will be done this day to the glory of thy holy name in heaven and on earth. All this I offer as a

---

(A) I also renew the vows of my religious profession, and renounce all riches, pleasures, and all the glory of this world, to devote myself entirely to thee. I also thank thee a thousand times for the grace of calling me to a religious state of life.

homage

homage juſtly due to thy infinite excellence, in thankſgiving for all thy benefits, in ſatisfaction for all my ſins, and to obtain of thee all the ſuccours I am in need of to pleaſe thee and to work out my ſalvation. I offer it to the glory of Jeſus Chriſt, in honour of the bleſſed Virgin, and of all the angels and ſaints. I offer it unto thee for the whole catholick church, for the ſouls in purgatory, and for all publick and private neceſſities. I put myſelf, O Lord, under thy divine protection, and under that of thy ſaints and angels whom I beg to intercede with thee in my behalf. Preſerve me, I beſeech thee, this day from all evil both of ſoul and body, and eſpecially from every thing that diſpleaſes thee. Grant me grace to diſcharge as I ought the duties of my calling, and to accompliſh in all things thy moſt holy will. I now from this moment renounce all that may be diſpleaſing to thee, and I renew my good reſolutions of loving and ſerving thee in the moſt perfect manner I am able. *Amen*.

An Act of Adoration of the Bleſſed Sacrament for the Morning.

ADORABLE victim! who doſt offer thyſelf daily on our altars to the majeſty of God thy Father for the love of mankind; and who after having ſuffered infinite pains and toils for the ſpace of thirty-three years, and at laſt the moſt cruel and ignominious death of the croſs, haſt condescended to shroud thyself under these sacramental veils with the intent of offering thyself up to thy Father as a victim, in order to apply to us the merits of thy sacred passion, to reconcile us to him, to obtain grace for us, and to comfort us in our miseries; I here come to pay thee homage and adoration. I adore thee therefore with the most profound sentiments of reverence, and with the most religious awe and veneration I am capable of. I join my adorations to those of the angels and faithful here present, and of the church militant and triumphant: I transport myself in spirit and desire, into all parts of the earth, which thou honourest with thy sacramental presence; there to revere and adore thee with the like religious sentiments. I return thee my most humble thanks for all thou hast done and suffered for my salvation during thy mortal life, particularly for thy institution of this divine sacrifice and admirable sacrament, and for thy bounty in having so often given thyself to me therein to be the food and nourishment of my soul. I make an offering to thy Father, by and with thee and in union with the whole church, of all the Masses which will this day be celebrated over the whole earth. I offer, moreover, by thy hands to thy heavenly Father thy whole church, with each of her children and myself in particular, that we may all be sanctified by our union with the victim which thou offerest. I offer, in fine, every soul in purgatory, to be cleansed from her stains, and delivered from her punishment by virtue of the blood thou hast

of the Blessed Sacrament.

hast shed for her salvation. O my Jesus! I do here profoundly abase myself at thy feet; and howsoever annihilated thou appearest in this sacrament, I do acknowledge thee for the God of heaven and earth, for the sovereign monarch of the world, before whom every knee in heaven, on earth and in hell must bow. All power, O Jesus! having been given thee by thy Father, exert it, I beseech thee, in enlarging the pale of thy church, in destroying the power of the devil; in strengthening me this day against his attacks, and in forming for thyself hearts which adore and seek God in spirit and in truth, and which are according to his own heart. I am come hither to thee, O Jesus! at the beginning of the day, as to the beginning and overflowing source of all graces, to obtain all such as I stand in need of for spending it in a holy manner: pour them forth, I beseech thee, into my heart, impart to it all the virtues whereof thou art the shining pattern on our altars, and fill me with thy spirit, that I may take no step this day but by his direction: my own spirit I leave at the foot of thy altar, whenever I depart from hence, that it may there attend on thee, and pay thee incessant adoration. But before I leave thee, O my Saviour! give me, I pray thee, thy holy blessing, that it may serve me as a shield and bulwark of defence against any thing fatal or disastrous that might happen to me. *Amen.*

Adoration at Noon.

I AM come, O my king and my God! to renew my homage and adorations: it is by thee that I began the day, and it is by thee also I desire to continue it. Thou art the centre, as well as beginning of all things; all perfections centre in thee. It is in thy adorable person, as in this centre, that I seek for repose and comfort, being desirous of no other than what is found in thee. I come likewise for a fresh supply of strength and vigour in order to finish the day, and to repair the faults I have committed in the former part of it. Grant me, Lord, all the succours that are necessary to me for these purposes, and come into my heart to be thyself my strength and my support. *Amen.*

Adoration at Night.

I AM come to finish the day by rendering thee my most humble adorations, O my king! and my God! who art the beginning and end of all things. I thank thee for all the graces thou hast vouchsafed me this day. I beg pardon for all the sins I have committed in it, which I pray thee to blot out by the merits of thy precious blood: it is to thee that I ascribe all the glory of any good work which I may have performed this day through thy grace,

and

and I place it in thy hands to be presented by thee to thy Father. Preserve me, O Lord, this night from all evil both of soul and body, and take possession of my heart and all my powers to defend me against my enemies. I leave my spirit and my heart at the foot of thy altars, as well by night as by day, ever to adore thee with thy holy angels. Grant me, I beseech thee, thy blessing that it may serve as a shield to me against all the darts of the enemy.

Those who perform their adoration to Jesus Christ in the Blessed Sacrament five or seven times in the day, may at each time consider him under one or other of the qualities of King, Redeemer, Shepherd, Father, Friend, Physician and Spouse ; or may pay homage to the perfections by which he appears most distinguished in this mystery; as, his Goodness, Power, Wisdom, Holiness, Greatness, Truth, Munificence ; or in fine, may honour the virtues he there sets us the example of, as, the love of God, charity towards our neighbour, humility, obedience, mortification, poverty, patience, prayer, and resignation into the hands of his Eternal Father.

Eleva-

Elevations to Jesus Christ in the Blessed Sacrament, to implore his assistance on different occasions.

To beg his Counsel or Direction.

ANGEL of *the great counsel*, and most charitable Counsellor of all that apply to thee, I come to ask thee for light and direction in the affair that is proposed to me. Let me therefore, I beseech thee, know what ought to be done in it, and what is most agreeable to thy will. Manifest to me, by means best known to thee, what it is that thou requirest of me; teach me in what manner I am to conduct myself in it, and the means I am to make use of that every particular may succeed to thy glory and the welfare of my soul. I offer to thee a heart prepared to follow thy divine direction, and to execute thy orders, because it is in thee that I place all my hopes, and desire nothing more in it than the accomplishment of thy will. Let therefore thy divine light shine on me, and do not abandon me to my own darkness. *Amen.*

To implore his affiftance at the Beginning of an Undertaking.

I COME to thee, O Jefus! before I fet about this undertaking, to confecrate it through thy hands to the glory of thy Father, and to implore thy fuccour, that it may be executed in a manner agreeable to him. Thou knoweft that without thee I can do nothing: give me then all neceffary affiftance whereby I may accomplifh therein the will of thy heavenly Father, obferve faithfully all the laws of juftice, and keep myfelf free from all fin in the execution of it: or rather take the charge of the whole upon thyfelf; conduct all by thy wifdom, execute all by thy power, and bring every thing to a happy iffue to the glory of thy Father, and, for thy infinite goodnefs fake, to the eternal falvation of my foul. *Amen.*

On a profperous Event.

ETERNAL fpring, whence all good things flow, I am come to return thee thanks for the fuccefs my affairs have been attended with. Whatever pleafure natural inclination may find in it, I neverthelefs rejoice in it only for the glory that redounds from it to thee, becaufe thy goodnefs in regard to me is there difplayed, and thy holy will accomplifhed. Clofe up my heart, O Jesus! against all earthly consolations, and grant that it may take pleasure in thee alone: suffer not the temporal blessings thou bestowest on me to link me to creatures, or be to me an occasion of sin; neither let them be the reward of the little good I do, but make me worthy of receiving the rewards of heaven. *Amen.*

On a disastrous Issue.

A PERSON in affliction naturally has recourse to a faithful friend for comfort. I am that afflicted person, O Jesus! and come to seek from thee consolation, because thou art the comforter of the afflicted and relief of the distressed. Thou seest how dejected my heart is from what has befallen me: give me strength, I pray thee that I may be able to bear my affliction with fortitude, and to receive it in thy spirit. I adore the divine justice which has overtaken me; I receive with submission and respect all its chastisements; I return thanks for them as for so many signal favours and testimonies of God's love; I accept them in the spirit of homage with the view of honouring thy labours and sufferings. I offer them through thy hand, and in union with thy sufferings, to my heavenly Father, in satisfaction for my sins. I sincerely acknowledge that I have deserved much greater; I praise his goodness for having treated me with so much lenity, and readily

submit

submit to whatever other chastisements he may be pleased to inflict on me hereafter. I only beg of him strength to bear them in the manner I ought, and the undeserved favour of not being punished to eternity. *Amen.*

Under Temptations.

LORD, thy enemies and mine have risen up against me, they seek my soul to destroy it, and use their utmost efforts to drag it into the bottomless pit; I am come to cast myself at thy feet to implore thy succour.

Ah! suffer not that person whom thou hast redeemed at the price of thy blood to become their prey; be thou my protector and my refuge, receive me into thy hands to shield me from their rage; confound their devices, destroy their power, disappoint their malice. Thy glory, O my Saviour! is concerned in not suffering those that belong to thee, to fall into the hands of thy enemies: support me therefore, I beseech thee, in the severe conflicts I have to sustain against them, and make me victorious over all their efforts. *Amen.*

On finding ones self lukewarm and dry in Devotion.

MY soul droops and is fallen into a state of langour and faintness, O my Jesus! it feels nothing but disgust and aversion to what is good. My understanding is without light, my will without fervour, my limbs without strength, I am come to thee for remedy. Yes, I am come to beg a drop of that sweetness which renders virtue agreeable, or at least which enables us to bear up with courage against its difficulties. I am come to light up, by the sacred fire of thy heart, the fire which is almost extinct in mine; to borrow light from thy spirit for chasing away my darkness, and to obtain strength from thee for the support of my weakness. Ah! succour me, I beseech thee, O my Saviour! enlighten me, strengthen me, change my lukewarmness into fervour, that I may not slacken but continually advance with alacrity in thy service. *Amen.*

When one has fallen into some Fault.

I HAVE defiled myself, O my Saviour! by the fault I have lately committed, I have wounded myself by my fall; I come to thee that thou mayst wash away my filth and heal my wounds. Cast me, I pray thee, into the bath

bath of thy moſt precious blood, that I may be waſhed and cleanſed; and apply the ſame as a ſovereign balm to my wounds to heal them. Grant, I beſeech thee, that by virtue of this blood my ſins may be blotted out and my ſtrength reſtored. I am heartily ſorry for my paſt infidelities; I aſk a thouſand pardons for them; blot them out of thy remembrance, I pray thee, O Jeſus! and reinſtate me in joy, peace and the ſtrength of thy Holy Spirit, that I may begin again to ſerve thee with freſh ardour. *Amen.*

In the Day Time.

IN whatever ſituation I am, in whatever buſineſs I may be engaged, and at whatever diſtance I may be from thy altars, O my Jeſus! my heart ſhall be ever with thee, by the help of thy grace: it ſhall be always intent upon conſidering the wonders of thy power, the inventions of thy wiſdom, the riches of thy love in this divine myſtery of our altars: it ſhall there inceſſantly adore, praiſe and glorify thy holy name; it ſhall always ſigh and pant after thee, as the thirſty ſtag pants (Pſ. 41. 1.) after the water brooks, and its moſt earneſt deſires ſhall be to take its fill of that *fountain of living water*, no other than thyſelf, *that ſpringeth up unto eternal life.* Amen.

On waking in the Night Time.

I WILL lift up my hands and my heart by night towards thy sanctuary, O Jesus! to pay thee my adorations, and to bless and thank thee for thy goodness in watching over me while I rest, that thou mayst repel the attacks of my enemies, and obtain favours of thy Father in my behalf. With the spouse in the Canticle, (Cant. 3. 1.) by night I will seek thee in my bed, and I will beg the grace of possessing thee in the midst of my heart. This heart is wholly thine, O Jesus! it loves thee, it adores thee and blesses thee for ever. *Amen.*

A Preparation for Death.

HOW I dread thee, O death! how I am terrified when I take a view of thee in the midst of the gloomy region in which thou dwellest! How I dread those horrid and hellish monsters, who when my soul is about leaving the body will found the signal thereof, for assembling in a frightful multitude to come and seize on her, and drag her before the tribunal of the sovereign judge to accuse her in his presence! How I dread appearing before this terrible judge, whom even his angels cannot behold without trembling! How, in fine, am I filled with horror and dread at seeing myself so destitute of good works, and so loaded with sin and iniquity! Our first parent durst not present himself before the angel that represented the Lord, on account of his being naked: how then shall I make my appearance before the God of majesty, so naked and bare of good works as I am; I ought to say, so loaded with crimes and *covered with iniquity*. O my divine redeemer! who hast instituted the adorable Sacrament of the Eucharist, not only to shew forth thy death (1. Cor. 11. 26.) until thy last coming, but to provide us also with all necessary succours whereby to prepare ourselves for our own; I am here come to cast myself at the foot of thy altar, to beg of thee those graces and helps I stand in need of for making a christian and a holy end. Thou art here, my Jesus, our paschal victim by the virtue of which we happily quit the Egypt of this world, are rescued out of the hands of our bitter enemies who are eagerly bent on our destruction, and find a safe passage through a sea of difficulties and obstructions into the land thou hast promised us for our inheritance. This it is that induces me to come humbly to implore thy assistance in the dangerous passage out of this life into the next, and earnestly to beseech thee to favour me with all those good dispositions, both remote and immediate, which are needful for a happy death.

In order thereto, grant I beseech thee, O my Saviour! that treading faithfully in thy steps, I may lead, a life as much sequestered from creatures as my circumstances will allow:

a hidden

a hidden life, abforpt in God ; a life fuited to the condition of a victim, entirely fpent in a conftant adoration of thy Father's excellencies; in a profound annihilation of myfelf ; in an uninterrupted penitential ftate and humiliation on account of my fins ; in continual fighs and groans by reafon of my wretchednefs ; in continual prayers and fupplications to thee for a fupply of my wants; in an inviolable obedience to the will of my Creator with regard to my duties ; in a privation of earthly comforts, ever dying to the world, to fin and to concupifcence, ever living to God, and to things heavenly and eternal ; ever abforpt in the contemplation of the perfections of God, and ever confuming in the holy ardours of charity. May my condition in this world be therefore like thine in this facrament, the fame in fome meafure as if I was not in it; having eyes, as if I did not fee what paffed in it ; having ears, without giving attention to what is faid in it ; a tongue, without fpeaking of that which paffes in it; hands unemployed about any thing that is done in it; feet without running after any thing that is fought for in it; finally, a heart without any inordinate attachments to any thing that is loved or admired in it.

To furnifh me with the immediate difpofitions for a good death, grant me, O divine redeemer ! thofe fuccours for the obtaining whereof thou haft inftituted this auguft facrament. Vouchfafe to give thyfelf to me as a Viaticum before I leave this world, in order to
prepare

prepare and strengthen my soul for her great and important journey from time to eternity; to be my guide in it to conduct her, my light to enlighten her, my strength to support her, my protector to defend her, my advocate to plead her cause before thy Father and to obtain favour for her. Leave her not forlorn and destitute of succour at the dreadful hour when she will find herself forsaken by all creatures. Wash her clean from her sins in the bath of thy blood; clothe her with thy justice, adorn her with thy virtues, enrich her with thy merits, and grant her the grace of a perfect reconciliation with thee and admission unto thy heavenly kingdom. Protect my soul under the shadow of thy wings when she shall go forth from her body; hide her within thy sacred wounds, as thou dost those who have placed their hope in thee; cherish her as one of thy sheep in thy bosom, that it may not be in the power of any one to rob thee of her; and bear her as one of thy children in thy hands.

But to contribute something on my side to these dispositions with the help of thy grace, I approach, O Jesus! this mystery of faith, confessing that I most stedfastly believe all that thou commandeft me to believe with regard to this sacrifice of *thanksgiving*, and to return thee my most humble thanks for all the blessings of nature and grace which thou hast bestowed on me during the whole course of my life: I approach this sacrifice of *propitiation* with the view of acknowledging before thee all my iniquities, with a lively sorrow for them for the love of thee,

thee, and of humbly intreating thy pardon. I approach this *peace-offering*, to the merits of which thy Father can refuse nothing, declaring that it is in it all-powerful efficacy that I place my whole confidence: I come to this divine *holocaust* to pay unto the Lord all the homage, adoration and worship both of heaven and earth, of time and eternity, which is therein concentered: I come to this myftery of love, to offer to God, in union with the love of my Jefus, that of his holy angels, faints and juft perfons upon earth; all the love of my own heart, and to confecrate unto him my whole being and all that I poffefs in the world: Laftly, I come to this bitter chalice wherein my Saviour chofe to die myftically by anticipation on the eve of his paffion, with the view of preparing myfelf for death: To this fountain of life (wherein life eternal is beftowed on the worthy receiver) in queft of the principle and fcource of my eternal happinefs.

Perhaps, O my Saviour! the prefent day may be the laft of my life; if fo, may thy will be done. With an intire fubmiffion I accept of death, as to the day, the hour, and the manner thy providence has ordained. I here come to make a previous facrifice of it to thy Father in union with thine: I come to declare to him, that the world I have formerly been fo fond of, is of no farther concernment to me; that I leave it with pleafure for the fake of going to my God; that my defires and inclinations are weaned from this earth, and that henceforward my only ardour and folicitude

shall

shall be to go to behold him and enjoy him for ever.

It is thou, O Jesus! who haft the keys of death, and allotteſt to mankind that kind of death which thou pleafeſt; grant me I befeech thee, a death that is holy and precious in thy fight, that it may bring to a happy conclufion the bufinefs of my falvation. Thou eternal *high-prieſt of good things to come,* who makeſt an offering to thy eternal Father of our death with thine; wafh and purify, I befeech thee, the victim before it is offered; cleanfe my foul from all the fins wherewith fhe has pollutted herfelf during her life before thou takeſt her out of this world. She deteſts them all with infinite abhorrence, is grieved for them, is confounded and humbled in the fight of God on their account; fhe offers to thy Father, for the expiation of them, all the grief and anguifh thou felt, all the tears thou fheddedſt, all thy fighs and groans during thy mortal life, and all the blood thou fpilt at thy death, and doſt ſtill myſtically fpill upon our altars. Give ear, O Eternal Father! give ear I befeech thee, to the voice of that blood that cries aloud for mercy in my favour; fee how the whole earth is befprinkled, covered and overflowed in fome meafure, by the myſtical effufion of it on our altars; and by its merits forgive me my offences. But do thou, O my foul! give ear alfo to the voice of this divine Saviour, who calls out to thee by the mouth of holy Job: *O earth! cover not thou my blood, nor let my cry find a hiding place in thee* (Job. 16. 19.) as if he had said:

said: Thou, who by the nature of thy being art no better than earth, cover not the blood of thy adorable redeemer by thy irregular affections for earthly things; hinder not his voice from rising to the throne of his Father in thy favour, by the hardness of thy heart and thy obstinacy in sin.

It is this precious blood, O my God! I once more repeat it, that is the only foundation of my hope, and the ground-work of all my merit. It is not in virtue of my own justice or good works that I hope for the pardon of my sins and admission into heaven, but by virtue of the blood of my Saviour; it is by sprinkling the blood of this innocent Lamb upon the threshold of my door, (Ex. 12. 22.) that I hope to escape the sword of the destroying angel. It is by binding a line of scarlet thread in the window, as Raab (Jos. 2. 28.) did, that is, by cleaving to Jesus Christ crucified with the most tender affections of my heart, and placing my whole confidence in the merits of his sacred passion, that I hope to escape being involved in the (Ibid. 6. 21.) sacking of Jericho, or the destruction of the wicked at the last day, and to have the happiness of being associated with the pleople of God, and of entering with them into the land which has been promised them for an everlasting inheritance and possession. *Amen.*

Manner of adoring the blessed Sacrament.

I. WE are to entertain a firm and lively faith in the truth of this mystery, that is, of the true and real presence of Jesus Christ in this sacrament; and at the same time the highest esteem of its excellence; that the bare calling it to mind may fill us with veneration, and that we may conceive a holy awe and be seized with a religious dread and terror, whenever we appear in its presence.

II. To burn continually with a heavenly flame for the divine object contained in this sacrament; and to be animated with an affectionate and grateful sense of his goodness which he exhibits to us therein.

III. To place our whole confidence in Jesus Christ concealed under the veils of this mystery; to have recourse to him in all our wants, as the best friend in prosperity, to entertain ourselves with him on the subject of our joy, and to return him thanks for our success; in adversity, to pour forth our tears before him, and to implore his assistance; in our doubts, to beg light and advice, and in our undertakings, support and protection.

IV. To place all our comfort and happiness in conversing with Jesus Christ in the blessed Sacrament, and to be as assiduous as possible in this holy exercise. When we retire, to leave always our heart and mind at the foot of his altars to attend on him; to entreat the angels to adore and praise him during our absence, and to beg his blessing at our departure.

V. To make Jesus Christ in this mystery the subject of our recollected thoughts in the day time. To have always our thoughts and desires fixed in a great measure on this divine sacrament. To admire incessantly the love he there evinces for us; to praise and thank him for the graces and favours he there bestows on us; to adore the humiliations to which he there subjects himself for our sakes; to enter in spirit into his divine heart to join in all its operations; to adore him in the night when we awake, and implore his succour amidst the several occurrences of the day.

VI. To go and pay our adorations to him regularly three times a day, morning, noon and night. Those who are more at leisure may go oftener, as was the practice of some saints. Those who are not and cannot conveniently attend, may adore him in spirit at home as often as their devotion prompts them to it. One may sometimes prostrate one's self on the ground with a profound reverence to pay him adoration.

VII. To hear Mass every day with devotion, and never to fail while we assist at it of doing these three things: 1. To offer this adorable sacrifice to the Eternal Father with Jesus Christ and his church, and with the same intentions they offer it. 2. To offer ourselves in unity of victim with them. 3. To make a spiritual Communion by an ardent desire of receiving Jesus Christ into our hearts.

VIII. To

VIII. To communicate often with fervour and devotion, and to take all possible care to prepare ourselves worthily for Communion in order to be benefited thereby.

IX. When the Blessed Sacrament is any where exposed, to go thither to perform our adorations to Jesus Christ; and to assist with reverence at processions and at the Benediction of the Blessed Sacrament.

X. To accompany devoutly the Blessed Sacrament when it is carried to the sick.

XI. Not to fail on Thursdays, or even oftener to perform the act of Atonement before the Blessed Sacrament.

XII. To do something for the service of the altar; which may tend to the honour of this adorable Sacrament.

XIII. To make some present to Jesus Christ on our altars, as sacred ornaments, flowers, &c. according to our abilities.

XIV. To procure Masses to be said in honour of the Blessed Sacrament, as on the first Thursday of every month, or oftener.

XV. To honour priests in consideration of the sacred body of Jesus Christ, which they consecrate and distribute to the faithful.

XVI. To devote our bodies, our souls and our whole lives, all that we are and all that we possess to the Holy Sacrament. To renew this consecration daily. To offer up our actions and recite some prayers every day by way of homage to Jesus Christ in this mystery, and as an acknowledgement and thanksgiving for his being

being ever employed in the bufinefs of our falvation.

XVII. To imitate the admirable examples he there fets us of charity, humility, obedience, mortification, patience, retreat, filence, prayer, and other virtues.

XVIII. To render on certain days a particular homage to certain virtues which Jefus Chrift eminently difplays in this myftery; as on Sunday, to the Love he bears in it to his Father: on Monday, to his Charity towards men: on Tuefday, to his Obedience: on Wednefday, to his Humility: on Thurfday, to his Poverty: on Friday, to his Patience: on Saturday, to his Refignation to the will of his Father. We may honour thefe virtues, by adoring, admiring and praifing them, by offering them to the Eternal Father, by thanking Jefus Chrift for practifing them out of love for us, and by doing the like with the view of paying them all due homage and veneration.

THE LITANY OF THE BLESSED SACRAMENT.

LORD have mercy on us.
Chrift have mercy on us.
Lord have mercy on us.
 O God the Father, creator of the world, have mercy on us.
 O God the Son, redeemer of mankind, have mercy on us.
 O God the Holy Ghoft, have mercy on us.
O holy

O Holy Trinity, three persons in one God, have mercy on us.

Jesus, God and man, in two natures one divine person, have mercy on us.

Jesus, our wonderful God, who for us vouchsafest to subject thy almighty self to the power of man, and immediately descend upon our altars, when the priest pronounces the words of consecration, have mercy on us.

Jesus, our incomprehensible God, whose immensity the heaven of heavens cannot contain, and yet vouchsafest personally to reside in our churches and dwell among us in a little tabernacle, have mercy on us.

Jesus, our sovereign king, on whose throne above, all the glorified spirits continually wait, and yet vouchsafest here in our solemn processions to be accompanied by such mean attendants as we, have mercy on us.

Jesus, our heavenly physician, who dwellest in the place of immortal bliss, and yet disdainest not to come in person to our houses of clay, visiting us in our beds of sickness, and giving us thyself to comfort our sorrows, have, &c.

Jesus, our glorious God, who sittest at the right hand of thy eternal Father, adored by innumerable angels, and encompast with the splendors of inaccessible light, have, &c.

Jesus, our glorious God, who, condescending to the weakness of our nature, coverest all thy glories under the familiar forms of bread and wine, and permittest thyself to be seen, touched and tasted by such inconsiderable wretches as we, have, mercy on us.

Jesus, our gracious God, who concealing the awful brightness of thy majesty under those low and humble veils, sweetly invitest us to approach thy person, and open our miseries before thy eyes, and deliver petitions into thy hands, have mercy on us.

Jesus, our gracious God, who to communicate thy divine nature to us miserable sinners, humbleft thyself to enter into our mouths, and descend into our breasts, and by an inconceivable union, become one with us, have, &c.

Jesus, the bread of life that came down from heaven, of which, whosoever eats, shall live eternally, have mercy on us.

Jesus, the heavenly manna, whose sweetness nourishes thy elect in the desart of this world, have mercy on us.

Jesus, the food of angels whose deliciousness replenishes our hearts with celestial joys, have mercy on us.

Jesus, the lamb without spot who every day art sacrificed, yet always remainest alive, every day eaten yet still continuest entire, have, &c.

Jesus, the good shepherd, who fearedst not to lay down thy life for thy sheep, nor sparest to feed them with thy own body, have, &c.

Jesus, who in this high and venerable mystery, art thyself both priest and sacrifice, have, &c.

Jesus, who in this sacred memorial of thy death, hast abridged all thy wonders into an accumulative miracle, have, &c.

Jesus, who in this admirable sacrament hast contracted all thy blessings into one stupendous bounty, have, &c.

the Blessed Sacrament. 355.

Jesus, who by this blessed fruit of the tree of life, restored us again to immortality, have, &c.

Jesus, who by sanctifying the most familiar and necessary of thy creatures, to build us up into a pure desire of thee, teachest us the only right use of all the rest, have, &c.

Jesus, who by becoming thyself the daily food of our souls in this life, preparedst us to live on thee eternally in the next, have, &c.

Jesus, who in this divine banquet of charity, givest us possession of thy grace here, and a secure pledge of thy glory hereafter, have, &c.

Have mercy, O Lord, and pardon our sins.

Have mercy, O Lord, and hear our prayers.

From presuming to fathom the omnipotence of God, by any discourse of human understanding, deliver us, O Lord.

From presuming to interpret the great secrets of thy will, by the uncertain rules of our private opinions, deliver us, O Lord.

From all distraction and irreverence in assisting at this awful sacrifice, deliver, &c.

From neglecting to come to this holy table, and from coming negligently, deliver, &c.

From unworthy and unfruitful receiving this adorable sacrament, deliver, &c.

From hardness of heart, and ingratitude for so unspeakable a blessing, deliver, &c.

By thy irresistible power which changes the course of nature as thou pleasest, deliver, &c.

By thy unsearchable wisdom, which disposes all things in perfect order, deliver, &c.

By

By thy infinite goodness, which freely bestows on us thyself in this incomprehensible mystery, deliver, &c.

By thy blessed body broken for us on the cross, and really given us in the holy communion, deliver, &c.

By thy precious blood shed for us on the cross and substantially present in the chalice of benediction, deliver us, O Lord;

We sinners beseech thee hear us,

That we may always believe thy sacred word, and submit our reason to the decision of thy church, we beseech thee hear us,

That by this sacred oblation we may solemnly protest thy infinite perfections in thyself and supreme dominion over all things, we beseech, &c.

That by this sacred oblation, we may humbly acknowledge our perpetual dependance on thee, and absolute subjection to the disposure of thy will, we beseech, &c.

That we may eternally adore thy goodness, who having no need of us, hast contrived such wonderful endearing motives to make us love thee and be happy, we beseech, &c.

That we may thankfully comply with thy gracious condescendence to be united to us, by a fervent desire of becoming one with thee, we beseech, &c.

That before we approach this royal banquet, we sincerely procure our reconcilement to thee, and be perfectly in charity with all the world, we beseech, &c.

That,

That, in the inftant of receiving thy facred body, our fouls may fill with reverence and love, to attend and entertain fo glorious a gueft, we befeech, &c.

That, returning from this great and holy Eucharift we may recollect all our thoughts to praife and blefs thee, and immediately apply our utmoft endeavours to the real amendment of our lives, we befeech, &c.

That, by this heavenly prefervative, our hearts may be healed of all its infirmities, and ftrengthened againft all relapfes, we befeech, &c.

That, as by faith we adore thee here under thefe facred veils, we may hereafter fee thee face to face, and in that blifsful vifion eternally rejoice, we befeech thee to hear us,

O Lamb of God who takeft away the fins of the world fpare us, O Lord.

O Lamb of God who takeft away the fins of the world, hear us, O Lord.

* O Lamb of God who takeft away the fins of the world, have mercy on us.

The ANTIPHON.

THE glorious king of heaven and earth, to fhew the riches of his bounty, has prepared a folemn and fplendid feaft, and by this gracious invitation, calls even the meaneft of his fubjects to fit down at his table: *Come to me all you that labour and are oppreft, and I will refrefh you : for my flesh is meat indeed, and my blood is drink indeed.*

V. Thou hast given us, O Lord, bread from heaven, *Alleluia.*

R. Replenished with all sweetness and delight, *Alleluia.*

V. O Lord hear our prayers.

R. And let our supplications come unto thee.

The PRAYER.

O God, who in this wonderful sacrament hast left us a perpetual memorial of thy passion; grant us, we beseech thee, so to reverence the sacred mysteries of thy body and blood, that we may continually perceive in our souls, the fruit of thy redemption; who with the Father and the Holy Ghost, livest and reignest, ever one God, world without end. *Amen.*

F I N I S.

Just Published

By the PRINTERS hereof,

SERMONS of PERE BOURDALOUE, S. J Tranflated from the French—2 vols. 13s.

The GENERAL HISTORY OF THE CHRISTIAN CHURCH, from her BIRTH to her final TRIUMPHANT STATE in HEAVEN, being an Explanation of the APOCALYPSE of St. JOHN, by SIG. PASTORINI.
" *Bleffed is he who heareth and readeth the*
" *Words of this Prophecy.*"
In this Book is a clear Hiftory of the Chriftian Church, not only of the paft, but alfo a Prophecy of what will happen.—We have reafon to believe the *future*, from the paft according exactly with the Events which have happened fince it was written, which though upwards of 30 years fince, points with perfpicuity to the prefent ftate of Europe—8vo. 6s. 6d.

*** As there are fome *fpurious* Editions of this Book in circulation, the Buyer is defired to note that the GENUINE is printed by J. MEHAIN.

The LIFE of the HOLY MOTHER, ST. TERESA, Foundrefs of the Difcalceated Carmelites, according to the Primitive Rule—8vo. 5s. 5d.

VESPERS, or EVENING OFFICE of the CHURCH, for every Day in the Year, in Latin and Englifh, for the ufe of the Laity, elegantly printed, and embellifhed with fuperb En-

Books published by the Printers hereof.

The entire Office and proper Masses for the Dead, Burial Service, &c. &c. in Latin and English—2s. 2d.

A Treatise on Confidence in the Mercy of God, by J. J. Linguet, Bishop of Soissons, 3s. 3d.

A Contrite Heart, with Motives and Considerations to Prepare it—"*A Contrite and humble Heart, O Lord, thou wilt not despise.*" Written by St. Pacin, Bishop of Barcelona, 1s. 1d.

The Spiritual Director of Devout and Religious Souls, by St. Francis de Sales, 1s. 1d.

The Imitation of Christ, by Thomas a-Kempis, 1s. 1d.

The Poor Man's Controversy, by J. Marmock, O. S. B. 1s. 7dh.

Spiritual Combat, 1s. 7dh.

Daily Exercise, 4s. 4d.

Ditto, 1s. 7dh.

Sinner's Guide, by Father Lewis of Granada, 6s. 6d.

Ward's Cantos, 6s. 6d.

Office of Holy Week, with plates, 2s. 8dh.

The Garden of the Soul, by the Rev. Dr. Challenor, 1s. 1d.

Catholic Piety, or a Manuel of chosen Prayers, &c. 1s. 1d.

Virgin's Nosegay, 1s. 1d.

Life of Christ, 1s. 1d.

De Sales Introduction to a Devout Life, 2s. 8dh.

Sinner's Complaint, 3s. 3d.

Sincere Christian, 2 vols. 6s. 6d.

Devout Christian. 2 vols. 6s. 6d.

www.ingramcontent.com/pod-product-compliance
Lightning Source LLC
Chambersburg PA
CBHW020326240426
43673CB00039B/932